ADOBE® PREMIERE® PRO CS5
CLASSROOM IN A BOOK®

The official training workbook from Adobe Systems

Adobe

WHAT'S ON THE DISC

Here is an overview of the contents of the Classroom in a Book disc

The *Adobe Premiere Pro CS5 Classroom in a Book* disc includes the lesson files that you'll need to complete the exercises in this book, as well as other content to help you learn more about Adobe Premiere Pro CS5 and use it with greater efficiency and ease. The diagram below represents the contents of the disc, which should help you locate the files you need.

Lesson files

Each lesson has its own folder inside the Lessons folder. You will need to copy these lesson folders to your hard drive before you can begin each lesson.

Adobe Press

ADOBE PRESS

Find information about other Adobe Press titles, covering the full spectrum of Adobe products, in the Online Resources file.

Online resources

Links to Adobe Community Help, product Help and Support pages, Adobe certification programs, Adobe TV, and other useful online resources can be found inside a handy HTML file. Just open it in your Web browser and click on the links, including a special link to this book's product page where you can access updates and bonus material.

CONTENTS

GETTING STARTED

Adobe® Premiere® Pro CS5, the essential editing tool for video enthusiasts and professionals, enhances your creative power and freedom. Adobe Premiere Pro is the most scalable, efficient, and precise video-editing tool available. Whether you're working with DV, HD, HDV, AVCHD, P2 DVCPRO HD, XDCAM, AVC-Intra, or RED, the superior performance of Adobe Premiere Pro lets you work faster and more creatively. The complete set of powerful and exclusive tools lets you overcome any editorial, production, and workflow challenges to deliver the high-quality work you demand.

About Classroom in a Book

Adobe Premiere Pro CS5 Classroom in a Book® is part of the official training series for Adobe graphics and publishing software. The lessons are designed so that you can learn at your own pace. If you're new to Adobe Premiere Pro, you'll learn the fundamental concepts and features you'll need to use the program. This book also teaches many advanced features, including tips and techniques for using the latest version of this software.

The lessons in this edition include opportunities to use features such as the new Ultra keyer, improved editing efficiency, tapeless media, and the ability to send a sequence to Adobe® Encore® CS5 without rendering or intermediate exporting to be output to DVD, Blu-ray Disc, or Adobe® Flash® Professional CS5. Performance has been significantly enhanced with the new Mercury Playback Engine, which provides both software- and hardware-assisted performance breakthroughs. Adobe Premiere Pro CS5 is available for both Windows and Mac OS.

Prerequisites

Before beginning to use *Adobe Premiere Pro CS5 Classroom in a Book*, make sure your system is set up correctly and that you've installed the required software and hardware. You should have a working knowledge of your computer and operating system. You should know how to use the mouse and standard menus and commands and also how to open, save, and close files. If you need to review these techniques, see the printed or online documentation included with your Windows or Mac OS system.

Installing Adobe Premiere Pro CS5

You must purchase the Adobe Premiere Pro CS5 software separately from this book. For system requirements and complete instructions on installing the software, see the document Adobe Premiere Pro ReadMe.html on the software DVD.

Install Adobe Premiere Pro from the Adobe Premiere Pro CS5 software DVD onto your hard disk; you cannot run the program from the DVD. If you purchased the download version of Adobe Premiere Pro, follow the instructions included with the download for launching the installation process. Follow the on-screen instructions. The installation process also installs Adobe® Encore® CS5, Adobe® OnLocation™ CS5, Adobe® Bridge CS5, and some shared components.

Make sure your serial number is accessible before installing the application; you can find the serial number on the registration card, on the back of the DVD case, or in your user account online if you purchased the download version.

Adobe Premiere Pro CS5 trial

Adobe offers a 30-day trial of Adobe Premiere Pro CS5. You can download this trial from the Adobe product website. After 30 days, the software will stop functioning. If you decide to purchase Adobe Premiere Pro, you can enter your purchased serial number into the trial version you have installed to convert it to a full version of Adobe Premiere Pro CS5.

● **Note:** The Adobe Premiere Pro CS5 trial is fully functioning and is a great way for you to try the features. However, a few features are disabled in the trial version.

Specifically, the trial version of Adobe Premiere Pro CS5 does not include some features that depend on software licensed from parties other than Adobe. For example, some codecs for encoding MPEG formats are available only with the full version of Adobe Premiere Pro.

Optimizing performance

Editing video is memory- and processor-intensive work for a desktop computer. A fast processor and a lot of memory will make your editing experience much faster and more efficient; 2 GB of memory is the minimum, and 8 GB or more is better for high-definition (HD) media. Adobe Premiere Pro CS5 takes advantage of multicore processors on Windows and Macintosh systems and will run on Macintosh computers with multicore Intel processors.

A dedicated 7200 RPM or faster hard drive is recommended for standard-definition (SD) or high-definition video (HDV) media. A RAID 0 striped disk array or SCSI disk subsystem is recommended for HD. Performance will be significantly affected if you attempt to store media files and program files on the same hard drive.

The Mercury Playback Engine in Adobe Premiere Pro can operate in software-only mode or GPU acceleration mode. The GPU acceleration mode provides significant performance improvement. The GPU acceleration is possible with select video cards. You can find a list of these video cards on the Adobe website at *http://www. adobe.com/go/premiere_systemreqs*.

> ▶ **Tip:** A common disk configuration is to put the operating system and applications on drive 1, video and audio files on drive 2, and export files on drive 3. For HD work, drive 2 should be a RAID 0 striped disk array or SCSI disk subsystem.

Copying the lesson files

The lessons in *Adobe Premiere Pro CS5 Classroom in a Book* use specific source files, such as image files created in Adobe® Photoshop® CS5 and Adobe® Illustrator® CS5, audio files, and videos. To complete the lessons in this book, you must copy all the files from the *Adobe Premiere Pro CS5 Classroom in a Book* DVD (inside the back cover of this book) to your hard drive. You will need about 3.5 GB of storage space in addition to the 12 GB you need to install Adobe Premiere Pro CS5.

Although each lesson stands alone, some lessons use files from other lessons, so you'll need to keep the entire collection of lesson assets on your hard drive as you work through the book. Here's how to copy those assets from the DVD to your hard drive:

1 Open the *Adobe Premiere Pro CS5 Classroom in a Book* DVD in My Computer or Windows Explorer (Windows) or in the Finder (Mac OS).

2 Right-click (Windows) or Control-click (Mac OS; if you're using a super mouse or pen, you can right-click) the folder called Lessons, and choose Copy.

3 Navigate to the location you set to store your Adobe Premiere Pro CS5 projects.

   The default location is My Documents\Adobe\Premiere Pro\5.0 (Windows) or Documents/Adobe/Premiere Pro/5.0 (Mac OS).

4 Right-click (Windows) or Control-click (Mac OS) the 5.0 folder, and choose Paste.

Following these steps will copy all the lesson assets to your local folder. This process may take a few minutes to complete, depending on the speed of your hardware.

How to use these lessons

● **Note:** You can control many aspects of Adobe Premiere Pro CS5 using multiple techniques, such as menu commands, context menus, and keyboard shortcuts. Sometimes more than one of the methods are described in any given procedure so that you can learn different ways of working, even when the task is one you've done before.

Each lesson in this book provides step-by-step instructions for creating one or more specific elements of a real-world project. The lessons stand alone, but most of them build on previous lessons in terms of concepts and skills. So, the best way to learn from this book is to proceed through the lessons in sequential order.

The organization of the lessons is workflow-oriented rather than feature-oriented, and the book uses a real-world approach. The lessons follow the typical sequential steps video editors use to complete a project, starting with acquiring video, laying down a cuts-only video, adding effects, sweetening the audio track, and ultimately exporting the project to DVD, Blu-ray Disc, or Flash.

Additional resources

Adobe Premiere Pro CS5 Classroom in a Book is not meant to replace documentation that comes with the program or to be a comprehensive reference for every feature. Only the commands and options used in the lessons are explained in this book. For comprehensive information about program features and tutorials, refer to these resources:

Adobe Community Help: Community Help brings together active Adobe product users, Adobe product team members, authors, and experts to give you the most useful, relevant, and up-to-date information about Adobe products. Whether you're looking for a code sample or an answer to a problem, have a question about the software, or want to share a useful tip or recipe, you'll benefit from Community Help. Search results will show you not only content from Adobe, but also from the community.

With Adobe Community Help you can:

- Access up-to-date definitive reference content online and offline

- Find the most relevant content contributed by experts from the Adobe community, on and off Adobe.com

- Comment on, rate, and contribute to content in the Adobe community

- Download Help content directly to your desktop for offline use

- Find related content with dynamic search and navigation tools

To access Community Help: If you have any Adobe CS5 product, then you already have the Community Help application. To invoke Help, choose Help > Premiere Pro help. This companion application lets you search and browse Adobe and community content, plus you can comment on and rate any article just like you would in the browser. However, you can also download Adobe Help and language reference content for use offline. You can also subscribe to new content updates (which can be automatically downloaded) so that you'll always have the most up-to-date content for your Adobe product at all times. You can download the application from www.adobe.com/support/chc/index.html

Adobe content is updated based on community feedback and contributions. You can contribute in several ways: add comments to content or forums, including links to web content; publish your own content using Community Publishing; or contribute Cookbook Recipes. Find out how to contribute: www.adobe.com/community/publishing/download.html

See http://community.adobe.com/help/profile/faq.html for answers to frequently asked questions about Community Help.

Adobe Premiere Pro CS5 Help and Support: www.adobe.com/support/premiere where you can find and browse Help and Support content on adobe.com.

Adobe TV: http://tv.adobe.com is an online video resource for expert instruction and inspiration about Adobe products, including a How To channel to get you started with your product.

Adobe Design Center: www.adobe.com/designcenter offers thoughtful articles on design and design issues, a gallery showcasing the work of top-notch designers, tutorials, and more.

Adobe Developer Connection: www.adobe.com/devnet is your source for technical articles, code samples, and how-to videos that cover Adobe developer products and technologies.

Resources for educators: www.adobe.com/education includes three free curriculums that use an integrated approach to teaching Adobe software and can be used to prepare for the Adobe Certified Associate exams.

Also check out these useful links:

Adobe Forums: http://forums.adobe.com lets you tap into peer-to-peer discussions, questions and answers on Adobe products.

Adobe Marketplace & Exchange: www.adobe.com/cfusion/exchange is a central resource for finding tools, services, extensions, code samples and more to supplement and extend your Adobe products.

Adobe Premiere Pro CS5 product home page: www.adobe.com/products/premiere

Adobe Labs: http://labs.adobe.com gives you access to early builds of cutting-edge technology, as well as forums where you can interact with both the Adobe development teams building that technology and other like-minded members of the community.

Adobe certification

The Adobe training and certification programs are designed to help Adobe customers improve and promote their product-proficiency skills. There are four levels of certification:

- Adobe Certified Associate (ACA)
- Adobe Certified Expert (ACE)
- Adobe Certified Instructor (ACI)
- Adobe Authorized Training Center (AATC)

The Adobe Certified Associate (ACA) credential certifies that individuals have the entry-level skills to plan, design, build, and maintain effective communications using different forms of digital media.

The Adobe Certified Expert program is a way for expert users to upgrade their credentials. You can use Adobe certification as a catalyst for getting a raise, finding a job, or promoting your expertise.

If you are an ACE-level instructor, the Adobe Certified Instructor program takes your skills to the next level and gives you access to a wide range of Adobe resources.

Adobe Authorized Training Centers offer instructor-led courses and training on Adobe products, employing only Adobe Certified Instructors. A directory of AATCs is available at http://partners.adobe.com.

For information on the Adobe Certified programs, visit www.adobe.com/support/certification/main.html.

Checking for updates

Note: To set your preferences for future updates, click Preferences. Select how often you want Adobe Updater to check for updates, for which applications, and whether to download them automatically. Click OK to accept the new settings.

Adobe periodically provides updates to software. You can easily obtain these updates through Adobe Updater, as long as you have an active Internet connection.

1   In Premiere Pro, choose Help > Updates. Adobe Updater automatically checks for updates available for your Adobe software.

2   In the Adobe Updater dialog box, select the updates you want to install, and then click Download and Install Updates to install them.

Accelerate your workflow with Adobe CS Live

Adobe CS Live is a set of online services that harness the connectivity of the web and integrate with Adobe Creative Suite 5 to simplify the creative review process, speed up website compatibility testing, deliver important web user intelligence and more, allowing you to focus on creating your most impactful work. CS Live services are complimentary for a limited time* and can be accessed online or from within Creative Suite 5 applications.

Adobe BrowserLab is for web designers and developers who need to preview and test their web pages on multiple browsers and operating systems. Unlike other browser compatibility solutions, BrowserLab renders screenshots virtually on demand with multiple viewing and diagnostic tools, and can be used with Dreamweaver CS5 to preview local content and different states of interactive pages. Being an online service, BrowserLab has fast development cycles, with greater flexibility for expanded browser support and updated functionality.

Adobe CS Review is for creative professionals who want a new level of efficiency in the creative review process. Unlike other services that offer online review of creative content, only CS Review lets you publish a review to the web directly from within InDesign, Photoshop, Photoshop Extended, and Illustrator and view reviewer comments back in the originating Creative Suite application.

Acrobat.com is for creative professionals who need to work with a cast of colleagues and clients in order to get a creative project from creative brief to final product. Acrobat.com is a set of online services that includes web conferencing, online file sharing and workspaces. Unlike collaborating via email and attending time-consuming in-person meetings, Acrobat.com brings people to your work instead of sending files to people, so you can get the business side of the creative process done faster, together, from any location.

Adobe Story is for creative professionals, producers, and writers working on or with scripts. Story is a collaborative script development tool that turns scripts into metadata that can be used with the Adobe CS5 Production Premium tools to streamline workflows and create video assets.

SiteCatalyst NetAverages is for web and mobile professionals who want to optimize their projects for wider audiences. NetAverages provides intelligence on how users are accessing the web, which helps reduce guesswork early in the creative process. You can access aggregate user data such as browser type, operating system, mobile device profile, screen resolution and more, which can be shown over time. The data is derived from visitor activity to participating Omniture SiteCatalyst customer sites. Unlike other web intelligence solutions, NetAverages innovatively displays data using Flash, creating an engaging experience that is robust yet easy to follow.

You can access CS Live three different ways:

1   Set up access when you register your Creative Suite 5 products and get complimentary access that includes all of the features and workflow benefits of using CS Live with CS5.

2   Set up access by signing up online and get complimentary access to CS Live services for a limited time. Note, this option does not give you access to the services from within your products.

3   Desktop product trials include a 30-day trial of CS Live services.

*CS Live services are complimentary for a limited time. See www.adobe.com/go/cslive for details.

1 TOURING ADOBE PREMIERE PRO CS5

Topics covered in this lesson

- What's new in Adobe Premiere Pro CS5
- Nonlinear editing in Adobe Premiere Pro CS5
- Standard digital video workflow
- Incorporating Adobe® Creative Suite® 5 Production Premium into the workflow
- Touring the Adobe Premiere Pro workspace
- Customizing the workspace

 This lesson will take approximately 40 minutes.

Before you make your first edit or apply your first transition, you will see a brief overview of video editing and how Adobe Premiere Pro fits into the video production workflow. You will also get an introduction to some of the new features of this release. Even those who are old hands at editing will find the tour useful for a glimpse of the enhancements and new features in Adobe Premiere Pro CS5.

New features in Adobe Premiere Pro CS5

As video editors, we've come a long way from clunky old videotape machines and expensive production equipment to professional-level editing on desktop computers. Adobe Premiere Pro CS5 extends our capabilities even further. To get started, we'll begin by looking at some of the exciting new features included with Adobe Premiere Pro CS5. We'll review the basic workflow most video editors follow and see how Adobe Premiere Pro fits within the different versions of Adobe Creative Suite. Finally, we'll introduce custom workspaces in Adobe Premiere Pro CS5.

Although this is not a complete list of every new feature in Adobe Premiere Pro CS5, it will give you an idea of some of the improvements you can look forward to as you learn this exciting application. We will use many of these features in the lessons throughout the book:

- **64-bit application**: Adobe Premiere Pro CS5 is now a 64-bit application. This allows greater use of RAM and better performance.

- **Mercury Playback Engine**: This is a combination of software and hardware acceleration of your video-editing experience. Edit HD video as smoothly as SD video. Play back many effects in real time without the need for rendering.

- **Expanded native tapeless workflows**: Adobe Premiere Pro CS5 offers native support for XDCAM HD 50, AVCCAM, DPX, and AVC-Intra as well as enhanced RED support, which builds on the existing support for P2, XDCAM EX and HD, and AVCHD.

- **Ultra keyer**: Adobe has added a new keyer to quickly and easily perform keying tasks.

- **Content analysis**: In addition to analyzing speech and converting it to searchable text, Adobe Premiere Pro CS5 can now detect and analyze faces.

- **Script-to-screen workflow**: Now you can collaborate on writing scripts with Adobe Story and then automatically create shot lists from your script in Adobe OnLocation CS5. When you import the project into Adobe Premiere Pro, metadata from OnLocation makes it easy to create a preliminary rough cut.

- **Direct export**: In addition to the batch exporter built into the Adobe Media Encoder, you can now prioritize an export and bypass the batch queue when desired.

- **Find gaps in sequences and tracks**: Now you can save time finding the gaps between clips in a sequence and easily remove them if desired.

- **Export to Final Cut Pro**: Adobe has introduced a round-trip workflow when exchanging projects with Final Cut Pro users.

- **Automatic scene detection for HDV video**: This allows Adobe Premiere Pro to automatically separate your footage from HDV into individual clips.

- **Native DLSR camera video support**: You can edit video from the latest DSLR cameras, such as the Canon 5D Mark II and EOS 7D; the Nikon D90,D300s, D3000; and others.

- **Create searchable web-DVDs**: In Encore CS5 you can create a more engaging experience with web-DVDs to now automatically include a search interface, making it easier for viewers to jump directly to content of interest.

Nonlinear editing in Adobe Premiere Pro CS5

Adobe Premiere Pro is a nonlinear editor (NLE). Unlike older videotape-editing systems, which require you to lay down edits consecutively and contiguously, Adobe Premiere Pro lets you place, replace, trim, and move clips anywhere you want in your final edited video.

Adobe Premiere Pro lets you do things nonsequentially. With Adobe Premiere Pro (and other NLEs), you can make changes by simply dragging clips or segments around within your final video. You can edit video segments separately and tie them together later. You can even edit the closing sequence first!

NLEs have another huge benefit over videotape-editing systems: immediate access to your video clips. No longer do you need to fast-forward or rewind through tons of tape to find that one elusive but essential shot. With Adobe Premiere Pro, it's a mouse click away.

Adobe Premiere Pro CS5 supports tapeless media formats including XDCAM EX and HD, XDCAM HD 50, AVCCAM, DPX, Panasonic P2, AVCHD, and AVC-Intra, and it offers enhanced RED support. With current digital video technology, media acquisition has also become nonlinear.

Presenting the standard digital video workflow

There is a basic workflow for creating videos with NLEs such as Adobe Premiere Pro. After a while, it'll become second nature to you. Generally, that workflow follows these steps:

1 Shoot the video.

2 Capture (transfer or ingest) the video to your hard drive. With tapeless media, Adobe Premiere Pro can read the media directly. Or, use Adobe OnLocation CS5 to record video right to your workstation hard drive (bypassing the capture step).

3 Build your edited video by selecting, trimming, and adding clips to the Timeline.

4 Place transitions between clips, apply video effects to clips, and composite (layer) clips.

5 Create text, credits, or basic graphics, and apply them to your project.

6 Add audio—be it narration, music, or sound effects.

7 Mix multiple audio tracks, and use transitions and special effects on your audio clips.

8 Export your finished project to videotape, to a file on your desktop computer, to streaming video for Internet playback, or to a DVD or Blu-ray Disc.

Adobe Premiere Pro supports each of these steps with industry-leading tools. Since this book is geared toward beginning and intermediate video editors, becoming proficient with these standard workflow tools is the primary goal of the upcoming lessons.

Enhancing the workflow with high-level features

Adobe Premiere Pro goes well beyond providing a full-featured toolset for standard digital video editing. It's loaded with extra features that can enhance the video production process and improve the quality of your finished product.

You're not likely to incorporate many of these features in your first few video projects. However, as you ramp up your skills and expectations, you'll begin to tap these high-productivity features. The following topics will be covered in this book:

- **Advanced audio editing**: Adobe Premiere Pro provides audio effects and editing unequaled by any other nonlinear editor or even by most audio-editing software. Create and place 5.1 surround-sound audio channels, make sample-level edits, apply multiple audio effects to any audio clip or track, and use the included state-of-the-art plug-ins as well as third-party Virtual Studio Technology (VST) plug-ins.

- **Color correction**: Correct and enhance the look of your footage with advanced color-correction filters.

- **Keyframe controls**: Adobe Premiere Pro CS5 gives you the precise control you need to fine-tune your visual and motion effects without requiring you to export to a compositing application.

- **Broad hardware support**: Choose from a wide range of capture cards and other hardware to assemble a system that best fits your needs and budget. Adobe Premiere Pro CS5 support extends from low-cost computers for digital video (DV) and compressed HDV format editing up to high-performance workstations capturing HD video. When it's time to upgrade your hardware to work with HD and film, you don't need to leave the familiar Adobe Premiere Pro interface—unlike with some proprietary systems that use different interfaces for different formats.

- **Mercury Playback Engine graphics card acceleration**: The Mercury Playback Engine operates in two modes: software only and GPU acceleration. The GPU acceleration mode requires a compatible graphics card in your workstation. See Adobe.com for a list of compatible graphics cards.

- **Multicam editing**: You can easily and quickly edit any production shot with multiple cameras. Adobe Premiere Pro displays all the camera tracks in a split-view monitor, and you can set the camera view edits by clicking the appropriate screen or by using shortcut keys.

- **Project Manager**: Manage your media through a single dialog box. View, delete, move, search for, and reorganize clips and bins. Consolidate your projects by moving just the media actually used in a project and copying that media to a single location. Then reclaim drive space by deleting unused media.

Incorporating other CS5 components into the editing workflow

Even with all the exciting extra features in Adobe Premiere Pro, the application cannot perform some digital video production tasks. These include the following:

- High-end 3D motion effects
- Detailed text animations
- Layered graphics
- Vector artwork
- Music creation
- Advanced audio mixing, editing, and effects processing

To incorporate one or more of these features into a production, you can turn to the other applications included in the Adobe Creative Suite 5 Production Premium product family. It has all the components you need to produce some absolutely amazing videos.

Here's a brief description of the nine other components in Adobe Creative Suite 5 Production Premium:

- **Adobe® After Effects® CS5**: The tool of choice for motion graphics and visual effects artists.

- **Adobe® Photoshop® CS5 Extended**: The industry-standard image-editing and graphic-creation product.

- **Adobe® Soundbooth™ CS5**: An easy yet powerful tool for audio editing, audio cleanup, audio sweetening, and music creation.

- **Adobe® Encore® CS5**: A high-quality DVD-authoring product designed to work closely with Adobe Premiere Pro, After Effects, and Photoshop CS5. Encore publishes to standard DVD, Blu-ray Disc, and interactive SWF files. Encore CS5 is included with Adobe Premiere Pro CS5 when it's purchased outside Creative Suite 5 Production Premium.

- **Adobe® Illustrator® CS5**: Professional vector graphics creation software for print, video production, and the Web.

- **Adobe® Dynamic Link**: A cross-product connection that allows you to work in real time with native After Effects files in Adobe Premiere Pro and Encore CS5 without rendering first.

- **Adobe® Bridge CS5**: A visual file browser that provides centralized access to your Creative Suite project files, applications, and settings.

- **Adobe® Flash® Professional CS5**: The industry standard for creating rich, interactive web content.

- **Adobe® OnLocation® CS5**: Powerful direct-to-disk recording and monitoring software to help you produce superior-quality results from your video camera.

Adobe CS5 Production Premium workflow

Your Adobe Premiere Pro/Adobe CS5 Production Premium workflow will vary depending on your production needs. Here are a few mini-workflow scenarios:

- Use Adobe OnLocation to record video directly to disk. Import scripts created in Adobe Story, and apply them to specific shots.

- Use Photoshop CS5 to touch up still images from a digital camera, a scanner, or an Adobe Premiere Pro video clip. Then use them in Adobe Premiere Pro.

- Create layered graphics in Photoshop CS5, and then open them in Adobe Premiere Pro. You can opt to have each layer appear on a separate track in the Timeline, allowing you to apply effects and motion to selected layers.

- Build custom music tracks using Adobe Soundbooth CS5, and then use them in Adobe Premiere Pro using Dynamic Link.

- Use Adobe Soundbooth to do professional-quality audio editing and sweetening on an existing Adobe Premiere Pro video or a separate audio file.

- Using Dynamic Link, open Adobe Premiere Pro video sequences in After Effects CS5. Apply complex motion and animation, and then send those updated motion sequences back to Adobe Premiere Pro. You can play After Effects compositions in Adobe Premiere Pro CS5 without first waiting to render them.

- Use After Effects CS5 to create and animate text in ways far beyond the capabilities of Adobe Premiere Pro. Use those compositions in Adobe Premiere Pro.

- Send video projects created in Adobe Premiere Pro into Encore CS5 using Dynamic Link, without rendering or saving an intermediate file. Use Encore to create a DVD, Blu-ray Disc, or interactive Flash application.

Most of this book will focus on a "standard" workflow involving only Adobe Premiere Pro. However, several lessons will demonstrate how you can incorporate Adobe CS5 Production Premium components within your workflow for even more spectacular results.

Touring the Adobe Premiere Pro workspace

You'll dive into nonlinear editing in the next lesson. At this point, you'll take a brief tour of the video-editing workspace. In this exercise, you'll use an Adobe Premiere Pro project from this book's companion DVD.

1 Make sure you've copied all the lesson folders and contents from the DVD to your hard drive. The suggested directory is My Documents\Adobe\ Premiere Pro\5.0\Lessons (Windows) or Documents/Adobe/Premiere Pro/5.0/ Lessons (Mac OS).

● **Note:** It's best to copy all the lesson assets from the DVD to your hard drive and leave them there until you complete this book; some lessons refer to assets from previous lessons.

2 Start Adobe Premiere Pro.

3 Click Open Project.

In Adobe Premiere Pro's welcome screen, you can start a new project or open a saved one.

4 In the Open Project window, navigate to the Lesson 01 folder in the Lessons folder, and then double-click the Lesson 01.prproj project file to open the first lesson in the Adobe Premiere Pro workspace.

All Adobe Premiere Pro project files have a .prproj extension.

● **Note:** You may be prompted with a dialog box asking where a particular file is. This will happen when the original files are saved on a hard drive letter different from the one you're using. You'll need to tell Adobe Premiere Pro where the file is. In this case, navigate to the Lessons/Assets folder, and select the file that the dialog box is prompting you to open. Premiere Pro will remember this location for the rest of the files.

The workspace layout

If you've never seen a nonlinear editor, the default workspace might overwhelm you. Don't worry. A lot of careful consideration went into its design and layout. The principal elements are shown here.

Each workspace item appears in its own panel. You can dock multiple panels in a single frame. Some items with common industry terms stand alone, such as Timeline, Audio Mixer, and Program Monitor. The main workspace elements are as follows:

- **Timeline**: This is where you'll do most of your actual editing. You create *sequences* (Adobe's term for edited video segments or entire projects) in the Timeline. One strength of sequences is that you can *nest* them—place sequences in other sequences. In this way, you can break up a production into manageable chunks.

- **Tracks**: You can layer—or *composite*—video clips, images, graphics, and titles in an unlimited number of tracks. Video clips in higher-numbered tracks cover whatever is directly below them on the Timeline. Therefore, you need to give clips in higher-numbered tracks some kind of transparency or reduce their size if you want to let clips in lower tracks show through. We'll cover compositing in several upcoming lessons.

- **Monitors**: You use the Source Monitor (on the left) to view and trim raw clips (your original footage). To place a clip in the Source Monitor, double-click it in the Project panel. The Program Monitor (on the right) is for viewing your project in progress.

- **Single- or dual-monitor view**: Some editors prefer working with only one monitor screen. The lessons throughout this book reflect a two-monitor workflow. You can change to a single-monitor view if you choose. Click the Close button on the Source tab to close that monitor. In the main menu, choose Window > Source Monitor to open it again.

- **Project panel**: This is where you place links to your project's assets: video clips, audio files, graphics, still images, and sequences. You can use *bins*—or folders—to organize your assets.

- **Media Browser**: This is where you can browse your file system to quickly locate a file to examine or import. We will show how to use the Media Browser in future lessons to locate and import video, stills, and audio assets.

- **Effects panel**: Click the Effects tab (docked, by default, with the History and Info tabs) to open the Effects panel (shown here). Effects are organized as Presets, Audio Effects, Audio Transitions, Video Effects, and Video Transitions. If you open the various effects bins, you'll note that they include numerous audio effects to spice up your sound; two audio crossfade transitions; video scene transitions, such as dissolves and wipes; and many video effects to alter the appearance of your clips.

- **Audio Mixer**: Click the Audio Mixer tab to the right of the Effect Controls tab to open the Audio Mixer. This interface looks a lot like audio production studio hardware, with its volume sliders and panning knobs—one set of controls for each audio track in the Timeline, plus a master track.

Effects panel   Audio Mixer

- **Effect Controls panel**: Click the Effect Controls tab, and then click any clip in the Timeline to display that clip's effect parameters in the Effect Controls panel. This will give you a small taste of many lessons to come. Three video effects are always present for every video, still, or graphic: Motion, Opacity, and Time Remapping. Each effect parameter (in the case of Motion: Position, Scale height and width, Rotation, and Anchor Point) is adjustable

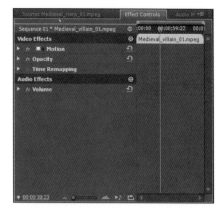

Effect Controls panel

over time using keyframes. The Effect Controls panel is an immensely powerful tool that gives you incredible creative latitude. It comes up in many of this book's lessons.

- **Tools panel**: Each icon in this panel represents a tool that performs a specific function, typically a type of edit. The Selection tool is context-sensitive, which means it changes appearance to indicate the function that matches the circumstances.

Tools panel

- **Info panel**: Click the Info tab to the left of the Effects tab. The Info panel that appears presents a data snapshot of any asset you've selected in the Project panel or any clip or transition selected in a sequence.

- **History panel**: Click the History tab to the right of the Effects tab to open the History panel. This panel tracks up to 32 steps you take in your video production and lets you back up if you don't like your latest efforts. When you back up to a previous condition, all steps that came after that point are also undone. In other words, you cannot extract a single misstep buried within the current list.

Customizing the workspace

You can customize the workspace to create a layout that works best for you:

- As you change the size of one frame, other frames change size to compensate.

- All panels within frames are accessible via tabs.

- All panels are dockable—you can drag a panel from one frame to another.

- You can drag a panel out of a frame to become a separate floating panel.

You can save your workspace as a custom workspace, and you can save as many custom workspaces as you like.

In this exercise, you'll try all these functions and save a customized workspace. Before changing the interface layout, though, you'll adjust its brightness.

1 Choose Edit > Preferences > Appearance (Windows) or Premiere Pro > Preferences > Appearance (Mac OS).

Tip: For those of you working in cave-like editing bays: As you approach the darkest setting, the text switches to white on gray. This is to accommodate those editors who work in editing bays in darkened rooms.

2 Drag the Brightness slider to the left or right to suit your needs. When done, click OK.

3 Click the Effects tab, and then position your pointer on the vertical divider between the Effects panel and the Timeline. Then, click and drag left and right to change the sizes of those frames.

Note: As you move a panel, Adobe Premiere Pro displays a drop zone. If the panel is a rectangle, it will go into the selected frame as an additional tab. If it's a trapezoid, it'll go into its own frame.

4 Place the pointer on the horizontal divider between the Effect Controls panel and the Timeline. Drag up and down to change the sizes of these frames.

5 Click the gripper area in the upper-left corner of the History tab, and drag it to the top of the interface, next to the Project tab, to dock the History panel in that frame.

▶ **Tip:** Dealing with a crowded frame: When the History panel is added to the frame with the Project panel, you may not be able to see all the tabs. In this case, a slider appears above the tabs. Slide it left or right to reveal all the tabs. You can also open a hidden (or any other) panel directly from a menu by choosing Window and then clicking a panel name.

Rectangular drop zone   Trapezoidal drop zone

6 Drag the Effect Controls drag handle to a point near the bottom of the Project panel to place it in its own frame.

As shown here on the left, the drop zone is a trapezoid that covers the lower portion of the Project panel. Release the mouse button, and your workspace should look something like the one shown here on the right.

7 Click the Program Monitor's drag handle, and hold down the Control (Windows) or Command (Mac OS) key while dragging it out of its frame. Its drop zone image is much more distinct, indicating you are about to create a floating panel.

8 Drop the Program Monitor anywhere, creating a floating panel. Expand it by dragging from the corner.

9 As you gain editing acumen, you might want to create and save a customized workspace. To do so, choose Window > Workspace > New Workspace. Type a workspace name, and click OK.

10 If you want to return the workspace to its default layout, choose Window > Workspace > Reset Current Workspace.

Review questions

1 Why is Adobe Premiere Pro considered a nonlinear editor?

2 Describe the basic video-editing workflow.

3 What is the Media Browser used for?

4 Can you save a customized workspace?

5 What is the purpose of the Source Monitor? What is the purpose of the Program Monitor?

6 How can you drag a panel to its own floating panel?

Review answers

1 Adobe Premiere Pro lets you place video, audio, and graphics anywhere on a sequence (in the Timeline), rearrange media clips within a sequence, add transitions, apply effects, and do any number of other video-editing steps in just about any order that suits you.

2 Shoot your video; transfer it to your computer; create a sequence of video, audio, and still-image clips on the Timeline; apply effects and transitions; add text and graphics; edit your audio; and export the finished product.

3 The Media Browser allows you to browse and import media files without having to open an external file browser.

4 Yes. Any customized workspace can be saved by choosing Window > Workspace > New Workspace.

5 You use the monitor panels to view your project and your original clips. When working with two monitors—Source and Program—you can view and trim your raw footage in the Source Monitor and use the Program Monitor to view the Timeline sequence as you build it.

6 Drag the panel with your mouse while holding down Control (Windows) or Command (Mac OS).

2 SELECTING SETTINGS, ADJUSTING PREFERENCES, AND MANAGING ASSETS

Topics covered in this lesson

- Selecting project and sequence settings
- Setting scratch disk options
- Adjusting user preferences
- Importing assets
- Taking a closer look at images
- Managing media in bins
- Finding assets with the Media Browser

 This lesson will take approximately 50 minutes.

Adobe Premiere Pro CS5 is eminently customizable and adaptable. All you need to do is adjust the sequence settings and preferences.

Getting started

In most of your Adobe Premiere Pro CS5 projects, you won't have to give more than a passing glance to project settings and preferences. Nevertheless, it's good to know the options available to you. You'll learn how to manage your assets from within the Project panel and delve into the Adobe Media Browser—a full-scale asset browser that works with all the media types you may need to import into Adobe Premiere Pro CS5.

Selecting project settings by sequence

The basic rule of thumb when selecting project and sequence settings is to match the settings to your source material and not to the final output. Maintaining the original quality of source material means you'll have more options later. Even if your goal is to create a low-resolution video to play on the Internet, wait until you finish editing, and then reduce the output quality settings to make your video Internet-ready.

You might have a mix of source media—wide-screen, standard, HDV, and P2, for example—among your project assets. With Adobe Premiere Pro CS5, you can create multiple sequences, each with a different media type or frame size, all in the same project.

Three types of settings

Adobe Premiere Pro CS5 has three types of settings:

- **Project settings**: These apply to the entire project, and most can't be changed once the project is created.

- **Sequence settings**: You set these when you create a new sequence and deal with the types of media you will be using.

- **Preferences**: These generally apply to all projects, and you can change them at any time.

Specifying project settings

To specify project settings for your Premiere Pro project, do the following:

1   Launch Adobe Premiere Pro CS5.

    The startup screen appears. The Recent Projects list should be populated with the projects you last opened. In this case, you'll be starting fresh.

2   Click New Project to open the New Project dialog, which contains the General tab and Scratch Disks tab.

General tab

The General tab contains these sections:

- **Action and Title Safe Areas**: It is recommended you leave the settings in this section at their default values. They do not affect the video in any way. They simply determine where guides are displayed on the Program Monitor and Source Monitor to help plan title placement and see where TV overlay molding may hide the edges of video.

- **Video and Audio**: Again, it is recommended that you leave the Display Format settings at their defaults unless you need to display video increments in feet or frames rather than timecode or you need to display audio in milliseconds rather than at the sample rate.

- **Capture**: The only setting in this section, Capture Format, is important to set correctly based on the media you plan to capture. The choices are DV or HDV.

- **Video Rendering and Playback**: This option may be active or inactive depending on the graphics card installed in your system. This feature will be discussed in detail in Lesson 8.

Scratch Disks tab

Scratch disks is a term used to describe the location on your computer hard drive where various files associated with video editing are stored. Scratch disks may be placed all on the same disk or on separate disks, depending on your hardware and workflow requirements.

The default for each type of file is Same as Project. This means all files will be stored in the same folder or subfolders of your project file. This is a very organized way to work; when you're finished with the project, deleting one folder will clean up the entire project.

In some scenarios, you may have good reasons to specify different locations for different files (scratch disks). For example, you may have a really fast hard drive in a RAID 0 configuration. This would be the best place to store your captured video files because they require the most system input/output (I/O).

● **Note:** Partitioning a single drive into multiple drives is not helpful for performance.

For the purposes of these lessons, it's recommended that you leave your scratch disks set to Same as Project. When you start capturing your own video clips, feel free to customize the scratch disks to your environment.

Typical drive setup

Although all files can exist on a single hard drive, a typical editing system will have three hard drives: drive 1, dedicated to the operating system and programs; drive 2 (the fastest drive), dedicated to captured video and video previews; and drive 3, dedicated to audio, miscellaneous still images, and exporting.

While on the Scratch Disks tab, set a location and filename for your new project, and click OK.

Sequence settings

You will be prompted to choose sequence settings every time you create a new sequence. This is because each sequence in Adobe Premiere Pro CS5 can have different settings. Since Adobe Premiere Pro assumes you need at least one sequence in your project, it prompts you for sequence settings when starting a new project.

The New Sequence dialog contains three tabs, which are as follows:

- **Sequence Presets**: This tab allows you to choose a preset for the most commonly used and supported media types. The media used for most of the lessons in this book are Sony XDCAM EX files at 720p resolution and 24 frames per second, so choose the XDCAM EX 720p24 preset. When you capture your own video clips, choose the preset that matches your media.

- **General**: The General tab allows you to customize the individual settings of a preset. If your media matches one of the presets, it's not necessary to make any changes on the General tab. In fact, it's recommended that you do not. However, if you need to create a custom preset, choose the one on the Sequence Presets tab that matches your media most closely, and then make the customization on the General tab. You may save your custom preset by clicking the Save Preset button near the bottom of the General tab.

- **Tracks**: Here you can specify how many video and audio tracks will be added when the sequence is created. You can also add audio or video tracks later.

For this chapter's project, give your initial sequence the name **Sequence 01** on the Sequence Presets tab, and click OK.

Custom preset for new projects

If you expect to use your modified project settings on multiple projects, you can save them for reuse by creating a customized new project preset. To do so, choose your settings, and then click the Save Preset button on the General tab. Give your customized project settings preset a name on the Sequence Presets tab, and click OK. The name will appear in the Custom folder under Available Presets.

If you're editing standard DV or native HDV, it's not necessary to use a custom preset. In this case, choose one of the standard presets on the Load Preset tab.

Adjusting user preferences

Preferences are different from sequence settings in that you typically set preferences once and have them apply to all your projects. You can change preferences and have them take immediate effect at any time.

Preferences include default transition times, timing and number of autosaves, Project panel clip label colors, and user interface brightness (you adjusted this in Lesson 1).

Note: Unlike Lesson 01.prproj, this project has no media files imported. It's blank. That's because you'll be importing assets into the project later in this lesson.

If you've been following along with this lesson, you should be sitting at the Adobe Premiere Pro blank workspace and can skip step 1. If you need to start fresh, load the Lesson 02-01.prproj project.

1 Start Adobe Premiere Pro, choose Open Project, navigate to the Lesson 02 folder, and choose Lesson 02-01.prproj.

2 Choose Edit > Preferences > General (Windows) or Premiere Pro > Preferences > General (Mac OS).

Note: You can select any of the Preferences submenus. All choices take you to the Preferences dialog, with the appropriate category selected. You can easily move from one category to another by clicking a category name in the list on the left.

Preferences categories

The various preferences categories rarely come into play until you've used Adobe Premiere Pro for a while, and most are self-explanatory. Here's a brief run-through:

- **General**: This category primarily sets default times for audio and video transitions, still-image duration, preroll/postroll for sequence, and clip behavior.

- **Appearance**: This sets the interface brightness. You saw this in Lesson 1.

- **Audio**: The Automation Keyframe Optimization setting is relevant when you use the Audio Mixer to change volume or panning. Adjusting the "Linear keyframe thinning" and "Minimum time interval thinning" settings to greater than 30 ms makes it easier to edit the changes later.

- **Audio Hardware**: This sets the default audio hardware device.

- **Audio Output Mapping**: This specifies how each audio hardware device channel corresponds to an Adobe Premiere Pro audio output channel. Generally, the default settings will work fine.

- **Auto Save**: This sets the frequency and number of autosaves. To open an autosaved project, choose File > Open Project, navigate to the Adobe Premiere Pro Auto-Save folder, and double-click a project.

- **Capture**: This sets four basic capture parameters.

- **Device Control**: The choices here are Preroll and Timecode Offset (usually used only during analog video capture).

- **Label Colors**: This lets you change the default Project panel medialink label colors.

- **Label Defaults**: This assigns specific label colors to different media types.

- **Media**: Here you'll find options for maintaining cache files and locations.

- **Memory**: These are options for reserving a specific amount of RAM for Adobe Premiere Pro. It is recommended that you start with the default settings.

- **Player Settings**: This is usually set to Adobe Media Player. However, some third-party capture cards may add their own video players, which you can choose to use here.

- **Titler**: This specifies the characters to be used for font and style samples in the Adobe Titler frame.

- **Trim**: This adjusts how many frames and audio time units are trimmed if you select Large Trim Offset (a quick way to chop off chunks of video) in the Trim Monitor.

● **Note:** When you finish reviewing the various options, click Cancel, or click OK if you made any changes you want to keep.

Any changes you make in the preferences take effect immediately and remain in effect the next time you start Adobe Premiere Pro. You can change them again at any time.

▶ **Tip:** An important preference to understand here is the "Default scale to frame size" setting. If this option is selected, any media you import will automatically scale to the frame size of the sequence. This may be desirable for importing a lot of still images. If you intend to do a lot of zooming or panning, you may not want stills to automatically scale. We'll look more closely at zooming and panning in Lesson 11.

● **Note:** Some sequences, such as those containing high-resolution source video or still images, require large amounts of memory for the simultaneous rendering of multiple frames. These assets can force Adobe Premiere Pro to cancel rendering and to give a Low Memory Warning alert. In these cases, you can maximize the available memory by changing the Optimize Rendering For preference from Performance to Memory. Change this preference back to Performance when rendering no longer requires memory optimization.

Importing assets

In Lesson 1, your project started with links to video clips (*assets*) that had already been placed in the Project panel. Adding those links to the Project panel—*importing assets*, in Adobe Premiere Pro parlance—is easy. But you should keep a few issues in mind. This exercise will cover the how-tos of importing and the issues you're most likely to encounter.

You'll import all four standard media types: video, audio, graphics, and still images. You'll see two importing methods and take a look at the properties of audio and graphic files.

You can continue where you left off, or you can open Lesson 02-01.prproj from the Lesson 02 folder.

You should see the standard Adobe Premiere Pro opening workspace. All the frames should be empty except for the Sequence 01 item in the Project panel and in the Timeline.

1   Choose File > Import.

▶ **Tip:** To select multiple files, hold down Ctrl (Window) or Command (Mac OS) while clicking the filenames.

2   Navigate to the Lessons/Assets folder, and select the .jpg, .mp3, .ai, and two .mpeg clips, as shown here. Then click Open. This will *import* (create links from) these files to the Adobe Premiere Pro Project panel.

3 In the Project panel, double-click the empty space below the newly added clips.

You'll import files from a different file folder, demonstrating that you don't have to keep all your assets in the same place. The Project panel simply lists links to your assets, wherever they may be.

● **Note:** This is a different and faster way to open the Import dialog. You can also press the keyboard shortcut Ctrl+I (Windows) or Command+I (Mac OS).

4 Navigate to the Lessons/Assets/More Assets folder. Select movie_logo.psd, and then click Open.

For the Adobe Photoshop file, an Import Layered File dialog appears.

5 Choose Sequence from the Import As menu, and click OK.

You could have selected one of the Merge Layer options to import the Photoshop image into a single layer. Choosing Sequence does two things:

● **Note:** Notice that when you choose to import the Photoshop file as a sequence, the dialog shows the layers of the Photoshop image and allows you to turn on and off individual layers.

- Adds a file folder to your Project panel with all the Photoshop CS5 layers listed as separate clips

- Creates a new sequence with all the layers on separate video tracks

● **Note:** Adobe Premiere Pro up-converts all audio to the project setting, thereby ensuring no quality is lost during editing. Floating-point data allows for even more precise and smoother edits.

6 Right-click (Windows) or Control-click (Mac OS) Medieval_Axe.mp3 in the Project panel, and choose Properties from the context menu to see information about the file.

7 Close the Properties dialog.

8 Another way to see information about an asset is with the Info panel. Click the Info panel located in the lower-left area of the workspace. Now click various assets in the Project panel to observe the properties being displayed in the Info panel.

● **Note:** If you are not in the Editing workspace, choose Window > Workspace > Editing.

Taking a closer look at images

● **Note:** You may be prompted with a dialog asking where a particular file is. This will happen when the original files were saved on a hard drive other than the one you're using or when the files were moved since the last time you used this project. You'll need to tell Adobe Premiere Pro where the file is. In this case, navigate to the Lessons/Assets folder, and select the file for which the dialog is prompting you.

Adobe Premiere Pro can import just about any image and graphic file type. You've already seen how it handles Photoshop CS5 layered files—giving you the option to import the layers as separate graphics within a sequence, import them as single layers, or merge the entire file into one graphic clip.

What's left to cover is how Adobe Premiere Pro handles Adobe Illustrator files and JPEG image files. You'll start this exercise where you left off. If you need to start fresh, just open Lesson 02-02.prproj from the Lesson 02 folder.

1 Right-click (Windows) or Control-click (Mac OS) Illustrator_file.ai in the Project panel, and choose Properties from the context menu.

This file type is Adobe Illustrator Artwork. Here's how Adobe Premiere Pro deals with Adobe Illustrator files:

- Like the Photoshop CS5 file you imported in step 4 in the previous exercise, this is a layered graphic file. However, Adobe Premiere Pro doesn't give you the option to import Adobe Illustrator files in separate layers. It merges them.

- It also uses a process called *rasterization* to convert the vector (path-based) Illustrator art into the pixel-based (raster) image format used by Adobe Premiere Pro.

- Adobe Premiere Pro automatically *anti-aliases*, or smoothes the edges of, the Illustrator art.

- Adobe Premiere Pro converts all empty areas into a transparent alpha channel so that clips below those areas on the Timeline can show through.

2 Close the Properties dialog.

Editing Illustrator files in Illustrator

If you right-click (Windows) or Control-click (Mac OS) Illustrator_file.ai again, you'll note that one option is Edit Original. If you have Illustrator installed on your computer, selecting Edit Original will open this graphic in Illustrator, ready to be edited. So, even though the layers are merged in Adobe Premiere Pro, you can return to Illustrator, edit the original layered file, and save it, and the changes will immediately show up in Adobe Premiere Pro.

3 To see more information in the Project panel, drag its right edge to the right as far as possible to reveal more columns.

4 Click one of the image assets again, and then press the Tab key to move from column to column. Note that you can enter text "spreadsheet style" into fields that are editable. This is also another way to see properties of the assets.

Customizing the Project panel columns

While you have the Project panel stretched wide, try dragging the column headers. You can move columns left or right to suit your style of work.

5 Drag the Project panel to its original size. If you have problems formatting the workspace the way it was originally, choose Window > Workspace > Reset Current Workspace.

6 Drag the video clip Medieval_Hero_02.mpeg to the Video 1 track in the Timeline. Click Play in the Program Monitor to view the video.

7 Drag explosion_still.jpg and Illustrator_file.ai to the Video 2 track above the video clip, as shown here.

8 Press the = key to zoom in on the Timeline or the - key to zoom out. Press the \ key to scale the Timeline to fit all clips on one screen. Zoom the Timeline so it appears close to what is shown here.

9 Drag the current-time indicator across the two graphic clips. Notice that the JPEG clip is too large (not all of it is visible) and that the Illustrator clip has a transparent background. JPEG files cannot have a transparent background.

● **Note:** As you drag the current-time indicator, look at the Program Monitor. You will see only a portion of the JPEG image because it is larger than the project preset dimensions. By default, Adobe Premiere Pro centers the images on the screen and displays them in their original resolution. The next step explains how to view them in their entirety, without changing the aspect ratio of the images.

10 Place the current-time indicator over the middle of the JPEG clip so it is visible in the Program Monitor. Right-click (Windows) or Control-click (Mac OS) explosion_still.jpg in the Timeline, and choose Scale to Frame Size to turn on that feature.

● **Note:** If you want all your images to be automatically scaled to the project frame size, you can set that as a preference in the General category in Preferences by selecting "Default scale to frame size." You must set the option before you import the images for it to take effect.

You should now see the entire image.

11 You can also manually scale the image from its full resolution using the Motion tool in the Effect Controls panel. The benefit of this method is that it allows you to pan or zoom up to the full image resolution. Right-click the JPEG again, and turn Scale to Frame Size off. Select explosion_still.jpg by clicking it once.

12 Expand the Motion effect in the Effect Controls panel.

13 Expand the Scale parameter, and adjust it larger or smaller. Watch the effect it has on the image. You can manually scale the image to any size you like. In a later lesson, we'll look at keyframing this parameter to create animation.

Image tips

Here are a few tips for importing images:

- You can import images up to 16 megapixels in size (4096x4096).

- If you don't plan to zoom or pan, try to create files with a frame size at least as large as the frame size of the project. Otherwise, you have to scale up the image, and it will lose some of its sharpness. Importing overly large files uses more memory and can slow down your project.

- If you plan to zoom or pan, create images such that the zoomed or panned area has a frame size at least as large as the frame size of the project.

Square vs. rectangular pixels

TV sets display rectangular pixels—slightly vertical rectangles (.9 aspect ratio) for NTSC and slightly horizontal rectangles for PAL. By contrast, computer monitors use square pixels. Images created in graphics software typically are square. Adobe Premiere Pro adjusts them to display properly by squashing and interpolating the square pixels to keep the images' original aspect ratios and to display them properly on TV sets. So when you create graphics or images with square pixels, create them with your TV standard in mind: 720x534 for NTSC (that frame size will become 720x480 after Premiere Pro squashes the square pixels into rectangles) and 768x576 for PAL.

Managing media in bins

The Project panel provides a means of accessing and organizing your assets—video clips, audio files, still images, graphics, and sequences. Each listed media asset is a link. The files themselves remain in their file folders, while the assets are stored in *bins*. Bins behave like folders as a way to organize and categorize your assets visually within Adobe Premiere Pro.

Importing and logically arranging your assets in the Project panel is simple. You can create new bins as well as bins inside bins.

In this exercise, you will check out some of the Project panel options and then rearrange the clips you have been working with. If you need to start fresh, open Project 02-02.prproj.

1 Click the Icon View button in the lower-left corner of the Project panel.

That changes the Project panel display from a list to thumbnails and icons.

2 Expand the Project panel by dragging its right edge to the right so you can see all the items.

3 Click Medieval_Axe.mp3 to select it, and then click the Play-Stop Toggle button on the thumbnail viewer.

You can click any other asset and play it. The Play-Stop Toggle button will be unavailable (dimmed) for still images and graphics.

4 Click Medieval_Hero_01.mpeg, and drag the slider under the thumbnail viewer a few seconds into the clip.

5 Click the Poster Frame button next to the preview to create a new thumbnail image for that clip.

● **Note:** The new thumbnail appears immediately in the Project panel. The thumbnail image has an audio display in it, indicating that this is a video clip with audio.

6 Click the New Bin button located near the bottom of the project panel to create a new file folder.

The new bin appears in the Project panel with its default name—Bin 01.

7 Change its name from Bin 01 to *audio*, and press Enter (Windows) or Return (Mac OS).

8 Create another bin, and name it *stills*.

9 Drag the audio clip to the audio bin thumbnail.

10 Drag the JPEG still and the Illustrator file to the new stills bin.

11 Return to List view (click the List View button to the left of the Icon View button).

12 Click somewhere in the Project panel to deselect any bin that might be selected.

13 Click the New Bin button to create a new bin. Name it *sequences*.

14 Open the movie_logo bin, and drag the movie_logo sequence to the sequences bin.

● **Note:** You need to deselect any bin at this point so that the bin you're about to add won't be a subfolder inside another folder. (Sometimes you might want to use subfolders to help organize the Project panel, but that's not what you're doing now.)

● **Note:** It's useful to organize your project assets in this type of bin structure. You may come up with your own way of organizing, but organizing by asset type, as demonstrated here, is a good way to start.

15 Create one more bin named *movies*, and drag the movie files to that bin.

16 Click somewhere in the Project panel to deselect any bin that might be selected.

17 Drag Sequence 01 to the sequences bin as well.

18 Click Name at the top of the file link list in the Project panel twice to put all the asset links and bins in alphabetical order.

Your Project panel should appear as shown here. If your bins aren't collapsed as in this figure, click the expand/collapse icon to the left of the bin name.

Exploring additional bin features

The bin feature in Adobe Premiere Pro CS5 is helpful when you have a lot of assets. It is possible to have thousands of assets (movie clips, image clips, audio clips, and so on) in your bins. Bins are very helpful in finding, moving, and organizing assets.

Having multiple bins open at once

In Adobe Premiere Pro CS5, you can open multiple bins at the same time in their own window or docked to a panel. This makes it easy to drag clips between two bins. Start this lesson where you left off in the previous section, or load Lesson 02-03.prproj from the Lesson 02 folder.

1 Double-click the stills bin you just created. Note that it opens in its own window. Be sure to click the bin icon, not the name of the bin.

2   Practice dragging clips from this new window to other bins and back.

3   Dock the new stills bin with another panel to try a different method of organizing your bins.

4   Close the stills bin by clicking the *x* on its tab. Note that the stills bin still exists in the main Project panel.

Finding assets

Adobe Premiere Pro CS5 has improved the searching capability within the Project panel. The Find tool is located near the top of the Project panel.

1   If your workspace has gotten messy, open Lesson 02-03.prproj.

2   Type the letters *med* in the Search box. Notice that the movies bin and audio bin automatically expand to reveal the clips that have the letters *med* in their names.

This feature is very simple yet is amazingly powerful for finding just the right clip quickly and easily.

3   When you're finished, clear all the text in the Search box so all the files are visible.

4   Click the Find icon at the bottom of the Project panel to experiment with a more detailed, specific search tool. This tool is helpful when you have a lot of assets and the search tool is not specific enough.

▶ **Tip:** You can clear the search criteria from the Search box by clicking the x to the right of the Search box input area.

Finding assets with the Media Browser

The Media Browser in Adobe Premiere Pro CS5 allows you to easily browse for files on your computer. Unlike the Import dialog (or Choose Object dialog) you used previously in this lesson, the Media Browser can stay open all the time and be docked where you find it convenient. In Lesson 3 you'll learn how useful the Media Browser is for finding and importing file-based media such as P2, AVCHD, and XDCAM assets.

The Media Browser is pretty self-explanatory. You'll learn to use it by importing the same assets you did earlier via the Import dialog (or Choose Object dialog).

1 Open Lesson 02-01.prproj in the Lesson 02 folder. This project should have no assets imported yet.

2 Expand the Media Browser by dragging its right edge to the right.

3 Using the Media Browser, navigate to the Lessons/Assets folder.

4 Select the same assets as you did before, and drag them to the Project panel.

▶ **Tip:** Filter the assets you're looking for by using the Files of Type menu in the Media Browser to filter them.

Review questions

1 What is the purpose of the General tab in the New Sequence dialog?

2 How can you cause Adobe Premiere Pro to import all JPEGs so that they're scaled to the dimensions of your current sequence?

3 Describe at least two ways to import assets.

4 Adobe Premiere Pro handles Photoshop and Illustrator layered graphic files differently. Explain the differences.

5 What is the advantage of importing high-resolution photos?

6 By default, what happens when you double-click a bin?

Review answers

1 The General tab is used to customize an existing preset or to create a new custom preset. If you are using a standard media type, the Sequence Preset option is all you should need to select.

2 In the General category of Preferences, check the "Default scale to frame size" box before importing the JPEGs.

3 Choose File > Import, double-click an empty space in the Project panel, or drag assets from the Media Browser to the Project panel.

4 Adobe Premiere Pro lets you import a Photoshop CS5 file in one of three ways: as a sequence with individual layers on separate video tracks, on an individual layer basis, or as a merged file. Adobe Premiere Pro imports Illustrator CS5 layered graphics only as merged files. It rasterizes and anti-aliases Illustrator vector-based art.

5 You can pan and zoom in on them and maintain a sharp-looking image. To see images at their full frame size, right-click (Windows) or Control-click (Mac OS) them in the Timeline, and deselect Scale to Frame Size.

6 The bin will open in its own window.

3 IMPORTING AND MANAGING TAPELESS MEDIA

Topics covered in this lesson

- Using a tapeless workflow
- Using the Media Browser
- Importing tapeless media including P2, XDCAM, and AVCHD
- Mixing media formats

 This lesson will take approximately 30 minutes.

Many popular video cameras record to disk or flash memory rather than tape. The advantages of this "tapeless" workflow include reliability, ingest speed, and flexibility in frame rates. Adobe Premiere Pro CS5 allows you to edit these formats natively without time-consuming conversions.

Getting started

Most of the lessons in this book use the XDCAM EX format for the demo assets. These are high-definition files that are a good example of media used in a tapeless workflow. Different camera manufacturers have created different media formats for storing video and audio information in files. But the processes (or workflow) of moving the files from the cameras to Adobe Premiere Pro CS5 are very similar. Working with the XDCAM EX files in these lessons will give you experience that will translate well to working with other tapeless media formats that you might encounter.

Using a tapeless workflow

A *tapeless workflow* (also known as a *file-based workflow*) is simply the process of importing video from a tapeless camera, editing it, and exporting it. Adobe Premiere Pro CS5 makes this especially easy because, unlike many competing non-linear editing systems, Adobe Premiere Pro CS5 does not require the media from these tapeless formats to be converted. Adobe Premiere Pro CS5 can edit tapeless formats (such as P2, XDCAM, AVCHD, and even DSLRs that shoot video) natively with no conversions.

Though P2, XDCAM, and AVCHD are all tapeless formats, they do have their differences. We'll review the basics of each format.

Panasonic P2

P2 is the video format recorded onto a P2 card by Panasonic P2 cameras. A P2 card is a PCMCIA flash memory card that is inserted into the camera for recording or into a PCMCIA slot in a workstation. Though Adobe Premiere Pro can read and edit directly from the P2 card, it's recommended that you copy the contents of the card to your local hard drive for best performance.

P2 cameras also have USB ports that allow the video to be transferred to an editing workstation via USB.

Notice that whether you move the files via the P2 card or transfer them via USB, the video does not need to be serially captured. It's transferred to the editing workstation at the speed allowed by the transfer I/O.

Several variants of the P2 format specify different frame sizes and frame rates. Some examples of P2 formats are DVCPRO, DVCPRO 50, DVCPRO HD, and AVC-I. Adobe Premiere Pro supports all the standard P2 variants.

A typical workflow for P2 media is as follows:

1 Shoot to the P2 card in the camera.

2 Move the P2 card to your workstation, and copy the files to your local hard drive.

3 Edit the files natively in Adobe Premiere Pro.

4 Export the project to Blu-ray Disc, to DVD, to the Web, or even back to the P2 native format.

Sony XDCAM

Sony XDCAM refers to a family of cameras that record to optical disc or SxS flash memory cards. Most of the cameras in the XDCAM and XDCAM HD lines record to optical disc. The XDCAM EX1 and EX3 models record to SxS flash memory cards.

You can remove the optical disc from your camera and place it in a deck attached to your workstation. Or you can insert the SxS flash memory card into a PCI Express card slot in your workstation and read it as a flash drive. In either case, it is recommended that you copy the files from the optical disc or SxS flash card to your local hard drive for best performance rather than attempting to edit directly from the source media.

Adobe Premiere Pro offers native support for optical disc XDCAM content recorded as standard-definition DVCAM and for all high-definition XDCAM HD formats recorded at 18 Mbps, 25 Mbps, and 35 Mbps.

Adobe Premiere Pro supports the Sony XDCAM EX, XDCAM HD, and XDCAM 422 formats.

A typical workflow for XDCAM EX media is as follows:

1 Shoot to the SxS card in the camera.

2 Move the SxS card to your workstation, and copy the files to your local hard drive.

3 Edit the files natively in Adobe Premiere Pro.

4 Export the project to Blu-ray Disc, DVD, or the Web.

AVCHD

AVCHD is a recording format generally used in consumer cameras to record high-definition video to a tapeless format. AVCHD is not limited to a single vendor's camera or family of cameras; it's used in many brands of consumer high-definition cameras including various models from Sony and Panasonic. Compared to HDV cameras, which are based on the MPEG-2 codec, AVCHD achieves higher compression and lower data rates using the H.264 codec.

Cameras using the AVCHD record onto one of three types of media:

- **DVD**: The camera burns video as it is recorded directly to a DVD in the camera using the AVCHD recording format.

- **Hard drive**: The camera records video directly to a hard drive inside the camera using the AVCHD recording format.

- **Flash memory**: The camera records video directly to a flash memory card inside the camera using the AVCHD format.

The AVCHD format is a good format to record and view video, but it has proven a challenge to edit because of its highly compressed nature. Adobe Premiere Pro CS5 has the ability to edit AVCHD video in its native format without converting it to an intermediate or alternate codec, but how smoothly the AVCHD edit process goes will depend largely on the power of the editing system you are using. The Mercury Playback Engine in Adobe Premiere Pro CS5 has greatly improved the performance of editing AVCHD media. The details of the Mercury Playback Engine will be discussed in more detail in Lesson 9.

A typical workflow for AVCHD media is as follows:

1 Shoot the AVCHD video to DVD, flash media, or hard drive. The media will vary depending on the type of AVCHD camera you are using.

2 Copy the AVCHD video clips to your workstation by placing the capture disc in your DVD drive, moving the flash card, or copying from your camera's internal hard drive to your workstation via USB.

3 Edit the files natively in Adobe Premiere Pro.

4 Export the project to Blu-ray Disc, DVD, or the Web.

Digital still cameras that shoot high-definition video

Some digital still cameras have the ability to shoot high-definition video and store it on a flash memory card. The video from these cameras is another form of tapeless media. No single format exists that different manufacturers' cameras use for encoding the video, but Adobe Premiere Pro CS5 has presets for digital SLRs that will work for most of the video formats produced by these cameras.

Using the Media Browser

If you're an experienced Adobe Premiere Pro user, you'll tend to want to use the traditional method of importing clips through the Project panel. You were introduced to the Media Browser in Lesson 2, and you will be using it in this lesson to locate and import the example clips. Although it's possible to import all the clips using the Import menu in the Project panel, using the Media Browser has advantages, as you will explore in this lesson.

Importing XDCAM media

You'll be using XDCAM EX 720p24 video clips for most of the lessons. This means the media is in XDCAM EX format with 720p resolution at a frame rate of 24 frames per second. Typically you would first copy the clips from the camera's flash memory card to your local hard drive before importing. This step was completed when you copied the included DVD lesson files to your hard drive in Lesson 1.

The clips are already on your hard drive. You're going to open a new Adobe Premiere Pro project and import the clips into the project.

1   After launching Adobe Premiere Pro, click New Project.

2   Name the new project *XDCAM Lesson*, and save it in the Lesson 03 folder.

3   Since you'll be importing XDCAM EX media, you need to choose the correct preset in the New Sequence dialog box. In this case, the video was shot at 1280x720 1.0 PAR at 24p. So, choose the XDCAM EX 720p24 preset, and click OK.

● **Note:** If you have problems creating the project, you can open Lesson 03.prproj in the Lesson 03 folder to start at this point.

4   Click the Media Browser tab if it is not already selected. You may also want to make the Media Browser wider by dragging the right edge of the panel to the right.

Note: The Media Browser filters out nonmedia files, making it easier to browse for video or audio assets.

5 Using the Media Browser, navigate to the Lessons/Assets folder.

6 Double-click the Medieval_villain_01.mpeg clip. It opens and plays in the Source Monitor but will not be imported into the Project panel. This feature allows you to preview the file easily before importing.

Note: If a clip's attributes do not match the sequence attributes, a red line will appear above the clip indicating it will need to render before it will preview in real time. You can render a clip by pressing Enter (Window) or Return (Mac OS) on the keyboard.

7 Right-click (or Control-click if you're a Mac user with a one-button mouse) the Medieval_villain_01.mpeg clip, and choose Import. The clip is now imported and added to the Project panel.

8 Select the other two Medieval_villain clips (Medieval_villain_02.mpeg and Medieval_villain_03.mpeg) by Shift-clicking them. Then right-click and choose Import to add them all to the Project panel.

9 Drag the three clips to the Timeline, and notice that no red render line appears when the attributes of your media match the attributes of your sequence. This means they will not need to render in order to preview them.

Importing P2 media

If you were shooting P2 video using a Panasonic P2 camera, you would remove the P2 card from the camera, connect a P2 reader to your editing workstation, and copy the video clips to your local hard drive.

P2 folder structure

A typical Panasonic P2 file structure contains a folder called CONTENTS. Within this folder are subfolders containing the *essence* (the actual audio and video media) and the metadata. The essence is split into components, each sorted into corresponding subfolders, as shown here.

- **AUDIO**: This folder contains up to 16 independent mono audio MXF files for each clip, using the video clip's filename with the channel number appended.

- **CLIP**: This folder contains clip metadata, stored as [filename].xml files.

- **ICON**: This folder contains a thumbnail icon or poster frame, stored as a BMP file.

- **PROXY**: This folder contains proxy files, stored as MP4 files and containing quarter-resolution MPEG-4 video at around 200 Kbps and one mono AAC audio track, along with a BIN file. Adobe Premiere Pro does not support these proxies.

- **VIDEO**: This folder contains video MXF files.

- **VOICE**: This folder contains voice annotations added after capture in WAV format.

This folder structure may seem overly complex, because the audio, video, metadata, and thumbnails are all in separate folders and long clips will often be split into multiple files. Adobe Premiere Pro handles this complexity very well. Using the Media Browser makes it easy to browse and select your media.

A word about P2 audio

The P2 format allows up to 16 independent mono audio files for each video clip depending on the setup and preferences set in the camera. Adobe Premiere Pro CS5 keeps track of what audio goes with what video clip and assembles them for you in the Timeline.

Importing AVCHD media

In the example you just completed, you used XDCAM EX media. AVCHD media is imported and used in a similar way. The difference comes in choosing the correct preset when starting the new sequence. The XDCAM, P2, or AVCHD folder structures may be different, but if you use the Media Browser as we recommend here, the workflow will be very similar.

Performance of AVCHD media

AVCHD media is a highly compressed format that creates a challenge when performing frame-accurate nonlinear editing. Adobe Premiere Pro CS5 is designed to handle native AVCHD media but requires a fast processor and a lot of memory to handle it efficiently. If you'll be working with high-definition video, including AVCHD, it's recommended that you scale your hardware to the high end of the Adobe hardware recommendations. You can further improve performance by using a compatible CUDA graphics card. The Mercury Playback Engine in Adobe Premiere Pro CS5 can leverage compatible CUDA cards to significantly boost performance. This is covered in more detail in Lesson 9.

Mixing media formats

It's not unusual to work on a project and end up with video clips from differ-ent cameras at different resolutions. This is no problem for Adobe Premiere Pro because you can mix clips of different frame sizes on the same Timeline. In this exercise, you'll do just that. You'll add a standard-definition video clip to the Timeline with other XDCAM EX high-definition clips.

1 Start where you left off, or open Lesson 03-01.prproj from the Lesson 03 folder.

2 Using the Media Browser, navigate to the Lessons/Assets folder.

3 Right-click the file Behind_the_scenes_SD.avi, and choose Import.

4 Drag the Behind_the_scenes_SD.avi clip to the end of the Timeline, and then play the Timeline.

Notice the SD clip is much smaller than the XDCAM EX clips. This is because the SD clip is a smaller frame size than the XDCAM clips. You can deal with this in a couple of ways. One is to enlarge the SD clip, which will make it a little soft or fuzzy. Another solution is to use the SD clip as a picture-in-picture (PIP) over an XDCAM clip. You'll try both methods in the following steps.

5 Select the Behind_the_scenes_SD.avi clip by clicking it once in the Timeline. If it's displayed too small to click, zoom into the Timeline by pressing the = key on your keyboard.

6 Drag the current-time indicator over the clip so it appears in the Program Monitor.

7 Right-click the Behind_the_scenes_SD.avi clip, and choose Scale to Frame Size. Play the Timeline to see the SD clip expanded to fill the frame.

Notice that the SD clip has a red line over it in the Timeline. This is because it has different attributes (frame size and frame rate) than the sequence. It may not play back in real time without first rendering it. So, choose sequence settings that match the majority of your source clips. You can render the Timeline by pressing Enter (Windows) or Return (Mac OS) on the keyboard.

8 Drag another copy of the Behind_the_scenes_SD.avi clip from the Project panel, and position it on top of the first XDCAM clip, in the Video 2 track. Play the Timeline, and notice the SD clip is already a picture-in-picture because of its smaller frame size.

Review questions

1 Does Adobe Premiere Pro CS5 need to convert P2, XDCAM, or AVCHD footage when it is imported?

2 What are two advantages of tapeless or file-based workflows?

3 What is one advantage of using the Media Browser to import tapeless media over the File > Import method?

4 Can different media types be added to the same sequence, or must separate sequences be created?

5 Name two of the three media types to which consumer AVCHD cameras record.

Review answers

1 No. Adobe Premiere Pro CS5 can edit P2, XDCAM, and AVCHD natively.

2 Speed (no serial capture), reliability (fewer moving parts to store the video), and flexibility (clips do not have to be captured or searched serially) are advantages of a tapeless workflow.

3 The Media Browser understands the P2 and XDCAM folder structures and shows you the clips in a friendly way.

4 Different media types can be added to the same sequence.

5 Consumer AVCHD cameras record to DVDs, hard drives, and flash memory cards.

4 SHOOTING AND CAPTURING GREAT VIDEO ASSETS

Topics covered in this lesson

- Shooting great video
- Capturing video clips
- Capturing an entire videotape
- Using batch capture and scene detection
- Capturing analog video
- Capturing HDV and other HD video

 This lesson will take approximately 45 minutes.

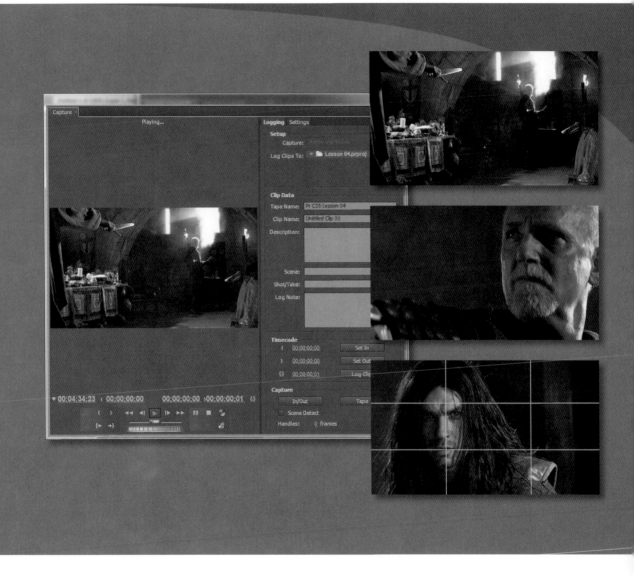

Your first task is to shoot some great-looking video. Then you'll use Adobe Premiere Pro CS5 to capture that video, meaning transfer it from your camcorder to your hard drive. Adobe Premiere Pro makes this process fast and easy.

Getting started

The purpose of this book is to help you use Adobe Premiere Pro to make professional-looking videos. To do that, you need to start with high-quality raw material. This lesson gives you tips for shooting great video and then describes how to get that video into Adobe Premiere Pro.

Tips for shooting great video

With your camcorder of choice in hand, it's time to venture out and shoot videos. If you're new to videography, following these tips will help you create better videos. If you're an old hand, think of this list of shooting axioms as a way to snap out of your routine and juice things up a bit:

- Get a closing shot.
- Get an establishing shot.
- Shoot plenty of video.
- Adhere to the rule of thirds.
- Keep your shots steady.
- Follow the action.
- Use trucking shots.
- Find unusual angles.
- Lean forward or backward.
- Get wide and tight shots.
- Shoot matched action.
- Get sequences.
- Avoid fast pans and snap zooms.
- Shoot cutaways.
- Use lights.
- Grab good sound bites.
- Get plenty of natural sound.
- Plan your shoot.

Get a closing shot

Your closing images are what stick in people's minds. You should be constantly on the lookout for that one shot or sequence that best wraps up your story.

Get an establishing shot

An establishing shot sets a scene in one image. Although super-wide shots work well (aerials in particular), consider other points of view: a shot from the cockpit of a race car, a close-up of a scalpel with light glinting off its surface, or a shot of paddles dipping frantically in roaring white water. Each grabs the viewer's attention and helps tell your story.

The establishing shot sets the scene: It's a wide shot of the villain in his medieval environment.

The close-up shot tells the story: The villain is speaking intensely to the hero.

Shoot plenty of video

Videotape is cheap and expendable, and with tapeless cameras that record to compact flash media and hard drives, storage space is usually ample and can always be reused. Shoot a lot more raw footage than you'll put in your final production. Five times as much is not unusual. Giving yourself that latitude might help you grab shots you would have missed otherwise.

Adhere to the rule of thirds

It's called the *rule of thirds*, but it's more like the rule of four intersecting lines. When composing your shot, think of your viewfinder as being crisscrossed by two horizontal and two vertical lines. The center of interest should fall along those lines or near one of the four intersections, not the center of the image.

Consider all those family photos where the subject's eyes are smack dab in the center of the photo. Those are not examples of good composition.

Another way to follow the rule of thirds is to look around the viewfinder as you shoot, not just stare at its center. Check the edges to see whether you're filling the frame with interesting images. Avoid large areas of blank space.

Keep your shots steady

You want to give viewers the sense they're looking through a window or, better yet, are there with your subjects on location. A shaky camera shatters that illusion.

When possible, use a tripod. The best "sticks" have fluid heads that enable you to make smooth pans or tilts.

If it's impractical to use a tripod, try to find some way to stabilize the shot: Lean against a wall, put your elbows on a table, or place the camcorder on a solid object.

Follow the action

This might seem obvious, but keep your viewfinder on the ball (or sprinter, speeding police car, surfer, conveyor belt, and so on). Your viewers' eyes will want to follow the action, so give them what they want.

One nifty trick is to use directed movement as a pan motivator. That is, follow a leaf's progress as it floats down a stream, and then continue your camera motion past the leaf—panning—and widen out to show something unexpected: a waterfall, a huge industrial complex, or a fisherman.

Use trucking shots

Trucking or dolly shots move with the action. For example, hold the camera at arm's length right behind a toddler as she motors around the house, put the camera in a grocery cart as it winds through the aisles, or shoot out the window of a speeding train.

Find unusual angles

Getting your camcorder off your shoulder, away from eye level, leads to more interesting and enjoyable shots. Ground-level shots are great for gamboling lambs or cavorting puppies. Shoot up from a low angle and down from a high angle. Shoot through objects or people while keeping the focus on your subject.

Lean forward or backward

The zoom lens can be a crutch. A better way to move in close or away from a subject is simply to lean in or out. For example, start by leaning way in with a tight shot of someone's hands as he works on a wood carving; then, while still recording, lean way back (perhaps widening your zoom lens as well) to reveal that he is working in a sweatshop full of folks hunched over their handiwork.

Get wide and tight shots

Our eyes work like medium-angle lenses. So, we tend to shoot video that way. Instead, grab wide shots and tight shots of your subjects. If practical, get close to your subject to get the tight shot rather than use the zoom lens. Not only does it look better, but also the proximity leads to clearer audio.

Shoot matched action

Matched action keeps the story flowing smoothly while helping illustrate a point.

Consider a shot from behind a pitcher as he throws a fastball. He releases it, and then it smacks into the catcher's glove. Instead of a single shot, grab two shots: a medium shot from behind the pitcher showing the pitch and the ball's flight toward the catcher, and a tight shot of the catcher's glove. It's the same concept for an artist: Get a wide shot of her applying a paint stroke to a canvas, and then move in for a close shot of the same action. You'll edit them together to match the action.

Get sequences

Shooting repetitive action in a sequence is another way to tell a story, build interest, or create suspense. A bowler wipes his hands on a rosin bag, dries them over a blower, wipes the ball with a towel, picks up the ball, fixes his gaze on the pins, steps forward, swings the ball back, releases it, slides to the foul line, watches the ball's trajectory, and then reacts to the shot.

Instead of simply capturing all this in one long shot, piecing these actions together in a sequence of edits is much more compelling. You can easily combine wide and tight shots, trucking moves, and matched action to turn repetitive material into attention-grabbing sequences.

Avoid fast pans and snap zooms

Fast pans and zooms fall into MTV and amateur video territory. Few circumstances call for such stomach-churning camera work. In general, it's best to minimize all pans and zooms. As with a shaky camera, they remind viewers they're watching TV.

If you do zoom or pan, do it for a purpose: to reveal something, to follow someone's gaze from his or her eyes to the subject of interest, or to continue the flow of action (as in the floating leaf example). A slow zoom in, with only a minimal change to the focal length, can add drama to a sound bite. Again, do it sparingly.

Keep on rolling along

Don't let this no-fast-moves admonition force you to stop rolling while you zoom or pan. If you see something that warrants a quick close-up shot or you need to pan suddenly to grab some possibly fleeting footage, keep rolling. You can always edit around that sudden movement later.

If you stop recording to make the pan or zoom or to adjust the focus, you might lose some or all of whatever it was you were trying so desperately to shoot. You will also miss any accompanying natural sound.

Shoot cutaways

Avoid jump cuts by shooting cutaways. A *jump cut* is an edit that creates a disconnect in the viewer's mind. A *cutaway*—literally, a shot that cuts away from the current shot—fixes jump cuts.

Cutaways are common in interviews where you might want to edit together two 10-second sound bites from the same person. Doing so would mean the interviewee would look like he or she suddenly moved. To avoid that jump cut—that sudden disconcerting shift—you make a cutaway of the interview. That could be a wide shot, a hand shot, or a reverse-angle shot of the interviewer over the interviewee's shoulder. You then edit in the cutaway over the juncture of the two sound bites to cover the jump cut.

The same holds true for a soccer game. It can be disconcerting to simply cut from one wide shot of players on the field to another. If you shoot some crowd reactions or the scoreboard, you can use those cutaways to cover up what would have been jump cuts.

Use lights

Lights add brilliance, dazzle, and depth to otherwise bland and flat scenes. Consider using an onboard camcorder fill light and—if you have the time, money, patience, or personnel—a full lighting kit with a few colored gels.

In a pinch, do whatever you can to increase available light. Open curtains, turn on all the lights, or bring a couple of desk lamps into the room. Keep in mind one caveat: Low-light situations can be dramatic, and flipping on a few desk lamps can destroy that mood in a moment.

Grab good sound bites

Your narrator presents the facts. The people in your story present the emotions, feelings, and opinions. Don't rely on interview sound bites to tell the who, what, where, when, and how. Let those bites explain the why.

In a corporate backgrounder, have the narrator say what a product does, and let the employees or customers say how enthusiastic they are about that product.

Your narrator should be the one to say, "It was opening night, and this was her first solo." Let the singer, who is recalling this dramatic moment, say, "My throat was tight, and my stomach was tied in knots."

In general, even though your interviews might take forever, use only short sound bites in your final production. Use those bites as punctuation marks, not paragraphs.

Exceptions for idiosyncratic characters

These admonitions are not carved in stone. Some characters you'll videotape are so compelling, quirky, or humorous that your best bet is to let them be the primary narrator. Then you'll want to consider what scenes you can use to illustrate their commentary. You don't want to fill your entire video with a "talking head."

Get plenty of natural sound

Think beyond images. Sound is tremendously important. Listen for sounds you can use in your project. Even if the video quality is mediocre, grab that audio.

Your camcorder's onboard microphone is not much more than a fallback. Consider using additional microphones: shotgun mics to narrow the focus of your sound and avoid extraneous noise, lavalieres tucked out of sight for interviews, and wireless mics when your camera can't be close enough to get just what you need.

Plan your shoot

When you consider a video project, plan what you need to shoot to tell the story. Whether you're videotaping your kid's soccer championship match, a corporate backgrounder, or a medical procedure, you'll need to plan your shoot to ensure success. Know what you want your final video project to say, and think of what you need to videotape to tell that story.

Even the best-laid plans and most carefully scripted projects might need some adjusting once you start recording in the field. No matter how you envision the finished project, be willing to make changes as the situation warrants.

Capturing video

Before you can edit your own video, you need to transfer it to your computer's hard drive. In Lesson 3 you learned how to transfer video from tapeless media to Adobe Premiere Pro. Tapeless media has become the most common video format. But there are still plenty of video cameras around that record to tape. This section will cover how to capture video recorded onto tape to Adobe Premiere Pro CS5.

To bring footage into an Adobe Premiere Pro project, you can either capture it or digitize it, depending on the type of source material. The most common video formats recorded onto digital tape are DV and HDV.

You *capture* digital video from a live camera or from tape to the hard disk before using it in a project. Adobe Premiere Pro captures video through a digital port, such as a FireWire or Serial Digital Interface (SDI) port installed on the computer. Adobe Premiere Pro saves captured footage to disk as files and imports the files into projects as clips.

Alternatively, you can use Adobe OnLocation to capture video. You will take a closer look at OnLocation in Lesson 18.

You *digitize* analog video from a live analog camera source or from an analog tape device. You digitize the analog video and convert it to digital form so your computer can store and process it. The capture command digitizes video when a digitizing card or device is installed in the computer. Adobe Premiere Pro saves digitized footage to disk as files and imports the files into projects as clips.

In the analog world, the capture process takes several steps: transfer, convert, compress, and wrap. Your camcorder transfers the video and audio as analog data to a video capture card. That card's built-in hardware converts the waveform signal to a digital form, compresses it using a codec (compression/decompression) process, and then typically wraps it in the AVI file format on Windows systems or in the QuickTime format for users working with Adobe Premiere Pro CS5 on the Mac.

Three DV/HDV-capturing scenarios

Adobe Premiere Pro offers tools to take some of the manual labor out of the capturing process. There are three basic approaches:

- You can capture your entire videotape as one long clip.

- You can log each clip's In and Out points for automated batch capturing.

- You can use the scene detection feature in Adobe Premiere Pro to automatically create separate clips whenever you press the Pause/Record button on your camcorder.

To do this exercise, you need a DV camcorder. Most DV camcorders have an IEEE 1394 cable that you hook up to your computer's IEEE 1394 connector. If your computer does not have an IEEE 1394 connector, it is recommended that you buy an IEEE 1394 card.

You can work with HDV or with a professional-level camcorder with an SDI connector and a specialized video capture card. Adobe Premiere Pro handles HDV and SDI capture with the same kind of software device controls used with a standard DV camcorder. SDI requires an extra setup procedure.

If you have an analog camcorder, you need a video capture card that supports S-Video or composite video connectors. The only option with most analog camcorders is to manually start and stop recording. Most analog capture cards do not work with remote device control or have timecode readout, so you can't log tapes, do batch capture, or use the scene detection feature.

● **Note:** Different manufacturers have different brand names for their IEEE 1394 cables. Apple calls this connector cable a FireWire cable while Sony calls it I.LINK.

Capturing an entire DV tape

To capture an entire tape, follow these steps:

1   Connect the camcorder to your computer.

2   Turn on your camcorder, and set it to playback mode: VTR or VCR. Do not set it to camera mode.

● **Note:** Windows might note that you've powered up your camcorder by displaying a Digital Video Device connection message. Mac OS may start a default associated application, such as iMovie.

Use AC, not a battery

When capturing video, power your camcorder from its AC adapter, not its battery. Here's why: When using a battery, camcorders can go into sleep mode, and the battery will often run out before you're done.

3 In Windows, an AutoPlay dialog may pop up. Click "View more AutoPlay options in Control Panel." Set the option to "Take no action." (The next time you fire up your camcorder, you should not see this connection query.) In Mac OS, if iMovie or another application starts up, see that application's Help for information about which application to open when a camera is connected.

4 Start Adobe Premiere Pro, click Open Project, navigate to the Lesson 04 folder, and double-click Lesson 04-01.prproj.

5 Choose File > Capture to open the Capture panel.

6 Look above the Capture panel preview pane to make sure your camcorder is connected properly.

7 Insert a tape into your camcorder. Adobe Premiere Pro prompts you to give the tape a name.

8 Type a name for your tape in the text box. Be sure not to give two tapes the same name; Adobe Premiere Pro remembers clip in/out data based on tape names.

9 Use the VCR-style device controls in the Capture panel to play, fast-forward, rewind, pause, and stop your tape. If you've never used a computer to control a camcorder, this will seem pretty cool.

Note: If you get a No Device Control or Capture Device Offline message, you'll need to do some troubleshooting. The most obvious fix is to make sure the camcorder is turned on and the cables are connected. For more troubleshooting tips, refer to the Adobe Community Help website.

A. Next Scene **B.** Set In Point **C.** Set Out Point **D.** Rewind **E.** Step Back **F.** Play
G. Step Forward **H.** Fast Forward **I.** Pause **J.** Stop **K.** Record **L.** Previous Scene
M. Go To In Point **N.** Go To Out Point **O.** Jog **P.** Shuttle **Q.** Slow Reverse
R. Slow Play **S.** Scene Detect

10 Try some of the other VCR-style buttons:

- Shuttle (the slider toward the bottom) enables you to move slowly or zip quickly—depending on how far you move the slider off-center—forward or backward through your tape.

- Single-frame Jog control (below the Shuttle slider)

- Step Forward and Step Back, one frame at a time

- Slow Reverse and Slow Play

11 Rewind the tape to its beginning or to wherever you want to start recording.

12 In the Setup area of the Logging tab, note that Audio and Video is the default setting. If you want to capture only audio or only video, change that setting.

Note: To help you identify these buttons, move the pointer over them to see tool tips.

Note: DV is the only format that allows you to select Audio only or Video only. When capturing HDV video, this drop-down box will be unavailable.

13 Click the Tape button in the Capture area of the Logging tab or the Record button in the Capture panel to start recording.

You'll see (and hear) the video in the Capture panel and on your camcorder. Since there is a slight delay during capture, you'll hear what sounds like an echo. Feel free to turn down the speaker on either your camcorder or your computer.

14 Click the red Record button or the black Stop button when you want to stop recording.

The Save Captured Clip dialog appears.

15 Give your clip a name (add descriptive information if you want), and click OK.

Adobe Premiere Pro stores all the clips you capture during this lesson in the Lesson 04 folder on your hard drive. You can change the default location by choosing Project > Project Settings > Scratch Disks.

Using batch capture and scene detection

When you perform a batch capture, you log the In and Out points of a number of clips and then have Adobe Premiere Pro automatically transfer them to your computer.

Use the logging process to critically view your raw footage. You want to look for "keeper" video, the best interview sound bites, and any natural sound that will enhance your production.

The purpose of using a batch capture is threefold: to better manage your media assets, to speed up the video capture process, and to save hard disk space (one hour of DV consumes roughly 13 GB). If you batch capture all your clips, you can use the combination of the Adobe Premiere Pro project file (which is relatively small) and the MiniDV tapes as a backup of your project. To reedit the project, simply open the project file and recapture the clips.

Use a clip-naming convention

Think through how you're going to name your clips. You might end up with dozens of clips, and if you don't give them descriptive names, it'll slow down editing.

You might use a naming convention for sound bites such as Bite-1, Bite-2, and so forth. Adding a brief descriptive comment, such as "Bite-1 Laugh," will help.

Here are the steps to follow:

1   In the Capture panel, click the Logging tab.

2   Change the Handles setting (at the bottom of the Logging tab) to 30 frames.

This adds one second to the start and finish of each captured clip, which will give you enough head and tail frames to add transitions without covering up important elements of the clip.

3   In the Clip Data area of the Logging tab, give your tape a unique name.

4   Log your tape by rewinding and then playing it.

5   When you see the start of a segment you want to transfer to your computer, stop the tape, rewind to that spot, and click the Set In button in the Timecode area of the Logging tab.

6   When you get to the end of that segment (you can use Fast Forward or simply Play to get there), click Set Out. The in/out times and the clip length will appear.

Three other ways to set In and Out points

You can use other means to set In points and Out points for selected clips: Click the brackets ({ or }) on the play controls, use the keyboard shortcuts (I for In and O for Out), or change the in/out time directly in the Timecode area by dragging left or right over the timecode.

7 Click Log Clip to open the Log Clip dialog.

8 Change the clip name, if needed, and add appropriate notes if you want; then click OK.

That adds this clip's name with its in/out times and tape name information to the Project panel (with "Offline" next to it). You'll go there later to do the actual capture.

9 Log clips for the rest of your tape using the same method.

Each time you click Log Clip, Adobe Premiere Pro automatically adds a number to the end of your previous clip's name. You can accept or override this automated naming feature.

10 When you've finished logging your clips, close the Capture panel.

All your logged clips will be in the Project panel, with the offline icon next to each.

11 In the Project panel, select all the clips you want to capture (see the following sidebar for three methods of doing that).

Three ways to select more than one item

There are usually three ways to select more than one file in a window. First, if the filenames are contiguous, click the top one, and then Shift-click the last one in the group. Second, you can click off to one side and above the top clip and then drag down to the last one to marquee-select a group. (The marquee-select method—creating the gray rectangle—was used in the previous figure.) Finally, if the filenames are scattered, click one first, and then Ctrl-click (Windows) or Command-click (Mac OS) each additional file in turn.

12 Choose File > Batch Capture.

A very simple Batch Capture dialog opens, allowing you to override the camcorder settings or add more handle frames.

13 Leave the Batch Capture options unselected, and click OK.

The Capture panel opens, as does another little dialog telling you to insert the proper tape (in this case, it's probably still in the camcorder).

● **Note:** Handles are extra frames at the beginning and end of a clip. For example, adding 30 frames as handles would add one second of video to the start and end of your clips. This can be useful for transitions.

14 Insert the tape, and click OK.

Adobe Premiere Pro now takes control of your camcorder, cues up the tape to the first clip, and transfers that clip and all other clips to your hard drive.

15 When the process is complete, take a look at your Project panel to see the results. The offline icon is now a movie icon, and your footage is ready to be edited.

Use scene detection

Instead of manually logging In and Out points, you might want to use the scene detection feature. Scene detection analyzes your tape's time/date stamp, looking for breaks such as those caused when you press the camcorder's Pause/Record button while recording.

When scene detection is on and you perform a capture, Adobe Premiere Pro automatically captures a separate file at each scene break it detects. Scene detection works whether you are capturing an entire tape or just a section between specific In and Out points.

To turn on scene detection, do either of the following:

• Click the Scene Detect button (below the Record button in the Capture panel).

• Select the Scene Detect option in the Capture area of the Logging tab.

Then you can either set In and Out points and click Record or cue your tape to wherever you want to start capturing and click Record. In the latter case, click Stop when done.

Your clips will show up in the Project panel. You don't need to batch capture them—Adobe Premiere Pro captures each clip on the fly. Adobe Premiere Pro then names the first captured clip by putting a "01" after the name you put in the Clip Name box and increments the number in each new clip name by one.

Tackling manual analog movie capture

If you need to transfer analog video—consumer-level VHS, SVHS, Hi-8, or professional-grade video such as Beta SP—you need a video capture card with analog inputs. Most analog capture cards have consumer-quality composite connectors as well as S-Video and sometimes top-of-the-line component connections.

Check your card's documentation for setup and compatibility issues.

With analog video, you have only one capture option: to do it manually.

1 Open the Capture panel (File > Capture).

2 Use the controls on the camcorder to move the videotape to a point several seconds before the frame you want to begin capturing.

3 Press the Play button on the camcorder, and then click the red Record button in the Capture panel.

4 When your clip has been captured, click the Stop button in the Capture panel and on the camcorder. Your clip will show up in the Project panel.

Capturing HDV and HD video

Note: HDV video is not displayed in the Capture panel while the video is being captured.

You can capture HDV video in the same way as DV video: by connecting the HDV camcorder or deck to your computer via IEEE 1394. When you start a new HDV project, select the appropriate HDV project preset, and capture as described for DV video.

HD video requires an SDI card in your computer to connect the coaxial interface from the HD camcorder to your computer. The vendor that supplies the SDI card will typically install additional HD presets into Adobe Premiere Pro as part of its installation.

Review questions

1 Why are cutaway shots so useful?

2 What should you check if you see "Capture Device Offline" at the top of the Capture panel?

3 What does scene detection do when selected?

4 What is one benefit of using batch capture rather than manual capture?

5 During the capture process, how do you add extra frames to ensure you have enough footage for transitions?

6 Is the actual media captured to your hard disk during a batch capture?

Review answers

1 Cutaway shots of a crowd, faces, or landscapes are often useful for covering up a bad shot or providing a pleasant transition to another scene.

2 Check that your camcorder or deck is connected to the computer and that it is turned on and in VCR mode.

3 Enabling scene detection causes clips to be automatically logged at each point where the camcorder was stopped or paused.

4 If you batch capture all your clips, it is possible to save your Adobe Premiere Pro project file (which is relatively small), store your DV tapes, and be able to recapture the project easily if you ever need to reedit. This is a very efficient means of backup.

5 Type a number of frames in the Handles option in the Capture area of the Logging tab.

6 Only information about the clip, such as the tape name and In and Out points, is captured when creating the batch list. The clip will be displayed as "Offline" in the Project panel. The media is captured when you go to the Project panel and perform the batch capture of offline files.

5 CREATING CUTS-ONLY VIDEOS

Topics covered in this lesson

- Using a storyboard to build a rough cut
- Editing clips on the Timeline
- Moving clips to, from, and within the Timeline
- Working with Source Monitor editing tools
- Adjusting clips in the Trim panel
- Using other editing tools

 This lesson will take approximately 80 minutes.

Watch any TV news program, and virtually every
edit is a straight cut with no transitions. There's
an art to creating cuts-only videos, and Adobe
Premiere Pro CS5 gives you a full palette of tools
and techniques for creating cut edits.

Getting started

The first thing you do when you're creating a video is to lay down a cuts-only version. Later, you can apply transitions, effects, titles, and motion, as well as work on compositing. Whether or not you use these extra effects, building a cuts-only video is an art. You want to create a logical flow to your clips, make matching edits, and avoid jump cuts.

Adobe Premiere Pro offers several ways of achieving those ends. Depending on your circumstances, you might work in the Trim panel, use the Ripple Edit tool, or move clips on the Timeline using the Source Monitor or keyboard modifiers. You'll use all these techniques in this lesson.

Using a storyboard to build a rough cut

Film directors and animators frequently use walls of photos and sketches to visualize story flow and camera angles. These are known as *storyboards*, and they can be very useful in planning a project and making sure you get the shots or material you need.

Storyboards also help after the shoot ends. In the case of Adobe Premiere Pro, you can arrange clip thumbnails in the Project panel to get a basic feel for how your finished video will work. Then you can move all those clips to the Timeline for more precise editing.

This approach is useful in revealing gaps in your story. It's also a way to note redundancy and to quickly place a whole bunch of ordered clips on a sequence. When you're confronted with a Project panel loaded with clips, storyboards can help you see the big picture.

After creating your storyboard, you can place several clips in a sequence on the Timeline at one time. To begin, do the following:

● **Note:** As in most of the lessons in this book, you'll be using an XDCAM EX 720p sequence preset.

1 Open Adobe Premiere Pro.

2 Choose File > Open Project, navigate to the Lesson 05 folder, and double-click Lesson 05-01.prproj.

3 Notice that Lesson 05-01 has the clips you will be working with already imported into the Project panel.

4 Click the New Bin button in the Project panel, and name your new bin *Storyboard*.

5 Double-click the new Storyboard bin icon to open it in its own window. This makes it easy to move assets into this bin.

6 In the main bin, select the seven assets (do not select Sequence 01).

7 Right-click (Windows) or Control-click (Mac OS) one of the selected clips to open the context menu, and choose Copy. Note that you need to click the clip name, or you will deselect all the clips.

8 Select the Storyboard bin to make it the active window, and choose Edit > Paste.

Tip: Choosing Copy when you've highlighted multiple clips will copy the entire collection of clips.

All seven files now appear in the Storyboard bin. They remain in the main Project panel as well, because you copied them rather than dragged them.

9 Click the Icon View button in the Storyboard bin to switch to Icon view.

Note: When you copy clips from one bin to another, Adobe Premiere Pro does not make copies of the original files. Objects in the bins are just pointers to the actual files on your hard drive.

10 Click the panel menu icon, and then choose Thumbnails > Large.

11 Resize the Storyboard bin so you can see all the thumbnails.

Icon view

Arranging your project bin in Icon view allows you to view your clips in a story-board format. This is one way to start thinking about what clips you have and how you may arrange them to tell a story.

Arranging your storyboard

In this section, you'll learn how to arrange thumbnails into a logical order. Keep in mind that you will trim the clips later to make the edits work more smoothly.

In turn, view each clip in the Preview Monitor by clicking the clip to select it and then clicking the Play button in the preview area.

After viewing the clips, decide in what order you want them to run in your project.

Here's how to create the sequence after you've decided the order in which the clips should run:

● **Note:** Some of the videos are a little dark and can be hard to view critically in the Project panel's preview area. In those cases, double-click a clip to view it in the Source Monitor.

1   Continue where you left off in the previous section, or load Lesson 05-02.prproj from the Lesson 05 folder.

2   Drag the thumbnails within the Storyboard bin to position them in the order you want them to play.

To move a clip, simply drag it to a new location. The pointer changes, and a black vertical line indicates the new location for placement.

Automating your storyboard to a sequence

Now you're going to move your storyboard clips to the Timeline, placing them there contiguously, in sequential order. Adobe Premiere Pro calls this process *Automate to Sequence*. Here's how you do it:

1   Make sure the current-time indicator is at the beginning of the Timeline. Automate to Sequence places the clips starting at the current-time indicator location.

2   With the Storyboard bin window active, choose Edit > Select All to highlight all the clips. You can also marquee-select or use the Shift-click, Ctrl-click (Windows), or Command-click (Mac OS) method.

3   Click the Automate to Sequence button in the lower-left corner of the Project panel.

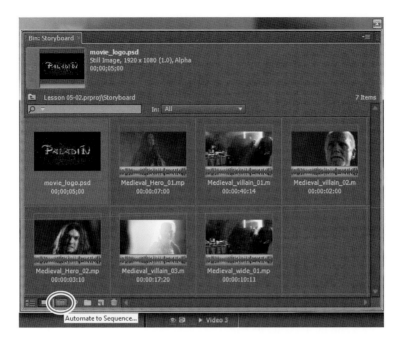

Note: You can also choose Automate to Sequence from the panel menu.

4 The newly opened Automate To Sequence dialog has several options. Choose the settings shown in the following image. The options include:

- **Ordering**: Sort Order puts clips on a sequence in the order you established in the storyboard. Selection Order places them in the order you selected them if you Ctrl-clicked (Windows) or Command-clicked (Mac OS) individual clips.

- **Placement**: This places clips sequentially on the Timeline.

- **Method**: The choices here are Insert Edit and Overlay Edit, both of which will be discussed later in this lesson. Because in this instance you are placing the clips on an empty sequence, both methods will do the same thing.

- **Clip Overlap**: Overlap presumes you'll put a transition such as a cross-dissolve between all clips. The goal in this lesson is to create a cuts-only video—that is, a video with no transitions—so set Clip Overlap to 0.

- **Transitions**: Because you'll opt for no transitions, make sure these two options (Apply Default Audio Transition and Apply Default Video Transition) are deselected.

- **Ignore Options**: Select the Ignore Audio check box to exclude the audio portion of the selected clips.

5   Click OK. This places your clips in the order you selected in Sequence 01.

6   Drag the Project panel out of the way. Click inside the Timeline to activate it, and press the spacebar to play your sequence.

● **Note:** If you have only one clip on the Timeline after this step, you may have missed step 2, in which we selected all clips in the bin.

View this sequence critically. Several edits are jump cuts or feel awkward. Some clips are too long. The next task is to fix those flaws.

Editing clips on the Timeline

You'll use a variety of editing tools to improve this storyboard rough cut, including the following:

- You'll trim a clip by dragging its end.

- You'll use the Ripple Delete command to remove a gap between clips.

- You'll use the Ripple Edit tool to save a step when you lengthen or shorten a clip.

Trimming a clip

To trim a clip, follow these steps:

1   Open Lesson 05-03.prproj from the Lesson 05 folder. The clips in this project may be in a different order than the order you selected. That's OK because you're going to edit the clips into a short movie that has some kind of plot.

2   Notice the Timeline now has two sequences, Sequence 01 and Completed. You may have as many sequences in a project as you like. An audio folder has also been added to the Project panel full of narration, music, and sound effects. Click the Completed sequence tab, and play the completed project.

● **Note:** To fully appreciate the cuts-only sequence, we've added the audio for you. The audio tracks are locked in this lesson to prevent you from accidentally moving or deleting the audio from the sequence. We'll focus on audio in a future lesson.

The video in the Completed sequence is the final cuts-only video you will make using the edit tools available in Adobe Premiere Pro. It's amazing how some well-timed cuts can transform your footage from a bunch of confusing clips into a short movie with a plot.

3   Practice zooming in and out of the Timeline by pressing the equal sign (=) to zoom in and the minus sign (-) to zoom out. Press the backslash (\) to make the entire sequence fit on the screen.

4 Click the Sequence 01 tab to switch to Sequence 01. You'll start editing this rough sequence so it looks like the Completed sequence. The first clip in the sequence is the title clip, which is the length you want here, so leave it as is.

5 Hover the pointer over the left edge of the second clip (Medieval_Hero_01. mpeg) until you see the right-facing Trim bracket.

● **Note:** As you move your pointer, you might notice that it changes into the Pen Keyframe tool. That happens when you hover the pointer over the thin yellow Opacity line. You'll work with the Opacity effect in upcoming lessons on compositing.

6 Drag the bracket to the right a couple seconds after the movie clapboard. Use the timecode in the Program Monitor display for reference. Drag the left edge to the right to +00:00:12:16.

This trim edit leaves a gap between the two clips on the Timeline. You'll remove this gap later.

● **Note:** Editing the length of this clip on the Timeline does not delete the video to the left. It's still there, just edited from the Timeline.

7 Release the mouse button. This will remove the extra footage from the beginning of the clip.

8 Now there is a long gap between the first clip and the second clip you just trimmed. Right-click (Windows) or Control-click (Mac OS) that empty gap, and choose Ripple Delete. All the clips that are downstream move to the left to fill the gap.

The second clip is still too long. You want only about one second of it to play.

9 Using the Edit tool, grab the right edge of the second clip on the Timeline, and drag it to the left until the duration in the Program Monitor reads 00:00:01:20, as shown here.

10 Now there is a long gap between the second clip and the third clip. Right-click (Windows) or Control-click (Mac OS) in that empty gap, and choose Ripple Delete. All the clips that are downstream move to the left to fill the gap.

Step further back using History

When working on most editing projects in Adobe Premiere Pro, you'll make multiple edits and, inevitably, a few mistakes. You can back up one step at a time by pressing Ctrl-Z (Windows) or Command-Z (Mac OS) or by choosing Edit > Undo. You can also use the History panel to move back several steps at once.

Frame-specific editing with Snap

Adobe Premiere Pro has a tremendously useful feature called Snap. It's a default setting, and in only a few instances will you want to turn it off. With Snap turned on, as you drag a clip toward another clip, the clip will jump to the edge of the adjacent clip to make a clean, unbroken edit. With Snap turned off, you'd have to slide the new clip very carefully next to the other clip to ensure there is no gap.

Snap is also useful when making precise edits. Using the Selection tool to trim a clip can be a bit clumsy, as you might have noted in step 6 in this section. Snap allows you to trim to the current-time indicator easily.

Locate the frame you want to trim by dragging the current-time indicator through your sequence to that frame's location (use the right arrow and left arrow keys to move to the specific frame). Use the Selection tool to drag the edge of the clip toward the current-time indicator line. When it gets near the line, it will snap to the current-time indicator, and you'll have made a frame-specific edit. You can use this technique in all sorts of circumstances.

If you want to toggle the Snap feature off or on, click the Snap button in the top-left corner of the Timeline (shown here), or use the S keyboard shortcut.

Using the Ripple Edit tool

A way to avoid creating gaps in the first place is to use the Ripple Edit tool. It's one of the many tools in the Tools panel.

Use the Ripple Edit tool to trim a clip in the same way you used the Selection tool in Trim mode. The two differences are that the Ripple Edit tool does not leave a gap on the sequence and that the display in the Program Monitor gives a clearer representation of how the edit will work.

When you use the Ripple Edit tool to lengthen or shorten a clip, your action ripples through the sequence. That is, all clips after that edit slide to the left to fill the gap or slide to the right to accommodate a longer clip.

You need to trim a lot of footage off the beginning and end of the third clip, but this time you'll use the Ripple Edit tool so no space is left behind:

1 Open Lesson 05-04.prproj to ensure you are starting at the same point.

2 Click the Ripple Edit tool (or press B on your keyboard).

3 Hover the Ripple Edit tool over the left edge of the third clip (Medieval_wide_01.mpeg) until it turns into a large, right-facing square bracket.

4 Drag to the right until the timecode reads +00:00:20:06, as shown here.

Notice that when you're using the Ripple Edit tool, the Program Monitor displays the last frame of the first clip on the left and the first frame of the second clip on the right. Watch the moving edit position on the left half of the Program Monitor.

5 Release the mouse button to complete the edit. The remaining part of the clip moves left to fill the gap, and the clips to its right slide along with it. Play that portion of the sequence to see whether the edit works smoothly.

6 You still need to trim the end of this clip because it needs to be exactly one second long. Use the Ripple Edit tool to grab the right side of the clip, and drag it to the left until its duration reads 00:00:01:00. Notice how the clips to the right (downstream) ripple to close the gap when you release the mouse button.

Note: The Ripple Edit icon looks very similar to the Trim pointer icon, but it's larger and a bit bolder.

Note: Make sure the current time indicator is out of the way so the clip doesn't snap to it before the appropriate edit is made.

At this point, your project should look just like the Completed sequence for the first seven seconds. You have several more edits to make to the rest of the sequence.

Moving clips to, from, and within the Timeline

One of the beauties of Adobe Premiere Pro is how easy it is to add clips anywhere in the project, move them around, and remove them altogether.

You can place a clip in the Timeline in two ways: by dragging it from the Project panel or by dragging it from another location in the Timeline. In the next exercise, you will move the yellow clip to the Video 1 track in two different ways:

- **Overlay:** The newly placed clip and its audio (if applicable) replace what was in the sequence at the point in the Timeline at which the clip is placed.

- **Insert:** The first frame of the newly placed clip cuts the current clip and, without covering up anything, slides the cut segment and all clips after it to the right. This process requires using a keyboard modifier—in this case, the Ctrl (Windows) or Command (Mac OS) key.

You can move a clip from a location in the Timeline in two ways:

- **Lift**: This leaves a gap where the clip used to be.

- **Extract**: This works like using the Ripple Edit tool in that other clips move over to fill the gap. This move also requires a keyboard modifier—holding down Ctrl (Windows) or Command (Mac OS) before clicking the clip to be removed.

Open the Lesson 05-colors project in the Lesson 05 folder to load the color clips shown in these figures. Use this sequence to practice each of these different edits. The colored clips make it easy to see exactly how each edit works.

Using the current-time indicator to establish the edit point

Now you need to edit the rest of the sequence to make it look and sound like the Completed sequence.

One method of establishing an edit point is to scrub the Timeline with the current-time indicator to find the point where you want to trim your clip. The current-time indicator can then act like a snap point to make the edit point easy to find.

1 To begin, open Lesson 05-05.prproj to make sure you are starting from the same point as this portion of the lesson. At this stage, the first three clips on Sequence 01 are trimmed the way you want. You need to work on the fourth clip (Medieval_villain_02.mpeg).

2 Scrub the current-time indicator over the clip to find the point just before the actor starts to slowly turn his head toward the camera. This should be at timecode 00:00:16:22. Leave the current-time indicator sitting at this point.

3 Grab the Ripple Edit tool, and drag the left edge of the clip to the right until it meets the current-time indicator. The Ripple Edit tool snaps to the current-time indicator, making it easy to set the edit at the correct spot.

This clip is still too long, and you have a couple additional clips to trim before Sequence 01 is done. You'll look at some other techniques for finishing it.

Adding clips to the Timeline with the Source Monitor

So far all the clips you've been editing have already been on the Timeline. It's possible to add clips to the Timeline and trim them at the same time. In this exercise, you'll perform an overlay edit that you practiced earlier with the color clips.

1 Continue where you left off, or open Lesson 05-06.prproj if you'd like to start fresh from here.

● **Note:** You also can drag the clip from the Project panel and drop it on the Source Monitor.

2 The next clip you are going to edit is Medieval_Hero_01.mpeg. Open it from the Storyboard bin in the Project panel by double-clicking it. This will open the clip in the Source Monitor where you can preview it and trim it.

3 Scrub the clip in the Source Monitor by dragging the Source Monitor current-time indicator back and forth. Also experiment with using the Source Monitor controls to move the current-time indicator in different increments. Set the Source Monitor current-time indicator to timecode 00:00:21:05.

4   You can trim the beginning of this clip right in the Source Monitor by setting
    the In point. With the Source Monitor current-time indicator at 00:00:21:05,
    click the Set In Point icon.

You want to drag this clip down over the top of the third clip, which is way too
long. First you need to identify where you want to drop it.

5   On the Timeline, scrub the current-time indicator so that it is at timecode
    00:00:11:03.

You'll be using the current-time indicator as a snap point again so you know
where to drop the new clip.

6   In the Source Monitor panel, grab the Drag Video icon, and drag it down to
    Video 1 track so that the new clip is overtop (or overlaying) the fourth clip,
    making sure the left edge of the clip you are dropping is snapped against the
    Timeline current-time indicator. Release the mouse button to overlay this new
    clip in the exact location you need it.

7   Play the Timeline to see how the clips flow and how close you are to finishing
    this sequence.

Modifier-key feedback

As you drag a clip from the Project panel to a sequence or from one place on a
sequence track to another, Adobe Premiere Pro displays a text message at the bottom of the user interface reminding you of the modifier-key options.

Working with Source Monitor editing tools

At the beginning of this lesson, you assembled clips on the Timeline by creating a storyboard and then automating the storyboard to the Timeline. You also practiced dragging clips from a bin directly to the Timeline. Both of these methods (or *work-flows*) are valid.

Now you'll look at one of the most common workflows for assembling clips onto the Timeline. It may seem awkward at first, but if you practice this method, you may find it to be the fastest, most efficient way to edit. It's helpful to trim clips before moving them from the Project panel to the Timeline. You just trimmed the In point of a clip and dragged it to the Timeline with the pointer. In this exercise, you'll set the In and Out points (trim the beginning and the end) of a clip and use the keyboard to send the clips to the Timeline.

1   Open Lesson 05-07.prproj.

    You need to trim the end of clip you just added to the Timeline.

2   Double-click the Medieval_Hero_01.mpeg clip you just added to the Timeline. In this case, double-click the clip in the Timeline, not the clip in the Project panel. This loads the clip from the Timeline into the Source Monitor.

3   Scrub the current-time indicator in the Source Monitor to timecode 00:00:25:21, and then click the Set Out Point icon (or use the keyboard shortcut 0). The Timeline is reduced to the length you set in the Source Monitor.

4   Delete the two clips on the Timeline to the right of the clip you just set. You're going to add the rest of the clips via the Source Monitor method.

5   Click the Timeline current-time indicator anywhere along the Timeline, and press Page Up or Page Down on your keyboard.

    The current-time indicator jumps to the next or previous edit point.

6   Press Page Up or Page Down until the current-time indicator is at the last edit point, which should be at timecode 00:00:15:20.

7   Double-click Medieval_wide_01.mpeg in the Storyboard bin in the Project panel to load that clip into the Source Monitor.

8   In the Source Monitor, type 00:00:26:21 in the timecode field, and click the Set In Point icon. Type 00:00:27:21 in the timecode field, and click the Set Out Point icon.

    You've just trimmed the clip to be one-second long at precisely the right location. Now you'll add it to the Timeline using the keyboard.

9   Make sure the Video 1 track is selected on the Timeline.

10 Click the Overlay icon on the Source Monitor. This sends the trimmed clip to the Timeline at the position of the current-time indicator.

● **Note:** When you perform an overlay edit like this, the current-time indicator automatically moves to the end of the new clip. It's set in the correct location to receive the next clip. Be careful not to move the current-time indicator to a different location; this is what determines where the new clip will be inserted on the Timeline.

More practice

This is the fastest way to edit. You can practice it some more with the rest of the clips; you have three more clips to add to the Timeline to finish this edit:

- **Seventh clip name**: Medieval_Hero_02.mpeg. In point: 00:00:31:18. Out point: 00:00:36:03.

- **Eighth clip name**: Medieval_villain_01.mpeg. In point: 00:00:30:20. Out point: 00:00:35:23.

- **Ninth clip name**: Medieval_villain_03.mpeg. In point: 00:00:43:17. Out point: 00:00:49:16.

The edit will go very fast using the method you just learned. Use this procedure for each clip:

1 Load the clip into the Source Monitor by double-clicking it on the Project panel.

2 Set the In and Out points, and then click the Overlay icon (or press the period key, which is the keyboard shortcut).

3 Repeat for the next clip.

The more you practice this method, the more natural it will be. Practice using keyboard shortcuts for setting In and Out points and sending them to the Timeline (insert or overlay), and you'll get faster and faster at editing. This is the preferred workflow for many professional editors.

▶ **Tip:** The keyboard shortcut to set the In point is the I key. The keyboard shortcut to set the Out point is the O key. The keyboard shortcut to send the trimmed clip to the Timeline in an overlay is the period (.) key; the keyboard shortcut to send the trimmed clip to the Timeline as an insert is the comma (,) key.

Adjusting clips in the Trim panel

The Trim panel is a useful tool. Its value is its large preview monitors, precise controls, and informative timecode displays. You will find that the editing tool icon changes automatically depending on its position in the panel.

Rolling-edit and ripple-edit behaviors

You apply the Ripple Edit tool to only one clip. It changes the length of your project, because the rest of the project slides over to accommodate the change. A rolling edit does not change the length of your project. It takes place at an edit point between two clips, shortening one and lengthening the other. It edits two adjacent clips at the same time.

1 Continue with the Lesson 05-07.prproj project.

2 Place the current-time indicator at the edit point between the last two clips in Sequence 01.

3 Choose Window > Trim Monitor (or press the T keyboard shortcut).

The Trim Monitor opens.

4 Hover the pointer over the left preview screen until it turns into a left-facing Ripple Edit pointer.

5 Trim the right edge of clip (the Out point) by dragging it left to about one second (watch the Out Shift timecode below the center of the left preview screen).

6 Use the same method to trim the right clip's In point to the right to about one second (use the In Shift timecode beneath the center of the right preview screen).

7 Click the precision trimming tools—the –1 and +1 numbers—to trim or lengthen the clips one frame at a time until you have the exact edit point you want.

Trim Monitor editing tools

Click in the left or right preview screen to make it active so that the precision trimming tools apply to it. You can tell which preview screen is active by the thin blue line beneath it.

8 Click the Play Edit button in the Trim Monitor to review your work.

9 Hover the pointer between the two preview screens. It turns into the Rolling Edit tool.

10 Drag the Rolling Edit tool left and right to change the Out and In points of the left and right clips, respectively. Notice how both clips move and the clips are in sync.

11 Close the Trim panel by clicking the Close button in its upper-right corner.

Using other editing tools

The Tools panel appears by default in the upper-left corner of the Adobe Premiere Pro workspace. As with any other panel, you can dock it or make it its own floating window. Generally, editors like to keep the tools near the Timeline, because that is where they're used most often.

Here's a brief rundown of the Tools panel's editing tools (the keyboard shortcut letters are shown in parentheses):

- **Selection (V)**: This is a multipurpose, all-around aid. You use it frequently to drag, drop, select, and trim clips.

- **Track Select (A)**: Not to be confused with the Selection tool, the Track Select tool enables you to select all clips to the right of wherever you position it on a video or audio track. You can Shift-click to select other tracks. After you've selected them, you can slide them, delete them, cut/paste them, or copy/paste them.

- **Ripple Edit (B)**: You've worked with this many times already. A ripple edit trims a clip and shifts subsequent clips in the track by the amount you trimmed.

- **Rolling Edit (N)**: A rolling edit trims adjacent Out and In points simultaneously and by the same number of frames. This effectively moves the edit point between clips, preserving other clips' positions in time and maintaining the total duration of the sequence. You did this in the Trim panel in a previous exercise in this lesson.

- **Rate Stretch (X):** You can stretch or shrink a clip, putting it in slow motion or speeding up the action.

- **Razor (C):** The Razor slices a clip in two. It can be useful when you want to use different effects that can't both be applied to a single clip.

- **Slip (Y):** By dragging with the Slip tool, you can change a clip's starting and ending frames without changing its duration or affecting adjacent clips.

- **Slide (U):** A slide edit shifts a clip along the Timeline while trimming adjacent clips to compensate for the move. As you drag a clip left or right with the Slide tool, the Out point of the preceding clip and the In point of the following clip are trimmed by the number of frames you move the clip. The clip's In and Out points (and, hence, its duration) remain unchanged. We'll cover the Slide tool, along with the Slip tool, in Lesson 9.

- **Pen (P):** Use the Pen tool to add, select, move, delete, or adjust keyframes on a sequence as well as create and adjust curves in the Titler, Effect Controls panel, and Program Monitor. You use the keyframes to change audio volume levels and panning, alter clip opacity, and change video and audio effects over time.

- **Hand (H):** Use the Hand tool to scroll an entire sequence by grabbing a clip and sliding it and the rest of the sequence to one side. It works the same as moving the scroll bar at the bottom of the Timeline.

- **Zoom (Z):** This works like the Zoom In and Zoom Out buttons in the lower-left corner of the Timeline and the viewing area bar at the top of the sequence above the time ruler. The default is Zoom In. Hold down Alt (Windows) or Option (Mac OS) to change that to Zoom Out. When you want to expand the view of a set of clips in the sequence, drag the Zoom tool around those clips.

Review questions

1 How can storyboards help you create your project?

2 What is the difference between a trim and a ripple edit?

3 What effect does holding the Ctrl key (Windows) or Command key (Mac OS) have when dragging a clip to an edit point?

4 How do you move a clip from one position on a sequence to another without covering up other clips and at the same time automatically filling the gap left by the removed clip?

5 What is the keyboard shortcut to set the In and Out points of a clip in the Source Monitor?

6 What can you accomplish using the Trim panel's Rolling Edit tool?

Review answers

1 Storyboards can give you an overall feel for the flow of your project, reveal gaps, help you weed out weaker shots, and avoid redundancy.

2 Trims leave gaps where the trimmed video used to be (or, if you lengthen a clip using the Trim tool, they cover that portion of the next clip). Ripple edits automatically fill gaps by sliding the clips following the edit to the left (filling the space left by the edit) or to the right (to compensate for a lengthened clip).

3 It changes the edit from an overlay to an insert edit.

4 Hold down Ctrl (Windows) or Command (Mac OS) as you extract the clip, and hold down Ctrl (Windows) or Command (Mac OS) again as you place the clip in its new position.

5 I is the shortcut for an In point, and O is the shortcut for an Out point.

6 Once you find a matching edit between two clips, you can fine-tune that edit using the Rolling Edit tool. It'll help you find just the right place to make a seamless edit.

6 ADDING VIDEO TRANSITIONS

Topics covered in this lesson

- Using transitions with restraint
- Trying some transitions
- Changing parameters in the Effect Controls panel
- Fine-tuning transitions
- Applying transitions to multiple clips at once
- Using audio transitions

 This lesson will take approximately 60 minutes.

Transitions can make a video move more smoothly or snap the audience to attention. Adobe Premiere Pro CS5 has nearly 80 transitions that are easy to use and customize. Fun stuff—but try to use restraint.

Getting started

Bridging your clips with transitions—dissolves, page wipes, spinning screens, and the like—is a nice way to ease viewers from one scene to the next or to grab their attention.

Adding transitions to your project is an art, though. Applying them starts simply enough; it's a mere drag-and-drop process. The art comes in their placement, length, and parameters, such as colored borders, motion, and start/end locations.

Most transition work takes place in the Effect Controls panel. In addition to the various options unique to each transition, that panel displays an *A/B timeline*. This feature makes it easy to move transitions relative to the edit point, change the transition duration, and apply transitions to clips that don't have sufficient head or tail frames. With Adobe Premiere Pro, you can also apply a transition to a group of clips.

Using transitions with restraint

Once you discover the cornucopia of transition possibilities that Adobe Premiere Pro offers, you'll be tempted to use them for every edit. They can be great fun. That said, it is highly recommended that you exercise restraint with transitions.

Watch some TV news stories. Most use cuts-only edits. It's unlikely you'll see any transitions. Why? Time is a factor, but most stations these days have ready access to nonlinear editors (NLEs) such as Adobe Premiere Pro, and it takes almost no time to add a transition when using an NLE.

The principal reason for the dearth of transitions is that they can be distracting. If a TV news editor uses one, it's for a purpose. Their most frequent use in newsroom editing bays is to take what would have been a jarring edit—such as a major jump cut—and make it more palatable.

That's not to say transitions don't have their place in carefully planned stories. Consider the *Star Wars* movies with all their highly stylized transitions, such as obvious, slow wipes. Each of those transitions has a purpose. George Lucas purposely created a look reminiscent of old serialized movies and TV shows. Specifically, they send a clear message to the audience: "Pay attention. We're transitioning across space and time."

Adding whimsy

Transitions can lighten up a story. Here are a few examples:

- Start on a tight shot of someone's hands cutting a deck of cards, and make a Swap transition—one image slides to one side and another slides over it—to another card-related shot.

- Start with a tight shot of a clock (analog, not digital), and use the aptly named Clock Wipe—a line centered on the screen sweeps around to reveal another image—to move to another setting and time.

- Get that James Bond, through-the-bloody-eye effect with the Iris Round transition.

- Take a medium shot of a garage door, and use a Push transition—one image moves off the top while another replaces it from below—to move to the next shot of the garage interior.

- With some planning and experimentation, you can videotape someone pushing against a wall while walking in place and use that same Push transition (after applying a horizontal direction to it) to have that person "slide" the old scene offscreen.

Adding visual interest

Transitions can give your video some pizzazz:

- Take a shot of a car driving through the frame and use a Wipe transition, synchronized with the speed of the car, to move to the next scene.

- Use the Venetian Blinds transition to move from an interior to an exterior.

- A Page Peel transition works well with a piece of parchment.

During this lesson, feel free to experiment with all that Adobe Premiere Pro has to offer.

Trying some transitions

Adobe Premiere Pro contains nearly 80 video transitions (plus three audio transitions, covered in more detail in Lesson 12). Some are subtle, and some are "in your face." The more you experiment with them, the more likely you are to use them well.

Applying a transition between two clips starts with a simple drag-and-drop process. That might be enough for many transitions, but Adobe Premiere Pro gives you a wide variety of options for fine-tuning transitions. Some transitions have a Custom button that opens a separate dialog with sets of options unique to each. And most offer tools that allow you to position the transition precisely.

1 Start Adobe Premiere Pro, and open Lesson 06-01.prproj.

2 Choose Window > Workspace > Effects.

This changes the workspace to the preset that the Adobe Premiere Pro development team created to make it easier to work with transitions and effects.

▶ **Tip:** Did your toolbar move when you changed to the Effects workspace? If you prefer to have your toolbar closer to the Timeline, feel free to dock it wherever you like. Many people like to dock the toolbar to the right or left of the Timeline where it is close to most of the work you will be doing.

3 Drag the three video clips from the Project panel to the Video 1 track, in the order shown here. Press the backslash key (\) to expand the view to show all the clips on one screen.

Clip Handles

You'll see little triangles in the upper-right and upper-left corners of the clips (shown here). They indicate the clips are at their original, full length. There are no additional frames past the beginning or end of the clip. For transitions to work smoothly, you need handles—some unused head and tail frames to overlap between the clips. Trimming both ends of the clips will give you those handles. Notice that when your clip has handles, there are no triangles displayed in the upper corners of the clip.

4 Select the Ripple Edit tool (or press B on your keyboard), and drag the end of the first clip to the left to shorten it by about 30 seconds (note the time in the pop-up menu).

5 Use the Ripple Edit tool to drag the beginning of the second clip to the right about 30 seconds into the clip.

6 Press the backslash key (\) to expand the Timeline.

● **Note:** Since you used the Ripple Edit tool, these two trims should have no gap. If there is a gap, right-click (Windows) or Control-click (Mac OS) the gap, and choose Ripple Delete.

7 Create handles at the end of the second clip and beginning of the third clip in the same way. Use the Ripple Edit tool to drag the end of the second clip 20 seconds to the left, and drag the beginning of the third clip 20 seconds to the right.

8 To make the transition you are about to apply easier to see, you need to zoom in closer to the Timeline. Put the current-time indicator at the edit point between clip 1 and clip 2 on the Timeline, and then press the equal sign (=) four times to zoom in fairly close.

9 The Effects panel should be docked with the Project panel. Select the Effects panel by clicking it, and then open the Video Transitions > Dissolve bin.

10 Drag Cross Dissolve to the edit between the first two clips of the sequence, but don't release the mouse button just yet.

11 While still holding down the mouse button, move the pointer to the left and right, and note how the pointer and the highlighted rectangle on the clips change (shown here). You can place the transition such that it ends at the edit point, is centered on the edit point, or starts there.

12 Place the transition at the middle of the edit point, and drop the transition there.

13 Put the current-time indicator to the left of the transition, and press the spacebar to play it.

The transition has a one-second duration by default.

Changing the default transition and duration

The default transition has two primary uses: It's used when automating a storyboard to a sequence or as a quick means to add a transition by using the keyboard short-cut, which is Ctrl+D (Windows) or Command+D (Mac OS). To set a different default transition, select the transition you want to use, open the Effects panel menu, and choose Set Selected As Default Transition. A red box will appear around that transi-tion. You can change the default duration by choosing Default Transition Duration, which opens the Preferences dialog.

14 Open the 3D Motion bin under the video transitions, and drag Flip Over to the beginning of the first clip. Note that the only placement option is to have the transition start at the edit point.

One very cool characteristic of transitions in Adobe Premiere Pro is that you can use them at the beginning or end of a clip. This is called a *single-sided transition. Double-sided transitions* go between clips.

15 Press the Home key or drag the current-time indicator to move the current-time indicator to the beginning of the Timeline, and play the transition. This is an interesting way to start a video.

Transitions on any track

Adobe Premiere Pro lets you place transitions between two clips (or at the beginnings or ends of clips) on any track in a sequence. A cool use of single-sided transitions is to put them in clips on higher tracks so they gradually reveal or cover up what's below them in the Timeline. You're using only a single track in these lessons to simplify things and because transition behavior on the Video 1 track is the same as on any other track.

16 Drag the Flip Over transition to the end of the third clip.

17 If it's not already open, click the Effect Controls tab to open the Effect Controls panel.

18 Click the Flip Over transition rectangle (the purple rectangle) at the end of the clip in the Timeline to switch on the display of its parameters in the Effect Controls panel.

19 Select the Reverse option (shown here) to have the Flip Over transition flip in the opposite direction at the end of the clip.

20 Open the Zoom bin under the Video Transitions, and drag the Cross Zoom transition over the Cross Dissolve transition between the first and second clips. That replaces Cross Dissolve with Cross Zoom. Play that transition.

21 Test some other transitions. It's a good idea to try at least one from every bin.

Sequence display changes

When you add a transition to a sequence, a short red horizontal line appears above that transition (shown here). The red line means that this portion of the sequence must be rendered before you can record it to tape or create a file of your finished project.

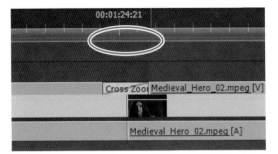

Rendering happens automatically when you export your project, but you can choose to render selected portions of your sequence to make those sections display more smoothly on slower computers. To do that, slide the handles of the viewing area bar (shown here) to the ends of the red rendering line (they will snap to those points), and press Enter (Windows) or Return (Mac OS). Adobe Premiere Pro will create a video clip of that segment (tucked away in the Preview Files folder with an indecipherable filename) and will change the line from red to green.

● **Note:** The viewing area bar may cover all clips on the Timeline by default. Pressing Enter (Windows) or Return (Mac OS) will render any areas that require rendering that are between the In and Out points of the viewing area bar. By adjusting the length of the viewing area bar, you can control what areas of the project are rendered.

Changing parameters in the Effect Controls panel

Up to this point you've seen the default action of each transition you've tested. That just scratches the surface of their possibilities. Tucked away in the Effect Controls panel is a passel of parameters, unique to each transition.

Here's how you adjust transition characteristics on the Cross Dissolve transition:

1 Open Lesson 06-02.prproj.

2 Drag the Cross Dissolve transition from the Effects > Video Transitions > Dissolve bin to the beginning of the first clip. If there is already a transition there, dropping a new one on top of it will replace it.

3 Click the transition rectangle in the upper-left corner of the clip in the sequence to display its parameters in the Effect Controls panel.

● **Note:** Another way to change the duration of the transition is to drag the edge of the transition on the Timeline. Drag the right edge of the transition left and right with the standard Selection tool to adjust its length.

4 Select the Show Actual Sources option (shown here), and drag the sliders beneath the Start and End preview screens.

You can use those sliders to have the transition start partially faded up and end less than completely faded up.

5 Change the duration in the Effect Controls panel to two seconds, and play the transition in the Timeline.

6 Play the transition at different lengths to see the effect.

7 Drag the Push transition from the Slide Transitions bin to the edit between the first and second clips. Play it in the Timeline, and notice the direction it pushes.

8   Change the direction to go from the top to bottom by clicking the transition and then clicking the north-to-south triangle in the Effect Controls panel (shown here).

9   Apply the Wipe transition (Wipe bin) between the second and third clips.

Three new options appear: Border Width, Border Color, and Anti-aliasing Quality.

10 Change Border Width to 20.

11 Click the upper-left direction triangle to change the direction to northwest to southeast.

12 Change the border color by clicking the Border Color swatch, and choose white.

13 Set Anti-aliasing Quality to High. Play the transition. Anti-aliasing adjusts the smoothness of the edges of the transition.

14 Select the Iris Round transition in the Iris bin, and apply it at the end of the last clip. Notice that when you drop a new transition on top of an old transition, it replaces the old transition.

This transition has a new option: a small positioning circle.

15 Select the Reverse option to make the iris closed rather than open.

16 On the End Preview screen, move the End slider to the left a little bit so you can see how the transition will look just before it completely closes.

Note: You can also use the Eyedropper tool located next to the color swatch to choose a color from the video clip.

Note: You can also watch the end position in the Program Monitor. You need to drag the Timeline current-time indicator through the transition to view it.

17 On the Start screen, move the positioning circle to make the transition finish on the villain's eye (watch the position of the transition change on the End Preview screen).

18 When you settle on a location, return the End slider all the way to the right. Play the transition.

Using A/B mode to fine-tune a transition

A/B editing is old-school, linear, film-style editing. Film editors frequently use two reels of film—an A-roll and a B-roll—which are usually duplicates made from the same original. The two-reel approach permits cross-dissolves from the A track to the B track.

The advantage of A/B editing in older versions of Adobe Premiere Pro was that it let you modify transition positioning and start and end points more easily than you could using single-track NLEs.

Here's the good news for both the A/B and single-track editing camps: Adobe Premiere Pro includes all that functionality in its Effect Controls panel.

Working with the Effect Controls panel's A/B feature

The Effect Controls panel's A/B editing mode splits a single video track into two subtracks. What would normally be two consecutive and contiguous clips on a single track are now displayed as individual clips on separate subtracks, giving you the option to apply a transition between them, to manipulate their head and tail frames (or handles), and to change other transition elements.

1 Open Lesson 06-03.prproj.

2 Click the Push transition that is applied between the first and second clips to display its parameters in the Effect Controls panel.

3 Open the A/B timeline in the Effect Controls panel by clicking the Show/Hide Timeline View button in the upper-right corner.

4 Drag the border (as shown here) between the A/B timeline and the transition parameters section to expand the view of the A/B timeline.

Timeline View button

5 Hover the pointer over the edit line at the center of the transition rectangle (as shown on the left).

That's the edit point between the two clips, and the pointer that appears there is the Rolling Edit tool (⊞)—the same Rolling Edit tool you encountered in the Trim panel in Lesson 5.

Note: You might need to expand the width of the Effect Controls panel to make the Show/Hide Timeline View button available. Also, the Effect Controls Timeline may already be visible. Clicking the Show/Hide Timeline View button in the Effect Controls panel toggles it on and off.

Note: As was the case when you used the Rolling Edit tool in the Trim panel, moving it left or right does not change the overall length of the sequence.

6 Drag the Rolling Edit tool left and right, and note how the changing Out point of the left clip and the changing In point of the right clip show up in the Program Monitor.

7 Move the pointer slightly to the left or right of the edit line, and notice that it changes to the Slide tool (⊕).

● **Note:** Using the Slide tool changes the start and end points of the transition without changing its overall length (the default duration is one second). The new start and end points show up in the Program Monitor, but unlike using the Rolling Edit tool, moving the transition rectangle by using the Slide tool does not change the edit point between the two clips.

8 Use the Slide tool to drag the transition rectangle left and right.

9 Click the Alignment menu, and click through the three available options: Center at Cut, Start at Cut, and End at Cut.

The transition rectangle moves to a new location as you make each change. These three locations mimic the options when you drag a transition to the Timeline. Also, if you manually change the transition location, the Custom Start alignment option becomes available.

10 Drag an end (it doesn't matter which end) of the viewing area bar to the edge of the A/B timeline.

This expands your view of the two adjacent clips so you can see the beginning of the left clip and the end of the right clip.

11 Drag the right and left edges of the transition to lengthen it.

Two other ways to change transition duration

You can also change the duration value by typing a new time or by clicking the duration time and dragging left or right to decrease or increase its value.

Note that as you lengthen the transition, the viewing area bar shrinks, thereby allowing you to drag its ends yet again to expand the area viewed in the A/B timeline.

Dealing with inadequate (or no) head or tail handles

Eventually you'll want to place transitions at edit points where you don't have adequate head or tail handles (footage beyond the In or Out point of your clip). This might be because you paused the camcorder too soon or didn't get it started fast enough. You might want to add a transition to ease what would be an abrupt cut edit. Adobe Premiere Pro deals elegantly with this situation.

1   Open Lesson 06-04.prproj. Notice that the two clips on the Timeline have no "heads or tails." You can tell this because of the little triangles in the corners of the clips; the triangles indicate the very ends of the clips.

2   Using the standard Selection tool, drag the right edge of the last clip to the left, and release. Notice that the little triangle at the end of that clip is no longer visible. Stretch the clip back to its full length.

3   Drag the Cross Dissolve transition to the edit point between the two clips.

    The "Insufficient Media" alert appears. Click OK.

4   Click the transition to display it in the Effect Controls panel, and note that the transition rectangle has parallel diagonal lines running through it, indicating the lack of head or tail frames.

5   Lengthen the transition to about three seconds by dragging the right and left edges of the transition rectangle. You may need to zoom in the Timeline by pressing the equal sign (=) to be able to grab the edge of the transition.

6   Drag the current-time indicator slowly through the entire transition, and watch how it works:

    • For the first half of the transition (up to the edit point), the B clip is a freeze frame while the A clip continues to play.

    • At the edit point, the A clip becomes a freeze frame, and the B clip starts to play.

    When played at regular speed (at the default one-second duration), few viewers would notice the freeze frames.

● **Note:** In this lesson's example, both the A and B clips have no head or tail handle frames. Frequently only one clip has no head or tail room. In those cases, Adobe Premiere Pro forces the placement of the transition to start or end at the edit point, depending on which clip lacks extra frames for the overlap.

Applying transitions to multiple clips at once

So far you've been applying transitions to video clips. However, you can also apply transitions to still images, graphics, color mattes, and even audio, as you will see in the next section of this lesson.

A common project that editors encounter is the photo montage. Often these montages look nice with transitions between photos. Applying transitions one at a time for 100 images would not be fun. Adobe Premiere Pro makes it easy to automate this process by allowing the default transition (that you define) to be added to any group of contiguous or noncontiguous clips:

1 Open Lesson 06-05.prproj. Notice there are 40 JPEG images of sunsets already imported into the Project panel.

2 Select all 40 JPEG images in the Project panel, and drag them to Sequence 01.

3 Play the Timeline by pressing the spacebar. You'll notice the JPEG clips are all five seconds long.

4 Press the backslash key (\) to zoom out the Timeline to make the whole sequence visible.

● **Note:** The selection of clips does not have to be contiguous. You can Shift-click clips to select only a portion of the clips on the Timeline.

5 With the Selection tool, draw a marquee around all the clips to select them.

6 Click the Sequence menu, and choose Apply Default Transition to Selection. This will apply the default transition between any clips currently selected.

7 Play the Timeline, and notice the difference a Cross Dissolve transition makes between images in a photo montage.

More than one way to batch transitions

The method described in this exercise is the most flexible way to add the default transition to multiple clips. However, Adobe Premiere Pro provides another method via the storyboard feature: Automate to Sequence. You explored this feature in Lesson 5 but did not apply the transitions. Feel free to repeat that exercise, and this time apply the default transition to all clips when you automate to the Timeline.

Adding audio transitions

Transitions are not just for video. Adding a crossfade transition to the end of an audio clip is a really fast way to add a fade-in or fade-out to an audio clip:

1 Open Lesson 06-06.prproj, play the Timeline, and notice the abrupt end volume of the soundtrack.

2 In the Audio Transitions bin in the Effects panel, click the Crossfade bin.

3 Drag the Constant Power transition to the end of the audio clip in the Audio 2 track. Play the Timeline, and notice the transition has created a fade-out for the music track.

> The Constant Power transition placed between two audio clips as a transition will help blend two different audio clips together to make the audio transition less harsh.

4 Drag the length of the audio transition to be longer or shorter, and listen to the effect when you play the Timeline.

5 To polish the project, add a Cross Dissolve transition to the beginning and end of the sequence by moving the current-time indicator near the beginning and pressing Ctrl+D (Windows) or Command+D (Mac OS) to add the default video transition. Repeat this for the end of the clip. This will create a fade from black at the beginning and a fade to black at the end.

Transitions are fun and interesting to add to your project. However, overusing them is the giveaway of an amateur video. When choosing a transition, make sure it adds meaning to your project rather than showing off how many editing tricks you know. Watch your favorite movies and TV shows to learn how the pros use transitions.

▶ **Tip:** Shift+Ctrl+D (Windows) or Shift+Command+D (Mac OS) is the keyboard shortcut for adding the default audio transition to the edit point near the current-time indicator on the selected audio track—a very fast way to add a fade-in or fade-out to an audio track.

Review questions

1 Describe two ways to apply the default transition to multiple clips.

2 How do you track down a transition by name?

3 How do you replace a transition with another one?

4 Some transitions start as small squares, circles, or other geometric shapes and then grow to reveal the next clip. How do you get those transitions to start with large geometric shapes that shrink to reveal the next clip?

5 Explain three ways to change the duration of a transition.

6 What is an easy way to fade audio at the beginning or end of a clip?

Review answers

1 Use the Automate to Sequence feature, or select clips already on the Timeline and choose Sequence > Apply Default Transition to Selection.

2 Start typing the transition name in the Contains text box in the Effects panel. As you type, Adobe Premiere Pro displays all effects and transitions (audio and video) that have that letter combination anywhere in their names. Type more letters to narrow down your search.

3 Drag the replacement transition on top of the transition you're rejecting. The new one automatically replaces the old one.

4 Select the Reverse option in the Effect Controls panel. That switches the movement from starting small and ending full-screen to starting full-screen and ending small.

5 Drag the edge of the transition rectangle in the Timeline, do the same thing in the Effect Controls panel's A/B timeline, or change the Duration value in the Effect Controls panel.

6 An easy way to fade audio in or out is to apply an audio crossfade transition to the beginning or end of a clip.

7 CREATING DYNAMIC TITLES

Topics covered in this lesson

- Strengthening your project with titles
- Changing text parameters
- Building text from scratch
- Putting text on a path
- Creating shapes
- Making text roll and crawl
- Applying text effects such as sheens, strokes, shadows, and fills
- Copying titles to other Adobe applications

 This lesson will take approximately 90 minutes.

The Adobe Premiere Pro CS5 Titler is a multifaceted, feature-rich text- and shape-creation tool. Your Titler-designed text and objects can run superimposed over video as static titles, as rolling credits, or as stand-alone clips.

Getting started

On-screen text helps tell your story. You can reinforce your message by using superimposed text (aka *supers*) to give a location or an interviewee's name and title, to show on-screen bullet points, and to display opening titles and closing credits.

Text can present information much more succinctly and clearly than narration. It can also reinforce narrated and visual information by reminding viewers about the people in your piece and the message you're trying to convey.

The Adobe Premiere Pro CS5 Titler offers you a full range of text- and shape-creation options. You can use any font on your computer. Your text and objects can be any color (or multiple colors), any degree of transparency, and a variety of shapes. Using the Path tool, you can place your text on the most convoluted curved line you can imagine.

The Titler is an engaging and powerful tool. Its infinite customizability makes it possible for you to create a look unique to your productions.

Strengthening your project with titles

Consider this opening sequence: a telephoto shot of scorched desert sand with rippling heat distorting the scene. Dry, desiccated, lifeless sagebrush. A lizard slowly seeking shade beneath a small stone. And a small plume of dust in the distance. That's attention-getting stuff.

Now a narrator intones, "The summer heat beats down on the Bonneville Salt Flats." That's effective, but even better is a title: "Bonneville Salt Flats." Then, as the plume of dust moves toward the camera, another super displays this text: "Speed Trials—Summer 2005." Then a rocket-shaped vehicle screams across the scene.

Rather than interrupt the building suspense with a sonorous narrator, save the voice-over for later. Instead, use titles to set up your story.

Here are other instances in which text can be an effective alternative to voice-overs:

- Instead of using a voice-over to say, "Sue Smith, vice president of manufacturing for Acme Industries," put that information in a super at the bottom of the screen. This type of title is also known as a *lower third*, because it's positioned in the lower third of the screen.

- Instead of narrating a collection of statistics, use bullet points that pop up on-screen with each new item.

Text strengthens your project.

Changing text parameters

In this lesson, you'll start with some formatted text and then change its parameters. This approach is a good way to get a quick overview of the powerful features of the Adobe Premiere Pro CS5 Titler. Later in this lesson you'll build basic text from scratch.

1   Start Adobe Premiere Pro CS5, and open Lesson 07-01.prproj.

2   Double-click Title Start in the Project panel.

● **Note:** You may have to expand the window to see all the Title Properties options.

The Titler opens with a title already loaded over a video frame. Here's a quick rundown on the Titler's panels:

Title Tools panel   Titler main panel

Title Properties panel

Title Actions panel   Title Styles panel

- **Title Tools panel**: These tools define text boundaries, set text paths, and select geometric shapes.

- **Titler main panel**: This is where you build and view text and graphics.

- **Title Properties panel**: Here you'll find text and graphic options such as font characteristics and effects.

- **Title Actions panel**: You'll use these to align, center, or distribute text and groups of objects.

- **Title Styles panel**: Here you'll find preset text styles. You can choose from several libraries of styles.

3 Click several different thumbnails in the Title Styles panel to acquaint yourself with the styles available.

Each time you click a new style, Adobe Premiere Pro instantly changes the active or selected text to that style. When you're finished checking out some of the styles, choose the style Info Bronze (shown here). This style works with the mood of the scene in the video.

4 Click the Font Browser menu in the Titler. Note that the current font is Minion Pro.

5 Scroll through the fonts, and note that as you select a new font, you see immediately how it will work with your text.

6 Click the Font Family menu in the Title Properties panel on the right of the Titler. This is another way to change fonts in the Titler. Experiment with changing the font through this panel.

7 After you're done experimenting, change back to the Info Bronze style.

The changes show up immediately in the Titler panel.

8 Change the font size to 140 by typing the new value into the Font Size field or by dragging the Size number until it reaches 140. Click the center icon to center the text.

9 Select Small Caps in the Title Properties panel, if it is not already selected.

10 Change Leading to 5. Leading changes the vertical distance between lines of text.

11 Change Kerning to 5. Kerning changes the amount of space between selected characters.

12 Change Slant to 13.

13 Change Shadow Distance to 10, Shadow Size to 25, and Shadow Spread to 25.

14 Click the Horizontal Center and Vertical Center buttons in the Title Actions panel.

● **Note:** Many TV sets cut off the edges of the video frame. Keeping text within the title-safe margin (also called the title-safe zone), as shown by the rectangular fields in the title display area, ensures viewers will see all your text.

— Horizontal Center
— Vertical Center

Your screen should look like the one shown here.

15 Drag the Titler floating window to the right—far enough to be able to see the Project panel.

16 In the Project panel, double-click Title Finished to load it in the Titler.

17 Toggle between the two titles by using the drop-down menu in the Titler main panel.

Your text should look similar to the Title Finished text.

● **Note:** Adobe Premiere Pro CS5 automatically saves your updated title in the project file. It does not show up as a separate file on your hard drive.

18 Close the Titler by clicking the little *x* in the upper-right corner (Windows) or the Close button (Mac OS).

19 Drag Title Start from the Project panel to the Video 2 track on the Timeline, trim it so it fits above the video clip, and drag the current-time indicator through it to see how it looks over that video clip.

● **Note:** You can apply transitions to titles to fade them up or move them on or off the screen.

Using titles in other projects

You're likely to create common titles for location names and supers of interviewee names that you can use in multiple projects. However, Adobe Premiere Pro does not automatically save titles as separate files. To make a title available for use in another project, select the title in the Project panel, choose File > Export > Title, give your title a name, choose a location, and click Save. Later, you can simply import that title file the same way you would import any other asset.

Building text from scratch

The Titler offers three approaches to creating text, each offering both horizontal and vertical text-direction options:

- **Point text**: This approach builds a text bounding box as you type. The text runs on one line until you press Enter (Windows) or Return (Mac OS) or until you choose Title > Word Wrap. Changing the shape and size of the box changes the shape and size of the text.

- **Paragraph (area) text**: You set the size and shape of the text box before entering text. Changing the box size later displays more or less text but does not change the shape or size of the text.

- **Text on a path**: You build a path for the text to follow by clicking points in the text screen to create curves and then adjusting the shape and direction of those curves using the handles.

Selecting a tool from the left or right side determines whether the text will orient horizontally or vertically.

Because Adobe Premiere Pro automatically saves text to the project file, you can switch to a new or different title and not lose whatever you've created in the current title. That's what you'll do now:

1 Open the Lesson 07-02.prproj project.

2 To open the New Title dialog, choose File > New > Title, or press Ctrl+T (Windows) or Command+T (Mac OS).

Note: Adobe Premiere Pro CS5 allows you to have sequences with different video attributes, so the New Title dialog allows you to create the title with different frame sizes and aspect ratios. It defaults to the settings of the active sequence. Because the settings you want to use for the title are the same as the active sequence, leave these settings at the defaults.

3 Type *Castle Room* in the Name box, and click OK.

▶ Tip: Dragging the timecode with the text screen displayed can come in handy if you want to position text relative to the video contents or check how the text looks over your video.

4 Drag the timecode (directly below the Show Background Video button) to change the video frame displayed on the text screen.

5 Click the Show Background Video button to hide the video clip.

● **Note:** The video frame displayed behind the title is not saved with the title. It's there as a reference for positioning and styling your title.

Checkerboard pattern signifies transparency

The background now consists of a grayscale checkerboard, which signifies transparency. That is, if you place text created in the Titler on a video track above other video clips, the video on lower tracks will be visible wherever you see that checkerboard. You can also create text or geometric objects with some transparency. In that case, you'll see the checkerboard through an object, which means the video will show through but will appear as if it's covered with smoked or tinted glass.

6 Click the Birch White 80 style (the third style of the style group shown here).

7 Click the Type tool (shortcut T), and click anywhere in the Titler panel.

The Type tool creates point text.

8 Type *Castle Room*.

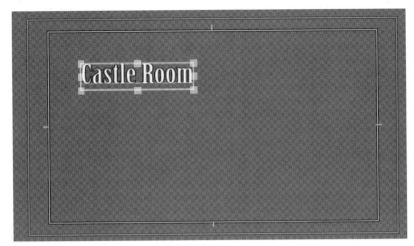

● **Note:** If you continue typing, you will note that point text does not wrap. Your text will run off the screen to the right. To make it wrap when it reaches the title-safe margin, choose Title > Word Wrap. To begin a new line, press Enter (Windows) or Return (Mac OS).

9 Click the Selection tool (the black arrow in the upper-left corner of the Title Tools panel). Handles appear on the text bounding box.

10 Drag the corners and edges of the text bounding box, and note how the text changes size and shape accordingly.

11 Hover the pointer just outside a corner of the text bounding box until a curved line pointer appears. Then drag to rotate the bounding box off its horizontal orientation.

● **Note:** In this case, the Selection tool keyboard shortcut (V) won't work, because you are typing inside a text bounding box.

More than one way to move a box

Instead of dragging bounding box handles, you can change values in the Transform settings in the Title Properties panel. Either type new values or position your pointer on a value and drag left or right. Your changes show up immediately in the bounding box.

12 After making sure the Selection tool is still active, click anywhere within the bounding box, and drag the angled text and its bounding box somewhere else on the Titler panel.

13 Edit that text by double-clicking anywhere in the text and typing.

You can drag to select text you want to remove or replace.

14 Delete all the text by using the Selection tool to select the text box (which puts handles on the text bounding box indicating the entire frame is selected) and pressing Delete.

Tip: Clicking and dragging with the Type tool will act just like the Area Type tool.

15 Click the Area Type tool, and drag a text bounding box into the Titler panel that nearly fills the title-safe zone.

The Area Type tool creates paragraph text.

Turning off safe margins

You can turn off the title-safe margins or action-safe margins by opening the Titler panel menu (or choosing Title > View) and then choosing Safe Title Margin or Safe Action Margin, respectively.

16 Start typing. This time, type enough characters to go beyond the end of the bounding box. Reduce the font size if needed so you can see a few lines of text at once.

Unlike point text, area text remains within the confines of the bounding box you defined. It wraps at the bounding box borders.

17 Press Enter (Windows) or Return (Mac) to go down a line.

18 Click the Selection tool, and change the size and shape of the bounding box.

The text does not change size. Instead, it adjusts its position on the bounding box baselines. If you make the box too small for all your text, the extra text scrolls below the bottom edge of the bounding box. In that case, a small plus sign (+) appears near the lower-right corner outside the bounding box.

19 Double-click within the text to edit it.

20 Switch to the Selection tool, click anywhere in the text bounding box, and press Delete to remove the text.

Vertical text

While you're testing your text, try the vertically oriented Vertical Type tool and Vertical Area Type tool. They create text with each character standing on top of the next one.

Putting text on a path

The Path Type tool is both elegant and tricky. It enables you to build paths that are simple or complex, or that are straight or curved, for your text to follow.

If you've worked with the Pen tool in Adobe Photoshop or Adobe Illustrator, you know how to use the Path Type tool. You define a path by creating a number of points in the Titler panel and dragging handles at each point to define curves. Here's how it works in Adobe Premiere Pro:

1 Continue with the same title opened for the previous exercise, or start a new title. Select the Path Type tool.

2 Click three different points in the Titler panel to form a triangle.

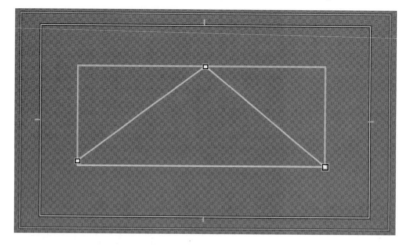

3 Click the Convert Anchor Point tool.

4 Click the Convert Anchor Point tool over the center point of your triangle (your pointer changes to a black arrow), and drag to the right to create anchor point handles. The longer the handle, the more the angle will flatten to a curve.

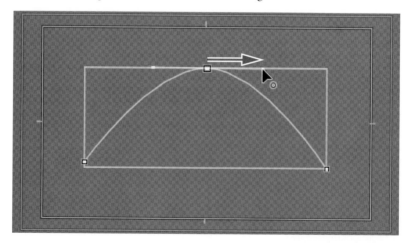

Try making the handles longer or shorter, or just move them around to see how they work.

5 Click the Text tool to select it.

6 Click anywhere inside the newly created bounding box.

A blinking text insertion point appears at the beginning of the curved line.

7 Type some text.

Your Titler panel should look something like the one shown here.

You should practice creating path text if you want to master the technique, but for now just try to get a basic idea of how it works.

Creating shapes

If you've created shapes in graphics-editing software such as Adobe Photoshop or Adobe Illustrator, you know how to create geometric objects in Adobe Premiere Pro. Simply select from the various shapes in the Title Tools panel, drag and draw the outline, and release the mouse button.

Shape-drawing tools:
A. Pen
B. Rectangle
C. Clipped Corner Rectangle
D. Wedge
E. Ellipse
F. Rounded Corner Rectangle
G. Rounded Rectangle
H. Arc
I. Line

Follow these steps to draw shapes in Adobe Premiere Pro:

1 Press Ctrl+T (Windows) or Command+T (Mac OS) to open a new title. Type *Shapes* in the Name box in the New Title dialog, and click OK.

● **Note:** Not all shape tools have keyboard shortcuts.

2 Select the Rectangle tool (R), and drag in the Titler panel to create a rectangle.

3 Click different title styles while the rectangle is still selected. Notice that title styles affect shapes as well as text. Click the first style (Caslon Pro 68) for a simple style with no shading, outlines, or shadows.

● **Note:** Pressing Shift creates shapes with symmetrical properties: circles, squares, and equilateral triangles. To maintain the original aspect ratio while resizing a shape you've already made, hold down the Shift key before making the change.

4 Shift-drag in another location to create a square.

5 Click the Selection tool, drag it in the Titler panel to marquee-select the two objects, and press Delete to make a clean slate.

● **Note:** You can adjust the amount of roundness of the rounded rectangles by adjusting the Fillet Size field in Title Properties.

6 Select the Rounded Corner Rectangle tool, and Alt-drag (Windows) or Option-drag (Mac OS) to draw from the center of the shape.

The center remains in the spot where you first clicked, and the figure changes shape and size around that point as you drag.

7 Select the Clipped Corner Rectangle tool, and Shift+Alt-drag (Windows) or Shift+Option-drag (Mac OS) to constrain the aspect ratio and draw from the center.

8 Select the Arc tool (A), and drag diagonally across the corner points to flip the shape diagonally as you draw.

9 Click the Wedge tool (W), and drag across, up, or down to flip the shape horizontally or vertically as you draw.

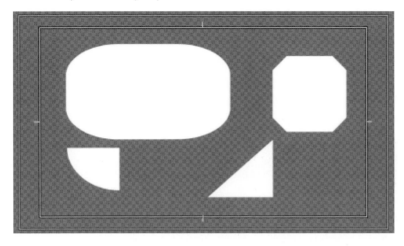

● **Note:** To flip the shape after you've drawn it, use the Selection tool to drag a corner point in the direction you want it to flip.

10 Change to the Selection tool, marquee-select by dragging a selection around the four objects, and press Delete to make another clean slate.

11 Select the Line tool (L), and drag to create a single line.

12 Select the Pen tool, and click in a blank area of the title canvas to create an anchor point (don't drag to create handles).

13 Click the Titler panel again where you want the segment to end (or Shift-click to constrain the segment's angle to a multiple of 45 degrees). This creates another anchor point.

14 Continue clicking with the Pen tool to create additional straight segments. The last anchor point you add appears as a large square, indicating it is selected.

15 Complete the path by doing one of the following:

- To close the path, move the Pen tool to the initial anchor point. When it is directly over the initial anchor point, a little circle appears underneath the Pen pointer. Click to make the connection.

- To leave the path open, Ctrl-click (Windows) or Command-click (Mac OS) anywhere away from all objects, or select a different tool in the Title Tools panel.

Experiment with the different shape options. Try overlapping them and using different styles. The possibilities are endless.

Aligning shapes

Sometimes you may need to create multiple shapes or titles and align them on the screen. The Titler has several alignment tools to make this job easy. You will explore a few here:

1 Delete your test shapes to create a blank Titler panel, or start a new title.

2 Draw a small circle using the Ellipse tool. You can constrain it to be a circle by holding down the Shift key while you drag the shape.

3 Style the circle by clicking the style HoboStd Slant Gold 80.

4 Make three exact copies by choosing the Selection tool and then Alt-dragging (Windows) or Option-dragging (Mac OS) the circle to three other locations within the title-safe area, roughly in a horizontal line.

5 Select all four circles by Shift-clicking each one.

Notice that when more than one object is selected, the Align tools become active.

6 Click the Vertical Center Align tool.

7 Click the Horizontal Center Distribute tool.

Vertical Center Align

Vertical Center

Horizontal Center

Horizontal Center Distribute

8 Click both the Horizontal Center and Vertical Center tools.

You should have four perfectly aligned circles centered in the title area.

Making text roll and crawl

Using the Titler, you can make rolling text for opening and closing credits and crawling text for items such as headline bulletins.

1 From the Adobe Premiere Pro menu bar, choose Title > New Title > Default Roll.

2 Name your title *Rolling Credits*, and click OK.

3 Select the Area Type tool and then type some text with the Orca White 80 style.

Create placeholder credits as shown here, pressing Enter (Windows) or Return (Mac OS) after each line. Type enough text to more than fill the screen vertically.

Note: With rolling text selected, the Titler automatically adds a scroll bar along the right side that enables you to view your text as it runs off the bottom of the screen (shown here). If you select one of the crawl options, that scroll bar will appear at the bottom to enable you to view text running off the right or left edge of the screen.

Roll/Crawl Options

4 Click the Roll/Crawl Options button.

You have the following options:

- **Still**: This changes the credits to a still title.

- **Roll (Scroll text vertically)**: This should be selected already, because this title was created to scroll vertically, as often seen in movie credits.

- **Crawl Left, Crawl Right**: These indicate the crawl direction (rolling text always moves up the screen).

- **Start Off Screen**: This controls whether the credits start completely off the screen and roll on or whether they begin at the location as typed in the Titler.

- **End Off Screen**: This indicates whether the credits roll completely off the screen.

- **Preroll**: This specifies the number of frames before the first words appear on-screen.

- **Ease-In**: This specifies the number of frames at the beginning to gradually increase the speed of the roll or crawl from zero to its full speed.

- **Ease-Out**: This specifies the number of frames to slow down the roll or crawl at its end.

- **Postroll**: This specifies the number of frames that play after the roll or crawl ends.

5 Select Start Off Screen and End Off Screen, and type 5 for Ease-In and Ease-Out. Click OK.

6 Close the Titler.

7 Drag your newly created Rolling Credits title to the Video 2 track of the Timeline above the video clip (if another title is there, drag this one directly on top of it to do an overlay edit).

8 With the Edit tool, grab the right edge of the Rolling Credits clip, and drag it to be the same length as the video clip in track 1.

● **Note:** The default length of rolling or crawling credits is five seconds. If you change the length of the credits clip, that changes the speed. A longer clip length means slower rolling credits.

● **Note:** Dragging a rolling title to increase its length will cause it to roll slower. Dragging the rolling title to decrease its length will cause it to roll faster.

9 With the sequence selected, press the spacebar to view your rolling credits.

Adding text effects: sheens, strokes, shadows, and fills

Reverse engineering can be a good learning tool. So, in this exercise, you will deconstruct one of the many built-in templates that come with Adobe Premiere Pro to learn how to work with the Titler's effects.

Unlike styles, templates are a combination of background graphics, geometric shapes, and placeholder text. They are organized into themes with enough variety for just about any circumstance.

Templates are tremendously useful. You can easily customize graphic themes to suit your needs or build your own templates from scratch and save them for future projects. Let's begin:

Note: You can also open the Titler and choose Title > Templates to get to the same Templates screen.

1   Choose Title > New Title > Based on Template.

2   Open as many template folders, and click through as many templates, as you like.

3   Open the Lower Thirds folder, select Lower Third 1024, and click OK.

Note: This is a good template to experiment with because it has a full range of effects, including a four-color gradient, reduced opacity (transparency), a sheen, a stroke, and shadows.

4   Click the Selection tool, and move it over the title.

Bounding boxes appear, delineating the three components of this title: the *Title One* text, a brown and yellow rectangle, and a black rectangle with a gradient fill superimposed over the right side of the brown and yellow rectangle.

5   Drag each bounding box in turn up the screen so you can see the template's three components.

Your Titler panel should look something like the one shown here.

6   Drag the top edge of the brown and yellow rectangle to expand it.

It is now selected, and its characteristics are displayed in the Titler Properties panel.

7   Collapse the Transform and Properties areas in the panel to make some room.

8   Expand Fill and then Sheen (shown here), Strokes, and Outer Strokes (no inner strokes are used in this template).

Note: Each color is slightly different from the other three, and the colors at the top are slightly darker than the bottom colors. This gives the rectangle extra depth.

9 Open the Fill Type menu for Fill, and select each option in turn to see what they do. When done, return to 4 Color Gradient.

10 Double-click one or two of the four color-stop boxes around the 4 Color Gradient display to open the Color Picker. Select new colors.

● **Note:** You can change the opacity (transparency) of any color applied to any object or text, be it fill, sheen, or stroke. You can give a geometric shape or text a solid-color stroke border and convert its fill color to 0 percent opacity to display only its edges.

Select a color from your video

Instead of using the Color Picker to change the color-stop color, you can use the Eyedropper tool (located next to the color swatch) to select a color from your video. Click the Show Video button at the top of the Titler panel, move to a frame you want to use by scrubbing the timecode numbers left or right, select the Eyedropper tool into your video scene, and click a color that suits your needs.

11 Change the color-stop opacities by clicking each color-stop color and changing its Opacity setting.

12 Click the Sheen color box, and change its color, opacity, size, angle, and offset.

● **Note:** Sheen is a soft-edged color that typically runs horizontally through shapes or text. In this case, it's the brown horizontal line that runs through the entire rectangle.

13 Click the two Outer Stroke disclosure triangles to expand the parameters.

Strokes are outer or inner borders on text or graphic objects. They have the same collection of properties available for text and other Titler objects. In this case, both strokes are 3 points wide, and they fall adjacent to one another.

14 Change the size of the two outer strokes to 10 points each.

As shown here, this more clearly displays the sheen applied to these borders.

15 Next to Inner Strokes, click Add.

The Inner Stroke properties box appears.

16 Select the Inner Stroke properties box to turn on the parameters, and experiment with this new stroke by changing its Size, Fill Type, Color, and Opacity settings.

17 Click the Title One text to select it, and then open its Shadow properties.

This text doesn't have an obvious shadow because the shadow size is only 2 points. It's more like an outer stroke.

18 Change all the characteristics to see how the Shadow feature works.

> **Note:** Adding a sheen or a shadow to an object is also easy. Just select the object in the Titler panel, select the appropriate properties box, and adjust the parameters.

> **Note:** The Shadow settings are self-explanatory, with the exception of Spread. Increasing the Spread value softens the shadow.

Experiment with effects

You can learn a lot by experimenting with effects. Open a new title, select a style, and draw an object. Do this with several distinctly different styles. Then open the Fill, Strokes, and Shadow properties, and make lots of changes to each object.

Create some new outer and inner strokes. Add sheens. Check a Texture box, and add any graphic image or Adobe Photoshop file to add some real pizzazz to your text and object.

The more you use the Titler, the more you'll come to appreciate its depth and creative possibilities.

Review questions

1   What are the differences between point text and area (or paragraph) text?

2   Why display the title-safe margin?

3   What's the difference between a style and a template when using the Titler?

4   Why might the Align tools be dimmed?

5   How do you use the Ellipse tool to make a perfect circle?

6   How do you apply a stroke or a sheen?

Review answers

1   You create point text with the Type tool. Its bounding box expands as you type. Changing the box shape changes the text size and shape accordingly. When you use the Area Type tool, you define a bounding box, and the characters remain within its confines. Changing the box's shape displays more or fewer characters.

2   Some TV sets cut off the edges of the TV signal. The amount lost varies from set to set. Keeping your text within the title-safe margin ensures that viewers will see all your title. This is less of a problem with newer digital TVs, but it is still a good idea to use the Title Safe zone to frame your titles.

3   You can apply a style to characters or objects you create in the Titler. Templates give you a starting point for creating your own full-featured graphic or text, backgrounds, styles, or shapes.

4   The Align tools become active if more than one object is selected in the Titler. The Distribute tools also become active when more than two objects are selected.

5   To create a perfect circle, hold down the Shift key as you draw using the Ellipse tool.

6   To apply a stroke or sheen, select the text or object to edit, and click its Stroke (Outer or Inner) or Sheen box to add a stroke or a sheen. Then start adjusting parameters, and they will show up on the object.

8 APPLYING SPECIALIZED EDITING TOOLS

Topics covered in this lesson

- Exploring timesaving editing tools
- Slicing and moving clips
- Replacing a clip and replacing footage
- Closing gaps with Ripple Delete
- Using Sync Lock and Track Lock
- Creating sequence In and Out points
- Using subclips from the Source Monitor or a sequence
- Editing multicamera footage

 This lesson will take approximately 60 minutes.

It's time to take a break from single-topic lessons and delve into some specialized editing tools and techniques. In this lesson, you'll use editing tools that can save you a lot of time.

Getting started

In this lesson, you'll try three specialized editing tools—Rolling Edit, Slide, and Slip—and two Program Monitor buttons, Lift and Extract. All of these can simplify certain tasks. Using the Track Select tool, you'll move entire Timelines or portions of Timelines with ease.

You'll also explore some new ways to move and replace clips on the Timeline and learn how to create subclips from long clips to help organize your project.

Then you'll dive into multicamera editing. If you ever have a multicamera video shoot—in which multiple cameras capture a single event simultaneously—this feature will save you a lot of time switching between camera angles during the editing process.

Exploring timesaving editing tools

You'll use the Rolling Edit, Slide, and Slip tools in a variety of situations, including when you want to preserve the overall length of your program while trimming and editing scenes within it. They come in handy for precisely timed projects such as 30-second advertisements. You saw the Rolling Edit tool in action in the Trim Monitor in Lesson 5.

You worked with extract edits and lift edits by using the drag-and-drop method. In this lesson, you'll use the Program Monitor's Extract and Lift buttons to remove selected groups of frames—even when they're spread out over one or more clips.

In some cases, it can be easier to make individual edits and forego these specialized tools, but it's good for any video editor to know how to use all of them. Here's a quick look at what they do and how they differ from one another:

- **Ripple edit**: A ripple edit trims a clip and shifts subsequent clips in the track by the amount you trim. You used this tool in Lesson 5.

A ripple edit changes the overall length of the project.

- **Rolling edit**: A rolling edit rolls the cut point between two adjacent clips, shortening one and lengthening the other by the same amount of frames, thereby retaining the overall length of the project.

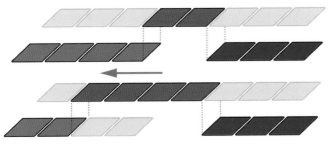

A rolling edit retains the overall length of the project.

- **Slide edit**: A slide edit slides the entire clip over two adjacent clips, shortening and lengthening those adjacent clips without changing the selected clip's length or In and Out points.

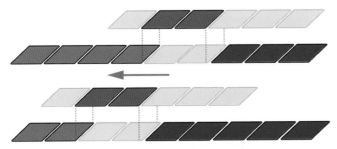

A slide edit changes the In and Out points of adjacent clips while retaining the original clip's edit points.

- **Slip edit**: A slip edit slips a clip under two adjacent clips. This changes the clip's starting and ending frames without changing its duration or its position on the timeline and without affecting adjacent clips.

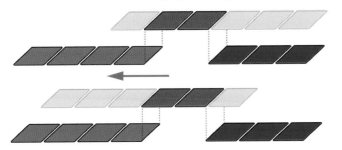

A slip edit changes the In and Out points of the selected clip while retaining the adjacent clip's edit points.

Note: Although the Slip and Slide tools are typically employed on the center clip of three adjacent clips, each tool functions normally even if the clip is adjacent to a clip on one side and a blank space on the other. For the Rolling Edit, Slip, and Slide tools to work as expected, you need to have sufficient unused head or tail frames to make the edits.

- **Extract edit**: An extract edit removes a selected range of frames and closes the gap by moving the following clips to the left.

- **Lift edit**: A lift edit removes a selected range of frames and leaves a gap.

Making rolling, slide, and slip edits

You'll begin with a rolling edit.

● **Note:** This lesson uses NTSC-DV video in 4:3 format, rather than the HD wide-screen format used in the other lessons.

1 Start Adobe Premiere Pro CS5, and open Lesson 08-01.prproj.

2 Open Sequence 01 in the Timeline, if it is not already open.

3 Set your workspace to Editing by choosing Window > Workspace > Editing.

    Three clips already appear on the Timeline, with enough head and tail frames to allow the edits you're about to make.

4 Select the Rolling Edit tool (⁑; keyboard shortcut N) in the Tools panel.

● **Note:** To ensure that you'll be able to make a precise, frame-specific edit, expand the view of the Timeline by pressing the equal sign (=) key.

5 Drag the edit point between Clip A and Clip B (the first two clips on the Timeline), using the Program Monitor split screen to find a better matching edit.

The Rolling Edit tool changes the Out and In points of adjacent clips.

Try rolling the edit point to the right to 00;20 (20 frames). You can use the Program Monitor timecode or the pop-up timecode in the Timeline (shown here, respectively) to find that edit.

6　Select the Slide tool (⟷; keyboard shortcut U), and position it over the middle clip.

7　Drag the second clip left or right.

● **Note:** This is just to demonstrate the edit. You don't need to find a specific edit point.

Take a look at the Program Monitor as you perform the slide edit. The two top images are the In point and Out point of Clip B. They do not change. The two larger images are the Out point and In point of the adjacent clips—Clip A and Clip C, respectively. These edit points change as you slide the selected clip over those adjacent clips.

Clip B In point (unchanged)　　Clip B Out point (unchanged)

Clip A Out point　　　　　　Clip C In point

The Slide tool moves a clip over two adjacent clips.

Note: Try both the Slide and Slip tools on Clips A and C. Both editing tools work on the first or last clips in a sequence.

8 Select the Slip tool (⊢⊣; keyboard shortcut Y), and drag Clip B left and right.

Take a look at the Program Monitor as you perform the slip edit. The two top images are the Out point and In point of Clips A and C, respectively. They do not change. The two larger images are the In point and Out point of Clip B. These edit points change as you slip Clip B *under* Clips A and C.

Clip A Out point (unchanged)   Clip C In point (unchanged)

Clip B In point   Clip B Out point

The Slip tool moves a clip under two adjacent clips.

Using the Program Monitor's Lift and Extract buttons

Next, you'll do a lift edit and then an extract edit:

1 Click the History tab, and choose New > Open to undo all the rolling, slide, and slip edits you just made.

2 Move the Timeline current-time indicator to about midway on the first clip.

3 Drag a viewing area bar handle (shown here) in the Program Monitor so its current-time indicator is roughly centered. This makes it easier to set In and Out points.

4 Use the Jog, Step Forward, and Step Back controls in the Program Monitor to advance the current-time indicator to where the second bike lands after the jump. This should be at 00;00;02;18.

5 Click the Set In Point button (I) in the Program Monitor.

6 Drag the Program Monitor current-time indicator over the second clip to find a good matching edit point, such as timecode 00;00;03;25.

7 Click the Set Out Point button (O) in the Program Monitor.

As shown here, your Timeline now has a light blue highlighted zone between the In and Out points, as well as a gray area in the time ruler with In and Out point brackets at each end.

Note: The Lift and Extract buttons look the same until you get really close to the screen. As shown here, Extract has tiny triangles indicating that adjacent clips will fill the gap left by the edit.

Gray highlight

Blue highlight

Set In   Set Out

Lift Extract

8 Click the Lift button.

That deletes the selected frames and leaves a gap.

9 Press Ctrl+Z (Windows) or Command+Z (Mac OS) to undo that edit.

10 Click the Extract button.

That performs the equivalent of a ripple delete. Play this edit to see how, by clicking only one button, you edited two clips.

Replacing a clip and replacing footage

Sometimes you may want to replace a clip with another clip and have the new clip fit in the same place and inherit all the effects of the original clip. For example, you may create an opening sequence for wedding videos that you use over and over for new projects. By replacing the clip with a new clip, you can save a lot of time by not having to rebuild the opening sequence from scratch.

Adobe Premiere Pro provides two ways to do this: Replace Clip and Replace Footage. You'll explore them both.

Using the Replace Clip feature

Let's start with the Replace Clip feature:

1   Open Lesson 08-02.prproj.

2   Play the Timeline. Notice that the same clip is played twice as a picture-in-picture (PIP). The clip has some motion effects that cause it to spin onto the screen and then spin off. You will learn how to create these effects in a later lesson.

  You want to replace the first PIP clip (bike low shot.mov) in the Video 2 track with a new clip called multicam_03.mov. But you don't want to have to re-create all the effects and timing. This is a great scenario for using the Replace Clip feature.

3   Locate the multicam_03.mov clip, and drag it on top of the first bike low shot.mov clip. Do not drop it yet. Notice that it is longer than the clip on the Timeline.

4   Press Alt (Windows) or Option (Mac OS). Notice that the replacement clip now becomes the exact length of the clip it is replacing. Release the mouse button to complete the Replace Clip function.

5   Play the Timeline. Notice the first PIP clip has the same effects but is using the new footage. The second PIP clip remains unchanged.

Using the Replace Footage feature

The Replace Footage feature in Adobe Premiere Pro replaces footage in the Project panel. This can be a huge benefit when you need to replace a clip that recurs several times in a sequence or multiple sequences. When you use Replace Footage, all instances of the clip you replace are changed anywhere the original clip was used in any sequence in the project.

1 Press Ctrl+Z (Windows) or Command+Z (Mac OS) to undo the Replace Clip function you just performed. Play the Timeline to see the original bike low shot. mov clip being used in both picture-in-picture instances.

2 Select the bike low shot.mov clip in the Project panel.

3 Right-click (Windows) or control-click (Mac OS) the bike low shot.mov clip, and choose Replace Footage from the menu that appears.

4 Navigate to the Lessons/Assets folder, select the bike rides into frame.mov file, and click Select (Windows) or Open (Mac OS).

5 Play the Timeline, and notice that both PIP clips were replaced with the new footage while they maintained their timing and effects.

● **Note:** You can use the Replace Clip and Replace Footage features with dissimilar media. For example, you can replace a video clip with a still image.

Using Sync Lock and Track Lock

In a typical editing project, you will have multiple layers of video clips. When you edit a sequence by doing ripple edits or inserts, you'll want all the video tracks to stay in sync. This means if one track moves, all the other tracks move the same amount.

However, sometimes you may want one track not to move when you're performing ripples or inserts. Adobe Premiere Pro provides two methods of protecting one or more tracks from being moved: Sync Lock and Lock Track.

Using Sync Lock

Let's start by trying the Sync Lock feature:

1　Open Lesson 08-03.prproj. Note that this sequence has four video tracks with a gap between clips.

2　Right-click (Windows) or control-click (Mac OS) the gap between clips on the Video 1 track, and choose Ripple Delete.

　The clips on the right move left to close the gap.

3　Press Ctrl+Z (Windows) or Command+Z (Mac OS) to undo the ripple delete.

4　Switch the Toggle Sync Lock icon (▤) off on the Video 4 track. Notice that by default all tracks have Toggle Sync Lock enabled.

5　Right-click (Windows) or control-click (Mac OS) the gap between clips on the Video 1 track, and choose Ripple Delete. All tracks stay in sync except the Video 4 track. This is because you turned Toggle Sync Lock off on this track.

6　Press Ctrl+Z (Windows) or Command+Z (Mac OS) to undo the ripple delete.

7　Select the Ripple Edit tool, grab the right edge of the first clip in the Video 1 track, and drag it an inch or so to the left. All tracks ripple except the clips in the Video 4 track.

8　Grab the right edge of the first clip in the Video 4 track, and drag it to the left. Notice that the clips are still editable in this track. Turning Toggle Sync Lock off does not prevent the clips in the track from being edited or deleted.

Using Track Lock

Now let's try editing with the Track Lock feature:

1　Press Ctrl+Z (Windows) or Command+Z (Mac OS) a few times until the project is back to the start point.

2   Make sure all tracks have Toggle Sync Lock on.

3   Click the Track Lock icon () in the Video 4 track. Diagonal lines appear through the track header.

4   Try doing a ripple delete as you did earlier, and notice the locked track is unaffected.

5   Try to edit or move clips in the Video 4 track. Notice that you cannot do anything to the clips in the Video 4 track.

Note: A locked track differs from a track with Toggle Sync Lock turned off in that a locked track cannot be changed.

Finding gaps in the timeline

Adobe Premiere Pro tools make it easy to keep unwanted gaps out of your Timeline by snapping clips to one another and other objects such as the current-time indicator. But sometimes an unwanted gap in the Timeline will appear. If the gaps are large, they are easy to find. But if the gaps are very small, you might miss them. Adobe Premiere Pro has a tool to help you find gaps in your Timeline.

1   Continue were you left off in the Lesson 08-03.prproj project. There should still be gaps on the Timeline.

2   Position the current-time indicator at the beginning of the Timeline.

3   From the menu, choose Sequence > Go to Gap > Next in Sequence.

4   Notice that your current-time indicator is snapped to the first gap in the sequence where you can decide what to do with the gap.

Editing with In and Out points around a clip

In Lesson 5 you set In and Out points on a sequence to perform some lifts and extracts. You can use the same In and Out points in a sequence to identify the location to insert a source clip that also has In and Out points marked. This is called a *four-point edit*.

Adobe Premiere Pro has two features called In and Out Around Clip and In and Out Around Selection. In this exercise, you will perform a four-point edit using In and Out Around Clip. This may seem like a complex edit, but once you get used to it, you may find it will save you a lot of time in certain editing situations. This is especially helpful when your start and end frame points are both important but you need to replace the frames in between. Let's begin:

1   Open Lesson 08-04.prproj.

2   Play the Timeline, and then click the second clip to select it.

The second clip on the Timeline is going to be replaced with a clip of a different camera angle. You want to remove the second clip and replace it with the In and Out sections of a new clip you will specify.

3   Move the current-time indicator anywhere over the second clip. Right-click in the Timeline area.

4   Choose Set Sequence Marker > In and Out Around Clip. The Timeline is now shaded above the second clip.

5 Double-click the multicam_02.mov clip in the Project panel to open it in the Source Monitor.

6 Drag the current-time indicator in the Source Monitor to 00;00;14;20, and set the In point by clicking the Set In Point bracket ({).

7 Drag the current-time indicator in the Source Monitor to 00;00;16;20, and set the Out point by clicking the Set Out Point bracket (}).

8 Click the Overlay icon in the Source Monitor (as shown here) to overlay the marked source clip on the clip you marked on the Timeline. A dialog appears, warning that the marked source clip is shorter than the destination clip. Accept the default to allow Adobe Premiere Pro to adjust the speed of the source clip to make it match the length of the destination clip.

9 Play the Timeline.

Creating subclips from the Source Monitor

If you have a very long clip, it's often helpful to break it down into smaller clips (*subclips*). You can rename these subclips and store them in the Project panel in bins as you choose. Creating subclips can help you organize your project and make it easy to find just the clip you need.

1   Open Lesson 08-05.prproj.

2   Double-click multicam_01.mov to open it in the Source Monitor.

3   Set the In point at the beginning of the clip. Set the Out point at around 08;00 seconds. This will represent the race portion of the clip.

4   Drag the marked clip from the Source Monitor to the Project panel while holding down Ctrl (Windows) or Command (Mac OS).

5   When you drop the clip in the Project panel, you will be prompted to give it a name. Name this subclip *Race*. Notice that subclips have a different icon than master clips.

Now you will make a subclip from the Timeline rather than the Source Monitor.

6   Drag the master clip multicam_01.mov to the Timeline in the Video 1 track.

7   Drag the right edge of the multicam_01.mov clip out to its full length.

8   Using the Selection tool (⬌), drag the left edge of the clip to the right until you see the bikers high-five each other in the Program Monitor. This will be the Hug section of the clip.

9   Drag the shortened clip from the Timeline to the Project panel while holding down Ctrl (Windows) or Command (Mac OS).

10 When you drop the clip in the Project panel, you will be prompted to give it a name. Call this subclip *Hug*.

Multicamera editing

The Adobe Premiere Pro multicamera editing feature is a tremendous time-saver when you're editing footage from a shoot or event captured with multiple cameras. Say you have four clips that recorded the same bike race from four different camera angles, but the four cameras started recording at different times. Your first task is to find the same point in time for all four clips so they will be in sync.

Creating the initial multicamera sequence

The first step is to create a multicamera sequence from your captured footage:

1 Open Lesson 08-06.prproj.

2 Double-click multicam_01.mov to open it in the Source Monitor.

3 Move the Source Monitor current-time indicator to where the bikers high-five after the race, which is at 00;00;16;16.

   You will use the high five as a clapper slate to set the sync point on all four clips.

4 Right-click (Windows) or Control-click (Mac OS) in the Source Monitor time ruler, and choose Set Clip Marker > Next Available Numbered.

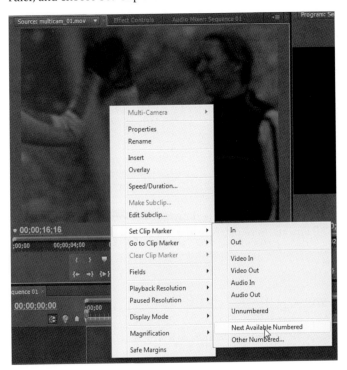

This adds a little marker triangle behind the Source Monitor current-time indicator (you'll need to drag the current-time indicator out of the way to see that marker).

5 Check that the Video 1 track header is targeted (highlighted). If not, click it as needed to target the track, and move the current-time indicator to the beginning of the sequence.

Note: You can put markers on clips or sequences. You use markers for a variety of purposes, most frequently to mark DVD chapter points in sequences. In this case, you will have Adobe Premiere Pro move the four clips so the markers you place on their sync points all line up vertically.

Using track targeting

When dragging clips from the Source Monitor to the Timeline, you target the track by dragging the clip to it. If you are adding clips to the Timeline by using the Source Monitor Insert or Overlay button, it is necessary to target your selected tracks or to tell Adobe Premiere Pro which track or tracks you want the clip to go to.

You must do two things to target the track or tracks you want to be the destination. Highlight (by selecting) the track or tracks you want to be the destination, and then target the track by dragging the source track indicator to the desired track. This may sound like a lot to do to target a single video or audio track, but this combination of tools can be very useful, such as when you have clips with multiple audio tracks attached.

Note: All four multicamera clips were recorded at the same time, so using the high five near the ends of the clips is a good way to sync them all up. Because they are at four different angles, you might have to look closely at some clips to see the exact frame where the bikers touch.

6 Click the Overlay button (Insert will work in this case too) in the Source Monitor to drop multicam_01.mov on the Video 1 track in the sequence.

7 Repeat the sync point location process, including adding the clip marker, for multicam_02.mov. I selected 00;00;16;29 as the sync point. Add the marker to this clip as you did on the first clip.

8 Click the Video 2 header to target that track, move the current-time indicator to the beginning of the sequence, and click the Overlay button in the Source Monitor.

Your sequence should look like the one shown here. Note the marker icons in the clips. You will line up those markers in a few steps.

9 Repeat this process for multicam_03.mov, marking it at 00;00;15;27, targeting the Video 3 track, and moving the Timeline current-time indicator to the beginning before clicking the Overlay button.

10 Repeat this process for multicam_04.mov, marking it at 00;00;17;06; however, there is no Video 4 track on the Timeline, so you can't target a track to overlay it to. Instead of moving the clip with the Overlay button, you can drag it to the Timeline. Click in the Source Monitor, drag to the gray blank space above the Video 3 track, and drop it. Adobe Premiere Pro creates the Video 4 track.

Your sequence should look like the one shown here. Notice that the markers do not line up. That is OK; you'll take care of that next. If you had trouble marking your clips, open Lesson 08-07.prproj to start at this point.

11 Marquee-select the four clips.

12 Check whether the Video 1 track is targeted (highlighted). If not, click its header to target it (it's not necessary, in this case, to target an audio track).

13 Choose Clip > Synchronize, select Numbered Clip Marker (Marker 0 is the only choice), and then click OK. The clips align to the marker on the clip in the Video 1 track.

All the markers are lined up vertically. The beginning of the clips above the Video 1 track were trimmed because they all had more video before the sync point than the clip in the Video 1 track. Now that all four clips are in sync, you can start switching camera angles.

Switching multiple cameras

Now you will nest that synced and trimmed sequence in another sequence, switch on the multicamera function, and edit this four-camera shoot:

1 Choose File > New > Sequence, and name it *Multi-cam*. Choose the preset DV – NTSC Standard 48kHz to match your source media for this project.

2 Drag Sequence 01 from the Project panel to the beginning of the Video 1 track on the Multi-cam sequence. This is called *nesting* a sequence in a sequence.

Note: The Multi-Camera > Enable command will be unavailable unless you have the video track selected.

3 Click the Video 1 track header to target it, click the nested sequence video clip to select it, and then choose Clip > Multi-Camera > Enable.

4 Choose Window > Multi-Camera Monitor.

The five-pane Multi-Camera Monitor opens.

5 Click the Play button in the Multi-Camera Monitor, and watch this video to get a feel for when to make your edits.

6 Move the current-time indicator to the beginning of the Timeline, click Play, and start clicking any of the four screens on the left side to switch among those cameras.

A red box appears around the selected camera each time you make an edit.

● **Note:** You can also press the number keys 1–4 to switch among the four cameras.

7 Use the playback controls to review your edited sequence.

Note that at each edit point a yellow box appears on that camera shot.

8 Close the Multi-Camera Monitor. You can always return to it by selecting it from the Program Monitor menu.

9 Take a look at the sequence in the Timeline.

As shown here, the sequence now has multiple cut edits. Each clip's label starts with *[MC#]*. The number represents the video track used for that edit.

● **Note:** After making your edits, you can always change them in the Multi-Camera Monitor or on the Timeline.

Finalizing multicamera editing

To change an edit in the Multi-Camera Monitor, do the following:

1 Open the Multi-Camera Monitor by choosing Window > Multi-Camera Monitor.

2 Click the Go To Previous (or Next) Edit Point button, or use the Page Up and Page Down key to move to an edit.

3 Click a different camera to change that edit.

Changing an edit in the Timeline

To change a multicamera edit in the Timeline, do the following:

1 Right-click (Windows) or Control-click (Mac OS) the clip you want to change.

2 Choose Multi-Camera from the context menu, and click the camera number.

Multicam tips

Here are a few helpful tips on multicam editing in Adobe Premiere Pro:

- You can use any of the Timeline editing tools to change the edit points of a multicam sequence.

- You can replay the multicam sequence with the Multi-Camera Monitor from any point to reedit the project.

- You can switch back to the sequence where the original clip is and apply effects or color correction (you'll learn about color correction in Lesson 16), and the effect will ripple to the nested multicam sequence.

● **Note:** This example of multicam footage did not include any audio.

- If you don't have a good visual clue in the video to sync multiple clips, look for a clap or loud noise in the audio track. It is often easier to sync video by looking for a common spike in the audio waveform.

▶ **Tip:** Audio is taken by Multicamera 1 by default. You can change this by going to the Multicamera menu and choosing "audio follows video."

Review questions

1 What's the basic difference between a slide edit and a slip edit?

2 What's going on when you use the Rolling Edit, Slip, or Slide tool and the clip frames stop moving in the Program Monitor and you can't move the edit point any further?

3 What is the difference between the Replace Clip feature and the Replace Footage feature?

4 What will happen to a subclip if you delete the master clip media from your hard drive?

5 Describe four ways to set sync points for multicamera clips.

Review answers

1 You *slide* a clip over adjacent clips, retaining the selected clip's original In and Out points. You *slip* a clip under adjacent clips, changing the selected clip's In and Out points.

2 You've reached the end of the line—the beginning or end of the original clip. There are no additional head or tail frames to enable you to move the edit any further.

3 Replace Clip replaces a single targeted clip on the Timeline with a new clip from the Project panel. Replace Footage replaces a clip in the Project panel with a new source clip. Any instance of the clip in any sequence in the project is replaced. In both cases, the effects of the replaced clip are maintained.

4 The subclip will go offline. Subclips do not copy the physical media of the master clip; they are references to it.

5 The four ways are clip start, clip end, timecode, and markers.

9 ADDING VIDEO EFFECTS

Topics covered in this lesson

- Sampling some basic video effects
- Applying effects to multiple clips
- Using keyframing effects
- Adding keyframe interpolation and velocity
- Applying lighting effects
- Creating custom presets

 This lesson will take approximately 90 minutes.

Adobe Premiere Pro CS5 features more than 140 video effects. Most effects come with an array of parameters, all of which you can *animate*—have them change over time—by using precise keyframe controls.

Getting started

Video effects let you add visual flair to your project or repair technical issues in your source footage. Video effects can alter the exposure or color of footage, distort images, or add artistic style. You can also use effects to rotate and animate a clip or adjust its size and position within the frame.

Adding video effects is easy: You can drag an effect to a clip, or you can select the clip and drag the effect to the Effect Controls panel. You can combine as many effects as you want on a single clip, which can produce surprising results. Moreover, you can use a nested sequence to add the same effects to a collection of clips.

Virtually all the video effect parameters are accessible within the Effect Controls panel, making it easy to set the behaviors and the intensity of those effects. You can add keyframes independently to every attribute listed in the Effect Controls panel to make those behaviors change over time. In addition, you can use Bezier curves to adjust the velocity and acceleration of those changes.

Adobe Premiere Pro has two types of effects: fixed and standard. Standard effects generally affect clip image quality and appearance, while fixed effects adjust clip position, scale, movement, opacity, speed, and audio volume. By default, fixed effects are automatically applied to every clip in a sequence, but they do not change the clip until they are manipulated.

When one of the supported video adapters is installed in the host computer, the Adobe Premiere Pro Mercury Playback Engine uses the graphics processing unit (GPU) to play back sequences. GPU acceleration offers the following benefits:

- You can stack multiple effects onto multiple video layers and play them back without rendering, often in real time.

- The 32-bit floating-point pipeline supports all the 32-bit effects available in Adobe Premiere Pro.

We don't have the space in this lesson to explain the more than 140 video effects included with Adobe Premiere Pro. Instead, you will look at a representative sample of what's available and learn how to apply the various types of parameters you'll encounter. To really get a feel for the possibilities of Adobe Premiere Pro, you'll need to do some experimenting.

Sampling some basic video effects

In this lesson, you will work with several effects, each offering something new in terms of its parameters or settings. Let's begin by creating a custom bin for your most frequently used effects.

1 Start Adobe Premiere Pro, open Lesson 09-1.prproj, and choose Window > Workspace > Effects to switch to the Effects workspace.

2 If necessary, click the Effects tab next to the Project panel to make it visible.

3 Open the Video Effects folder.

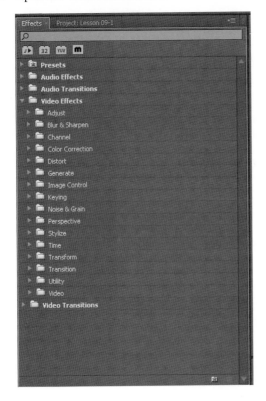

● **Note:** You'll see many Video Effects categories. Some effects are difficult to categorize and could reside in multiple categories or in categories by themselves, but this taxonomy works reasonably well.

4 Click the Effects panel menu, and choose New Custom Bin or click the New Custom Bin icon at the bottom of the panel.

The New Custom bin/folder appears in the Effects panel below Video Transitions.

5 Highlight the bin, and change its name to something like *My Favorite Effects*.

6 Open any Video Effects folder, and drag a few effects into your custom bin.

● **Note:** The effects remain in their original folder and also appear in yours. You can use custom folders to build effect categories that match your work style.

7 Choose Video Effects > Image Control > Black & White, and drag the Black & White video effect to the Medieval_villain_01.mpeg clip on the Timeline.

● **Note:** The Effect Controls panel contains three other effects: Motion, Opacity, and Time Remapping. These are fixed effects. Adobe Premiere Pro automatically makes them available for all video clips. If the clip has audio, you will also see the Volume fixed effect.

Applying this effect immediately converts your full-color footage to black and white—or, more accurately, *grayscale*. It also puts that effect in the Effect Controls panel.

8 If necessary, click the Effect Controls tab to open it. Toggle the Black & White effect off and on by using the button in the Effect Controls panel. Be sure the current-time indicator is on this footage clip to view the effect.

Toggling an effect on and off is a good way to see how an effect works with other effects. This toggle switch is the only parameter available with the Black & White effect. The effect is either on or off.

Resolve jarring shifts to grayscale

Moving between full-color and black-and-white clips can be jarring, so here's a fix: Use a cross-dissolve between clips or within the grayscale clip. To put one within the clip in this lesson, select the Razor Edit tool (C), cut the clip in two places, drag the Cross Dissolve transition to those edit points, select the first and third clip segments in turn, and switch off the Black & White effect on both. Now your sequence shifts gradually from color to black and white and then back to color. Undo those edits by clicking the History tab and clicking Apply Filter.

9 Check that the clip is selected so that its parameters are displayed in the Effect Controls panel, click Black & White to select it, and then press the Delete key.

10 Choose Video Effects > Blur & Sharpen > Directional Blur, and drag the Directional Blur effect to the Effect Controls panel.

Here is the other way to apply a video effect: Select the clip in the Timeline to display it in the Effect Controls panel, and drag the effect to the Effect Controls panel.

Finding effects

With so many Video Effects subfolders, it's sometimes tricky to locate the effect you want. If you know part or all of an effect's name, start typing it in the Contains text box at the top of the Effects panel. Adobe Premiere Pro immediately displays all effects and transitions that contain that letter combination, narrowing the search as you type.

11 In the Effect Controls panel, expand the Directional Blur effect's filter, and note there are options the Black & White effect did not have: Direction, Blur Length, and a stopwatch next to each option (the stopwatch icon is to activate keyframing, which we will cover later in this lesson).

12 Set Direction to 91 degrees and Blur Length to 4 to simulate the scene being filmed with a slow shutter speed.

13 Expand the Blur Length option, and move the slider in the Effect Controls panel.

Note: The specific options available in each effect vary; however, they all operate in a similar manner.

As you change that setting, it shows up in real time in the Program Monitor.

14 Open the Effect Controls panel menu, and choose Remove Effects. Click OK in the dialog box that pops up asking which effects you want to remove. You want to remove them all.

This is an easy way to start fresh.

15 Choose Video Effects > Distort, and select the Spherize effect. Drag it to the Effect Controls panel, and click its disclosure triangles to display its parameters.

Like the Motion fixed effect above it in the Effect Controls panel, Spherize has a Transform button that lets you directly control its location in the Program Monitor.

16 Move the Radius slider to about 170 so you can see the effect in the Program Monitor.

17 Click the word *Spherize* (the name of the effect) in the Effect Controls panel to switch on its Transform control crosshair in the Program Monitor, and drag the effect around in that screen.

● **Note:** Wave Warp has three menus. These are specific effect conditions that do not have numeric values associated with them, but even these can be keyframes; that is, you can switch from one discrete condition to another at any time in the clip's duration.

18 Delete Spherize, and choose Video Effects > Distort >Wave Warp. Drag the Wave Warp effect to the Effect Controls panel, and click its six disclosure triangles to display its eight parameters.

19 Make various selections from each of the three menus; then adjust some of the other parameters.

20 Play this clip.

This is one of the animated effects you'll find in Adobe Premiere Pro. Although virtually all Adobe Premiere Pro video effects let you animate them over time with keyframes, Wave Warp and a few others have built-in animations that operate independently of keyframes.

21 Reset the Wave Warp effect to its starting point by clicking the Reset button in its upper-right corner.

Applying effects to multiple clips

In this exercise, you will apply the same effect to two clips in the Timeline at the same time. Although you'll be using only two clips, you can use the technique to apply the same effect (or effects) to as many clips as you can select.

1 Remove any effects you have been testing from both clips on the Timeline by right clicking on the clips and selecting remove effects.

2 Select both clips on the Timeline by holding down the Shift key and clicking each one. You can also use the Marquee tool to select a group of clips.

3 Choose Video Effects > Generate, and drag the Lens Flare effect to either clip. The effect is applied to both selected clips.

Other ways to apply effects

You can also select an effect from the Effect Controls panel, choose Edit > Copy, select the Effects Controls panel of a destination clip, and choose Edit > Paste.

To copy all the effects from one clip so you can paste them to another clip, select the clip, choose Edit > Copy, select the destination clip, and choose Edit > Paste Attributes.

Adding keyframing effects

You can turn almost all parameters for all video effects into keyframes. That is, you can change the effect's behavior over time in myriad ways. For example, you can have an effect gradually change out of focus, change color, warp into a fun-house mirror, or lengthen its shadow.

1 Select the first clip on the Timeline.

2 Expand the display of the Effect Controls panel until its view is wide enough for the Show/Hide Timeline View button to become active.

▶ **Tip:** Depending on your screen size, you might want to turn the Effect Controls panel into a floating window.

3 Delete any effects on the clips, then choose Presets > Solarize > Solarize In, and finally drag the Solarize In preset to the Effect Controls panel.

4 Play the clip to see how this preset works. The clip starts at the maximum Solarize threshold value and reduces to 0 at the one-second point.

5 Drag the effect's second keyframe to the right; then play the clip again.

It takes longer for the Solarize effect to resolve to the normal image. Keyframes are not permanently fixed; you can change a keyframe's position without changing its value.

6 Delete the Solarize effect. Choose Video Effects > Stylize, select the Replicate effect, drag it to the Effect Controls panel, and click its single disclosure triangle to display its parameter.

7 With the Effect Controls panel active, press the Home or Page Up key or drag the timeline indicator to position the current-time indicator at the beginning of the clip.

8 Click the "Toggle animation" button, shown here.

Clicking this button does three things:

- Activates keyframing for the Replicate effect's Count parameter

- Adds a keyframe at the current-time indicator location and gives it Replicate's default starting value of 2 (a 2x2 grid of replicated clips)

- Displays two thin lines in the Effect Controls Timeline: the Value graph and the Velocity graph

● **Note:** Changing the effect's Count parameter automatically adds another keyframe at the current-time indicator's position in the Effect Controls Timeline; changing a parameter at a location without a keyframe automatically adds a new keyframe.

9 Drag the current-time indicator to about the one-second point. Locate the one-second point by looking in the Program Monitor or the Timeline time ruler. It's generally not easy to see an exact time in the Effect Controls Timeline unless you really widen its viewing area.

10 Change the Replicate effect's Count parameter to 4.

11 Drag the current-time indicator to about the three-second point.

12 Click the Add/Remove Keyframe button (between the two keyframe navigation buttons). Adobe Premiere Pro adds a keyframe with the same value as the previous keyframe. In this way, the effect will not change from the one-second to the three-second position.

13 Press Page Down, and then press the left arrow key to go to the end of the clip. The last frame of the clip appears.

14 Change the Count value to 10.

Your Effect Controls panel should look like the one shown here.

● **Note:** Pressing Page Down takes you to the frame following the last frame in a selected clip. That is by design. You can use the keyboard shortcut Page Down to go to the start of the next clip, not the final frame of the current clip.

15 Play the clip, and note how the effect builds to a 6x6 grid, holds for two seconds, and then changes to a 16x16 grid at the end.

Now you'll use two methods to change two keyframe values.

16 Click the Go To Previous Keyframe button twice to move to the second keyframe.

17 Use the slider to change the Count value to 2. That's one simple way to change a keyframe's value.

18 Click the Go To Next Keyframe button to move to the third (out of four) keyframe.

Note: You can drag the keyframe only up or down. It will not allow you to move it left or right to avoid inadvertently changing the keyframe's time position within the clip.

19 Hover the pointer over the corresponding keyframe on the Value graph (shown here). When it changes to the Selection tool, drag the keyframe as high as it will go to change its value to 16.

This is the other way to change a keyframe's value.

Note: If you don't move the current-time indicator to the clip you're applying an effect to, you won't see that clip or its effect in the Program Monitor. Selecting a clip does not move the current-time indicator to that clip.

20 Drag the title called Sir Drake from the Project panel to the track above the first video clip. Stretch the title clip to be the same length as the video clip beneath it.

21 Position the current-time indicator at the beginning of the Sir Drake clip, and select it to display its parameters in the Effect Controls panel.

22 Select the Magnify effect from the Video Effects > Distort menu, and drag it to the title clip or to the Effect Controls panel.

23 Set a keyframe at the beginning of the clip, with the Center value set to 10, 240.

24 Set a keyframe near the middle of the clip, with the Center value set to 740, 240.

Note: Make sure to activate keyframing in the Center option by clicking the "Toggle animation" button.

Note: Effects are great ways to animate or move a graphic or some text over a video clip.

25 Play this clip.

Extra credit: combining effects

Open Lesson 09-2.prproj to see multiple keyframed effects added to the title clip Sir Drake. Gaussian Blur, Lens Flare, and Basic 3D effects are applied to the same title clip so you can deconstruct the file. Each effect is keyframed over time.

- Gaussian Blur provides an interesting entrance and exit for the title.

- Lens Flare moves across the letters, giving the illusion of light and movement.

- Basic 3D gives the title a swivel movement that enhances the Lens Flare effect.

See whether you can re-create the effect from scratch.

Creating an effect preset

If you plan to reuse an effect with keyframes, save it as a preset. To do that, set your keyframes, parameters, and interpolation controls (these will be covered later); then click the effect name in the Effect Controls panel, open the panel menu, choose Save Preset, give the preset a name, note whether to scale it to the clip length or anchor it to the clip In or Out point, and then click OK. It'll show up in the Presets folder.

Order counts

Clip-based (nonfixed) video effects work from bottom to top in the Effect Controls panel, with the most recently applied effect appearing at the bottom of the effect list. For example, if you apply the Tint effect and then apply Black & White, the clip will appear as grayscale. Black & White trumps Tint because it appears below Tint in the Effect Controls panel effect list. If you apply Black & White first and then apply Tint, the clip will have the color you select in the Tint effect. Opacity and Motion, which are fixed effects, are always the final two effects applied—even when, in this case, you used a Motion preset and applied it first. If you want Motion to be applied in a different order, then use a clip-based motion effect, such as Basic 3D. You can drag effects up and down within the Effect Controls panel to change their order.

Adding keyframe interpolation and velocity

Keyframe interpolation changes the behavior of an effect parameter as it moves toward or away from a keyframe. The default behavior you've seen so far is linear—in other words, you have a constant velocity between keyframes. What generally works better is something that mirrors your experience or exaggerates it, such as a gradual acceleration or deceleration or super-fast changes.

Adobe Premiere Pro offers two ways to control those changes: keyframe interpolation and the Velocity graph. Keyframe interpolation is the easiest—basically two clicks—while tweaking the Velocity graph can become a full-time occupation. Getting a handle on this feature will take some time and practice on your part.

For this lesson, you'll use the Motion fixed effect. Its Position, Scale, and Rotation parameters all lend themselves to speed changes.

1 Open Lesson 09-3.prproj.

2 The title Sir Drake is over the Medieval_villain_01.mpeg clip. Click the title clip to select it.

3 Stretch the Effect Controls panel as wide as you can without covering up other workspace elements you need to see. If you put it in a floating window, leave room to view the Program Monitor.

4 Open the Effect Controls panel's Timeline (click the Show/Hide Timeline View button).

   You will be adding four Rotation keyframes: the first frame, the last frame, and two more frames spaced in between.

5 Position the current-time indicator at the beginning of the clip, expand the Motion effect, and click the Rotation effect's "Toggle animation" button. This adds a keyframe at the beginning of the clip with the default parameter value of 0.

6 Drag the current-time indicator to the three other positions, and click the Add/Remove Keyframe button in each spot.

   Your Effect Controls panel should look like the one shown here.

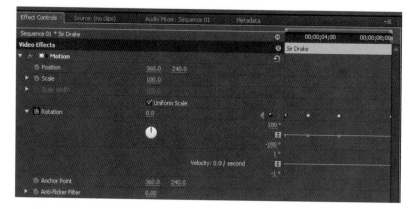

7 Look at the numbers highlighted in the previous figure. Expand the Rotation parameter if you haven't already.

   - **100 and −100**: These are default values for the highest and lowest Rotation parameter settings. They will change to accommodate the actual high and low Rotation values once you change the keyframe settings.

   - **1 and −1**: These are default relative velocity values. Since you have not changed any parameters, the velocity is a straight line with a value of 0.

8 Change the Rotation value for the second, third, and fourth keyframes by using three separate methods (navigate to the keyframes by using the Go To Next/Previous Keyframe buttons):

- **Second keyframe**: Click the Rotation value, and type *2x* (two full clockwise rotations).

- **Third keyframe**: Drag the keyframe on the Value graph to −1x0.0 degrees.

- **Fourth keyframe**: Drag the Rotation wheel left until the value displayed is something like −2x0.0 degrees. You can also select and type in the value.

Once completed, your keyframes and graphs should look like the ones shown here. If the graph lines are not entirely visible, click the "Toggle automatic range rescaling" button.

Parameter Value

Velocity/Direction

"Toggle automatic range rescaling" button

9 Drag the current-time indicator through the clip, and look at the Value and Velocity graphs and the numbers to the left of the graphs (shown in the previous figure). You should see the following:

- The top and bottom Value numbers have changed to 2x0 and −2x0 (two full rotations in both directions) to show the actual maximum and minimum parameter values. They remain unchanged as you move the current-time indicator.

- The Value graph shows the parameters' values at any given time.

- The top and bottom Velocity numbers on the left side of the graph indicate the spread of the parameters' velocity in degrees per second.

- The Velocity graph shows the velocity between keyframes. The sudden drops or jumps represent sudden changes in acceleration—*jerks*, in physics parlance. Points on the graph above the middle of the Velocity graph area represent positive (clockwise) speeds, and points below the center represent negative (counterclockwise) speeds. The farther the point or line is from the center, the greater the velocity (and you thought high-school algebra was a waste of time).

10 Press Enter (Windows) or Return (Mac OS) to render the work area; then play the clip.

The text spins clockwise twice, spins faster going counterclockwise three times, and then slows down for one last rotation.

11 Right-click (Windows) or Control-click (Mac OS) the first keyframe, and then choose Ease Out.

This does several things:

- The keyframe icon changes to an hourglass.

- The keyframe on the Value graph now has a Pen Tool handle, and the graph has a slight curve.

- The keyframe on the Velocity graph has a similar Pen Tool handle and a more obvious curve. That curve shows the velocity change over time— its acceleration.

12 Play that portion of the clip. The effect looks more realistic as the motion "eases."

13 Right-click (Windows) or Control-click (Mac OS) the next three keyframes, and apply (in this order) the Bezier, Auto Bezier, and Ease In interpolation methods.

Here's a rundown on the Adobe Premiere Pro keyframe interpolation methods:

- **Linear**: This method is the default behavior, which creates a uniform rate of change between keyframes.

- **Bezier**: This method lets you manually adjust the shape of the graph on either side of a keyframe. Beziers allow for sudden acceleration changes into or out of a keyframe.

- **Continuous Bezier**: This method creates a smooth rate of change through a keyframe. Unlike Bezier, if you adjust one handle, the handle on the other side of the keyframe moves in a complementary fashion to ensure a smooth transition through the keyframe.

- **Auto Bezier**: This method creates a smooth rate of change through a keyframe even if you change the keyframe parameter value. If you choose to manually adjust its handles, it changes to a Continuous Bezier point, retaining the smooth transition through the keyframe.

- **Hold**: This method changes a property value without a gradual transition (sudden effect change). The graph following a keyframe with the Hold interpolation applied appears as a horizontal straight line.

- **Ease In**: This method slows down the value changes entering a keyframe.

- **Ease Out**: This method gradually accelerates the value changes leaving a keyframe.

Your Effect Controls Timeline should look like the one shown here (the Value and Velocity graph-limit numbers might differ, depending on the size of your Effect Controls panel).

Note: By adding these smooth curves, the parameter values change over the course of the effect such that they sometimes might be greater than the highest keyframe parameter value or less than the lowest keyframe parameter you set.

14 Play the entire clip, and marvel (really) at how slick it looks.

Simply by adding keyframe interpolation, you've made your Motion effect look much more realistic.

15 Select the second keyframe—the Bezier hourglass—to activate it.

Pen Tool handles appear on the Value and Velocity graph keyframes as well as on the two adjacent sets of keyframes. That's because changing one keyframe's interpolation handles can change the behavior of the keyframes next to it.

16 Drag the handle on the Velocity graph keyframe (shown here).

This creates a steep velocity curve, meaning the title will accelerate quickly and then decelerate quickly, but it will still spin only twice between the first and second keyframes. You changed the velocity without changing the value.

17 Select the third keyframe—the Auto Bezier circle icon—to activate it.

18 Drag the handle, and note that the circular keyframe icon immediately switches to an hourglass, because manually adjusting an Auto Bezier keyframe makes it a Continuous Bezier keyframe.

Note: If you add another keyframe, it will have keyframe interpolation already applied to it. When you first add keyframes, you can grab their Value and Velocity graph handles and adjust the curves manually. Making any such adjustment will change the keyframe icon to the Bezier keyframe interpolation hourglass.

One additional velocity/interpolation issue

When working with position-related parameters, the context menu for a keyframe will offer two types of interpolation options: Spatial Interpolation (related to location) and Temporal Interpolation (related to time). You can make spatial adjustments in the Program Monitor as well as the Effect Controls panel. You can make temporal adjustments on the clip in the Timeline and in the Effect Controls panel.

These motion-related topics are covered in Lesson 10.

Adding lighting effects

This exercise combines hands-on, step-by-step tasks with experimentation. The purpose is to introduce you to a couple more advanced lighting effects and to encourage you to explore further.

1 Choose Help > Adobe Premiere Pro Help.

2 Type *Gallery of effects* in the Search field, and press Enter.

> **Note:** The other headings under Effect Reference match bin names in the Effects panel.

You will see examples of about a third of the video effects that come with Adobe Premiere Pro.

3 Search Adobe Premiere Pro Help for *Lighting effect*.

This gives you an explanation of each parameter—25 in all!—in the Lighting effect. Every Adobe Premiere Pro video and audio effect has such a listing in Adobe Premiere Pro Help. This also illustrates how complete and useful Adobe Premiere Pro Help is.

4 Quit Help, return to the Adobe Premiere Pro workspace, and open Lesson 09-4.prproj.

5 Choose Video Effects > Adjust, select Lighting Effects, and drag it to the clip in the Video 1 track.

6 Expand Lighting Effects and Light 1. You will leave off Lights 2 through 4.

7 Use the Color Picker under Light 1 to choose a yellow color from the torch flame in the Program Monitor.

8 Set the Major Radius and Minor Radius values to 24. Set the Intensity value to 50 and the Focus value to 10.

9 Toggle this effect on and off to see the significant difference it makes on the mood of the scene.

Lighting effects off   Lighting effects on

10 Remove all effects from the video clip, and move the current-time indicator to the beginning of the clip.

11 Drag the Leave Color effect from the Color Correction folder to the video clip.

12 Use the eyedropper tool next to the Color To Leave field to sample the yellow from the torch flame.

13 Set the Amount to Decolor slider to 100 percent. This will decolor everything except the color you chose with the eyedropper.

14 Set the Tolerance slider to about 35 percent.

15 Render and play the clip to see the effect. The whole scene should be black and white, with the exception of the yellow torch flame.

Creating custom presets

Adobe Premiere Pro allows you to save your favorite effect settings to your own custom preset so you don't have to re-create the settings every time. A preset may contain a single effect or multiple effects. Presets can be exported so you can share them with other editors, and of course you can import presets that have been exported from Adobe Premiere Pro.

In this exercise, you'll create a combination of effects and then save them as a custom preset:

1 Open Lesson 09-5.prproj.

2 Play the Timeline, and note that the title Sir Drake is just a static title. You will animate it like you were challenged to try on your own earlier in the lesson as extra credit on page 173.

3 Drag the Basic 3D filter from the Perspective bin to the title clip. Set a keyframe at the beginning of the clip with Swivel set to –25. Set an end keyframe with Swivel set to 25.

4 Drag the Lens Flare filter to the title clip. Set a keyframe at the beginning of the clip with Flare Center set to 20, 192. Set an end keyframe with Flare Center set to 700, 192.

5 Drag the Gaussian Blur filter to the title clip Sir Drake. Set a keyframe at the beginning of the clip with Blurriness set to 300. Set a second keyframe about one second in with Blurriness set to 0. Set a third keyframe about one second from the end with Blurriness set to 0, and finally set the end keyframe with Blurriness set to 700.

6 Play the clip. The title swivels slightly, the lens flare travels across the letters, and the whole title blurs in and out of existence. If you have problems setting up these filters, click the Finished sequence to see the completed effect.

Now that the combination of effects is working just how you want it to, you will save the combination of three effects as a single custom preset so you can use it again later.

7 Select the title clip so the three effects are visible in the Effect Controls panel. Collapse the three effects so each occupies only one line.

8 Hold down Ctrl (Windows) or Command (Mac), and click each of the three effects (Basic 3D, Lens Flare, Gaussian Blur) to select them all.

9 In the Effect Controls panel menu, choose Save Preset.

10 Name the preset, and click OK.

The preset appears in your Custom Preset folder.

11 Try dragging it to other titles to confirm that it works.

Review questions

1 What are the two ways to apply an effect to a clip?

2 List three ways to add a keyframe.

3 How do you make an effect start within a clip, rather than at the beginning?

4 Dragging an effect to a clip turns on its parameters in the Effect Controls panel, but you don't see the effect in the Program Monitor. Why not?

5 Describe how you can drag one effect to multiple clips.

6 Describe how to save multiple effects to a custom preset.

Review answers

1   Drag the effect to the clip, or select the clip and drag the effect to the Effect Controls panel.

2   Move the current-time indicator in the Effect Controls panel to where you want a keyframe, and activate keyframing by clicking the "Toggle animation" button; move the current-time indicator, and click the Add/Remove Keyframe button; and with keyframing activated, move the current-time indicator to a position, and change a parameter.

3   One of two ways, depending on the effect. Some effects, such as Fast Blur, have a 0 setting where they do not change the clip's appearance. In that case, add a keyframe where you want the effect to start, and then set it to 0. Other effects are always on to some degree. In those cases, use the Razor Edit tool to cut the clip where you want the effect to start, and then apply the effect to the segment on the right.

4   You need to move the Timeline current-time indicator to the selected clip to see it in the Program Monitor. Simply selecting a clip does not move the current-time indicator to that clip.

5   Select multiple clips on the Timeline by Shift-selecting or dragging a selection around them, and then drag the effect to the group of selected clips.

6   Ctrl-click (Windows) or Command-click (Mac OS) multiple effects in the Effect Controls panel, and then choose the Save Preset command from the menu that appears.

10

PUTTING CLIPS IN MOTION

Topics covered in this lesson

- Applying the Motion effect to clips
- Changing clip size and adding rotation
- Working with keyframe interpolation
- Creating a picture-in-picture effect
- Enhancing motion with shadows and beveled edges
- Using other motion-related effects such as Basic 3D and Camera View

 This lesson will take approximately 50 minutes.

The Motion fixed effect adds drama to static images and lets you change image sizes, fly them anywhere on (and off) the screen, and rotate them. You can further enhance motion characteristics by adding drop shadows and frames and creating picture-in-picture (PIP) effects.

Getting started

As you watch TV advertisements, you're bound to see videos with clips flying over other images or clips that rotate onscreen—starting as small dots and expanding to full-screen size. You can create those effects by using the Motion fixed effect or several clip-based effects with Motion settings.

You use the Motion effect to position, rotate, or scale a clip within the video frame. You can make those adjustments directly in the Program Monitor by dragging to change its position, or you can drag or rotate its handles to change its size, shape, or orientation.

You can also adjust Motion parameters in the Effect Controls panel and animate clips by using keyframes and Bezier controls.

Applying the Motion effect to clips

You adjust Motion effect parameters in the Program Monitor and the Effect Controls panel.

1   Open Lesson 10-1.prproj.

2   Choose Window > Workspace > Effects to switch to the Effects workspace.

3   Open the Select Zoom Level menu in the Program Monitor, and change the zoom level to 25%.

This helps you see and work with the Motion effect's bounding box.

4   Expand the Program Monitor frame (if necessary) so there are no scroll bars on
    the screen.

    Your Program Monitor should look like the previous figure.

5   Play the clip in the Timeline.

6   Click the clip to select it, and then click the Motion disclosure triangle in the
    Effect Controls panel to display its parameters.

7   Click Position's "Toggle animation" stopwatch button to turn off its keyframes.

8   Click OK when prompted that all keyframes will be deleted if you apply
    the action.

9   Click the Reset button (to the right of Motion in the Effect Controls panel).

    These two actions return Motion to its default settings.

Examining Motion settings

To examine some Motion settings, follow these steps:

1   Drag the current-time indicator anywhere in the clip so you can see the video
    in the Program Monitor.

2   Click the video frame in the Program Monitor.

A bounding box with a crosshair and handles appears around the clip (shown here) and activates the Motion effect in the Effect Controls panel. Clicking Motion or its Transform button in the Effect Controls panel will also activate the clip bounding box in the Program Monitor.

3 Click anywhere in the clip bounding box in the Program Monitor, drag this clip around, and note how the Position values in the Effect Controls panel change.

4 Drag the clip so its center is directly over the upper-left corner of the screen, and note that the Position values in the Effect Controls panel are 0, 0 (or close to that, depending on where you placed the center of the clip).

The lower-right corner of the screen is 1280, 720—the frame size of the 720p sequence setting used for this project.

5 Drag the clip completely off the screen to the left, as shown here.

● **Note:** Adobe Premiere Pro CS5 uses something like an upside-down x, y coordinate system for screen location. That coordinate system is based on a methodology used in Windows for so long that to change it now would create numerous programming head-aches. The upper-left corner of the screen is 0, 0. All x and y values respectively to the left of and above that point are negative. All x and y values respectively to the right of and below that point are positive.

6 Fine-tune that adjustment by changing the Position values in the Effect Controls panel to –640, 360.

Since 640 is half of 1280, this puts the right edge of the clip at the left edge of the screen frame.

7 Press Page Up or Home to put the current-time indicator at the beginning of the clip or drag the current time indicator there, and add a Position keyframe there by clicking Position's "Toggle animation" button.

8 Drag the current-time indicator to the middle of the clip, and change the Position values to 640, 360 (the center of the screen).

Changing the Position parameters adds a keyframe at the current-time indicator.

9 Press Page Down and then the left arrow key to position the current-time indicator at the end of the clip.

10 Change the Position values to 640, −360.

This places the clip completely above the screen and adds a keyframe.

11 Play the clip.

It moves smoothly onscreen and then slides off the top. You have created a path (if you don't see the path, click the word *Motion* in the Effect Controls panel to switch on its display). Make note of a few things (shown in the following figure):

- It's a curved path. Adobe Premiere Pro automatically uses Bezier curves for motion.

- The little dots describe both the path and the velocity. Dots closer together represent a lower speed; dots farther apart represent a higher speed.

- The little four-point stars are keyframes.

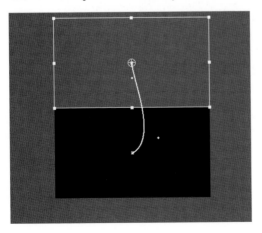

12 Drag the current time indicator to the position of the center keyframe. Drag the center keyframe in the Program Monitor (the four-point star/square) down and to the left.

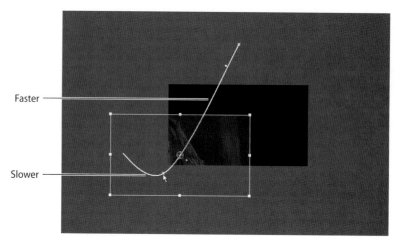

Notice that the dots get closer together to the left of the keyframe and farther apart to the right.

13 Play the clip. Note that it moves slowly until the first keyframe and then speeds up.

14 Drag the center keyframe again, this time down and to the right (use the figure shown here as a reference).

Now you've created a parabola with evenly spaced dots on both sides, meaning the velocity will be the same on both arms of the parabola.

15 Drag the center keyframe in the Effect Controls panel first to the left and then most of the way to the right.

16 Play this clip, and note how much slower it goes at the beginning and how much faster it goes at the end.

It should behave the same way it did when you opened Lesson 10-1.prproj.

● **Note:** By moving the center keyframe, you changed its location and thereby the distance the clip traveled between it and its adjacent keyframes. But you didn't change the time between keyframes. So, the clip moves faster between keyframes that are farther apart and slower for those closer to one another.

● **Note:** Now you are changing the time between keyframes but not changing their physical location in the screen. The little path/velocity dots in the Program Monitor spread out or slide closer together, but the keyframes do not change locations.

Changing clip size and adding rotation

Simply sliding a clip around only begins to exploit the possibilities of the Motion effect. What makes the Motion effect so useful is the capability to shrink or expand the clip and to spin it.

For example, you can start a clip full-screen (or zoom in even further) and then shrink it to reveal another clip. You can spin a clip onto the screen by having it start as a small dot and then spin it off the screen, having it grow as it moves away. You can also layer multiple clips, creating several PIP effects.

Before you dive into this exercise, look at Motion's six "keyframeable" options:

- **Position**: This is the screen location of the clip's anchor point (its center unless you change the anchor point).

- **Scale (Scale Height, when Uniform Scale is deselected)**: Scale refers to the relative size of the clip. The slider has a range from 0 to 100 percent, but you can set the numerical representation to increase the clip size to 600 percent of its original size.

> **Note:** The percent refers to the clip border perimeter, not the clip area. So, 50 percent is equal to 25 percent in terms of area, and 25 percent is equal to 6.25 percent in area.

- **Scale Width**: You must deselect Uniform Scale to make Scale Width available. Doing so lets you change the clip's width and height independently.

- **Rotation**: You can input degrees or number of rotations, for example 450° or 1 x 90. A positive number is clockwise, and a negative number is counter-clockwise. The maximum number of rotations allowed in either direction is 90, meaning you can apply up to 180 full rotations to a clip.

- **Anchor Point**: The Anchor Point setting is the center of the rotation, as opposed to the center of the clip. You can set the clip to rotate around any point on the screen, including one of the clip's corners, or around a point outside the clip like a ball at the end of a rope.

- **Anti-flicker Filter**: This feature is useful for images that contain high-frequency detail, such as fine lines, hard edges, parallel lines (moiré problems), or rotation. Those characteristics can cause flickering during motion. The default setting (0.00) adds no blurring and has no effect on flicker. To add some blurring and eliminate flicker, use 1.00.

1   Open Lesson 10-2.prproj, and open the Finished sequence.

2   Play the clip to see the animation.

    This is how the Motion effect will look by the end of this exercise.

3   Open the Practice sequence to start with the same clip but with no effects.

4   Place the current-time indicator at the beginning of the clip, expand the Motion effect, click Position's "Toggle animation" button to activate keyframing, and move the center of the clip to the upper-left corner (position 0, 0).

5 Expand the Scale parameter, click Scale's "Toggle animation" button to activate keyframing, and drag the slider to 0.

That sets the size to 0 for the beginning of the clip.

6 Drag the current-time indicator about a third of the way into the clip, and click the Reset button. That creates two keyframes that use Motion's default settings: the clip at full size and centered in the screen.

7 Drag the current-time indicator about two-thirds of the way into the clip, and click the Add/Remove Keyframe button for Position and for Scale.

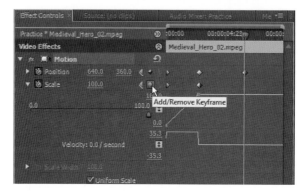

The clip will remain centered and at full-screen for the time between the two keyframes. You could also have clicked Reset again to use those default parameters and achieve the same effect.

8 Press Page Down and the left arrow key with the Timeline active to move the current-time indicator to the end of the clip, and change the Position parameters to 1280, 720 (lower-right corner).

9 In the Program Monitor, drag a bounding box corner handle to shrink the clip all the way down to the center crosshairs. That sets Scale back to 0.

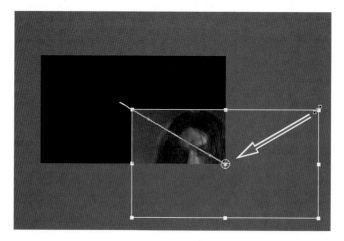

Changing clip size— like working with text

As you did in the Titler, you can change clip size by using the bounding box. Deselect Uniform Scale; then, to scale freely, drag a corner handle. To scale one dimension only, drag a side (not a corner) handle; to scale proportionally, Shift-drag any handle.

10 Play this clip.

The clip should grow from a tiny dot in the upper left, move to full-screen in the center, hold there for a while, and then shrink to a dot while moving to the lower-right corner.

Adding rotation and changing the anchor point

Now you'll add some rotation to the clip:

1 With the Timeline active, press Page Up or Home to move the current-time indicator to the beginning of the clip, and click Rotation's "Toggle animation" button.

That sets a keyframe for Rotation with 0.0° as the starting point.

2 Click the Go to Next Keyframe button next to either Position or Scale to move the current-time indicator to the second keyframe.

3 Hover the pointer just outside a handle of the bounding box in the Program Monitor until it becomes a curved double-arrow pointer, and then drag the bounding box clockwise two full rotations, as shown here.

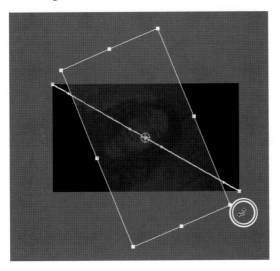

Note: You can fine-tune this move in the Effect Controls panel by setting Rotation to 2x0.0°.

4   Move the current-time indicator to the third keyframe, and click the Rotation Add/Remove Keyframe button. That adds a keyframe with the same value as the preceding keyframe.

5   Move the current-time indicator to the end of the clip.

6   Click the Rotation disclosure triangle to expand the Rotation parameter, and drag the Rotation circle counterclockwise twice. Note that you can't use the Program Monitor bounding box to adjust Rotation because the clip has been shrunk to a point.

That returns Rotation to its default setting of 0.0°. If you can't see the keyframe graphs, expand the Scale and Rotation parameters. Play this clip. It will rotate clockwise twice, hold, and then rotate counterclockwise.

7   Play this effect. It should look similar to the effect in the Finished sequence. A difference between this effect and what you see in the Finished sequence is that the rotation suddenly stops and starts. You'll fix that next.

If you like the effect, you can save it as a preset. Right-click (Windows) or Control-click (Mac OS) the Motion effect, and choose Save Preset.

● **Note:** When you save a preset, you can choose for the preset to scale the length of any clip or anchor to a specific In or Out point. In many cases, setting the effect to scale to the length of the clip is most effective.

Working with keyframe interpolation

The Motion effect moves clips around the screen over a period of time. Adobe Premiere Pro offers keyframe interpolation methods that suit both aspects of that motion: spatial and temporal.

Spatial interpolation refers to the motion path—where the clip appears onscreen. *Temporal* interpolation refers to changes in velocity.

In this exercise, you will use an interpolation method called Ease In and Ease Out. Using Ease In and Ease Out is a quick way to set a Bezier curve on a keyframe without manually dragging the keyframe handles.

1   Continue with the Practice sequence where you left off.

2   To adjust the interpolation of scale, position, and rotation all at once, drag a selection box around the second set of keyframes, as shown here. The selected keyframes will be blue.

3   Right-click any of the selected keyframes, and choose Ease In from the
    Temporal Interpolation menu.

4   Using the same technique, select the third set of keyframes, and choose Ease
    Out from the Temporal Interpolation menu.

5   Expand the Position, Scale, and Rotation parameters to display their graphs.
    You will see that choosing the Ease options changed the graph to a curve.

6   Play the clip, and note the subtle change to how motion starts and stops on the
    keyframes you changed.

Creating a picture-in-picture effect

The PIP technique is one of the most common uses of the Motion effect. It's also one of the easiest ways to see how you can *composite*, or layer, clips. You will begin formal work on compositing later in the book. This exercise will give you a taste.

To simplify things, you'll start with a sequence that has five layered clips in it, all ready to go. You will create PIPs and add drop shadows and beveled edges to the PIPs.

1 Open Lesson 10-3.prproj; then open the Finished sequence by double-clicking it in the Project panel, if it is not already displayed. Render and play that sequence to get an idea of what you can do.

   You should see five PIPs, each with a drop shadow and beveled edge.

2 Open the Practice sequence by double-clicking it in the Project panel.

   If you play this, you will see only the clip on the top track. It covers all the clips below it in the sequence.

3 In the Effects panel, expand Presets so you can see Effects > Presets > PiPs > 25% PiPs > 25% LR.

Note the following:

- All the PIP presets display clips at 1/16th their normal area (reminder: the 25% refers to clip perimeter, not area).

- LL, LR, UL, and UR refer to screen locations: lower left, lower right, upper left, and upper right.

- Each PIP set offers different types of PIP moves.

- Typically, you select a style and then adapt it to your needs. For example, you might change the preset start or end locations or the size.

The clip in the Video 1 track will remain as is; you want to use it as a background.

● **Note:** There is no 25% Center preset. You use one of the presets to create one. Simply change the start and end Position keyframes to 360, 240.

4   Drag the following PIP presets to the clips as follows:

- Clip in the Video 2 track: Apply the preset PiP 25% LR Spin In.

- Clip in the Video 3 track: Apply the preset PiP 25% UL Spin In.

- Clip in the Video 4 track: Apply the preset PiP 25% UR Spin In.

- Clip in the Video 5 track: Apply the preset PiP 25% LL Spin In.

- Clip in the Video 6 track: Apply the preset PiP 25% LL Spin In.

Next, you need to customize this motion so that this PIP shows up in the center rather than the lower-left corner.

5   Select the video clip in the Video 6 track, and expand its Motion settings in the Effect Controls panel.

6   Change the Position parameters to 640, 360. This centers the clip.

7   Play the clip to see the five PIPs you have added on top of a video background. If you have trouble with any of the steps, open the 5 PIP sequence to see how it should look.

Enhancing motion with shadows and beveled edges

PIPs are more interesting when their shrunken clips have drop shadows, beveled edges, or some other kind of border. In this exercise, you'll add these enhancements to a clip.

1   Open the 5 PIP sequence.

It has six layered clips (you might need to use the Timeline scroll bar to see all of them). The top five all have 25 percent motion presets applied. The clip on the bottom of the sequence in the Video 1 track will serve as the PIP background.

2 Drag the current-time indicator past the one-second point to display the five PIPs.

3 Choose Presets > Bevel Edges, and drag the Bevel Edges Thin effect to the clip on the Video 3 track in the sequence.

4 Zoom the Program Monitor view to 100 percent to get a better look at this effect.

The effect shows up in the center of the Program Monitor. After you adjust the Bevel Edges parameters, it will look as shown here. You may have to scroll around in the Program Monitor to see the PIP.

5 Click the Bevel Edges disclosure triangles in the Effect Controls panel, and change its parameters as follows:

- Increase Edge Thickness to 0.08.

- Change Light Angle to about 140° to illuminate the dark beveled edge at the bottom of the clip.

- Increase Light Intensity to about .4 to emphasize the beveled edges.

6 Click Bevel Edges in the Effect Controls panel to select the effect so you can create a preset with the parameters you just applied.

7 Open the Effect Controls panel, choose Save Preset, type **Lesson 10 Bevel Edges**, give it a description if you want, and click OK.

This new preset shows up immediately in the Presets folder.

● **Note:** If you had used keyframes with this effect, selecting one of the three types as you're saving the preset—Scale, Anchor to In Point, or Anchor to Out Point—would help identify the preset if you want to use it again.

8 Drag Lesson 10 Bevel Edges from the Presets bin to each clip in the Video 2, 4, 5, and 6 tracks (not to the clip in Video 1—that's the full-screen video you'll use as a background for the PIP). Or, you can Shift-select these tracks, and drag the preset over once.

9 Return the Program Monitor's Select Zoom Level menu to Fit, and then play this sequence.

All five PIPs have the same beveled-edge look.

Adding a drop shadow

To add a drop shadow, follow these steps:

1 Choose Video Effects > Perspective to drag a drop shadow onto the top clip. You may want to collapse the other effects in this panel to better see the Drop Shadow options.

2 Change the Drop Shadow parameters in the Effect Controls panel as follows:

- Change Direction to about 320°.

- Increase Distance to 30 so you can see the shadow (you might need to adjust the Select Zoom Level menu of the Program Monitor to see how this works).

- Change Opacity to 50% to darken the shadow (since the background clip is rather dark).

- Set Softness to 30 to soften the edges of the shadow. Generally, the greater the Distance parameter, the more softness you should apply.

Note: You want the shadow to fall away from any perceived light source. In this exercise, you set the light direction for bevel edges to about 320°. To make shadows fall away from a light source, add or subtract 180° from the light source direction to get the correct direction for the shadow to fall.

3 Apply these same values to the other four PIPs by using Copy and Paste. Right-click (Windows) or Control-click (Mac OS) the Drop Shadow effect in the Effect Controls panel, and choose Copy.

4 Select the clip in Video 2, right-click in a blank area of the Effect Controls panel, and choose Paste. This will paste the shadow filter to the selected clip. Repeat this for the other PIP clips.

5 Render and play this sequence. It should look like the Finished sequence.

Using other motion-related effects: Transform, Basic 3D and Camera View

Adobe Premiere Pro has several effects with some shared functionality, with subtle differences that dictate their respective use. In this section, you'll learn the differences between the Motion and Transform effects and between the Basic 3D and Camera View effects.

Transform

Let's start with Motion and Transform.

1 Open Lesson 10-4.prproj, and open the Motion and Transform sequence. As you'll see, there are two sets of two videos on the Timeline. Drag the current-time indicator over both to quickly view the content. Note that the Mac version of Premiere Pro CS5 doesn't have the Camera View filter, so you'll get an error message.

In both cases, a picture-in-picture is rotating twice over the background clip, while moving from left to right. Look carefully at the relationship of the shadow to each pair of clips. In the clips on the left, the shadow follows the bottom edge of the PIP and therefore appears on all four sides of the clip as it rotates, which obviously isn't realistic because the light source produces the shadow and it isn't moving. In the set on the right, the shadow stays on the lower right of the PIP, which is realistic.

2 Click the top clip of the set on the left, and view the effects applied in the Effect Controls panel: the Motion fixed effect and Drop Shadow effect. Now do the same for the pair on the right; you'll see that the Transform effect is producing the motion, with the Drop Shadow effect again producing the shadow.

In the screen comparison shown here, you can see that the Transform effect has many of the same capabilities as the Motion fixed effect but also adds Skew, Skew Axis, and Shutter Angle. As you just saw, the Transform effect also works more realistically with the Drop Shadow effect than the Motion fixed effects.

3   Observe the render bar above both sets of clip. If you have a Mercury Engine–compatible graphics card in your system, you'll note that the render bar is yellow on the left and red on the right.

This tells you that the Motion effect is GPU-accelerated, which makes previewing and rendering more efficient, while the Transform effect isn't.

4   Click the top clip on the right. In the Effect Controls panel, drag the Drop Shadow effect *above* the Transform effect, and drag through the pair of clips on the right again.

Note how the shadow now follows the PIP around as it rotates, which isn't the realistic look that you want. The order in which effects are listed matters, and different orders will often produce different results. When applying multiple effects to a clip, if you're not getting the look you want, drag the order around and see whether that produces the desired result.

Basic 3D and Camera View

The Basic 3D and Camera View effects share some common features with each other and also have their unique qualities. Since the Camera View effect isn't available on the Mac, ignore any commands, descriptions, or screenshots that relate to that effect.

1   Open Lesson 10-4.prproj if it isn't already open, and open the Basic 3D and Camera View sequence. As you'll see, there are two sets of two videos on the Timeline. Drag the current-time indicator over both to quickly view the content

In both cases, a picture-in-picture is rotating to the left in 3D space while tilting upward slightly. On the left, you'll see that a light that follows the motion—called a *specular highlight*—which you won't see on the right. Don't worry about the white box around the PIP on the right, you'll eliminate that in a moment.

2   Click the top clip of the set on the left, and view the effect applied in the Effect Controls panel: the Basic 3D effect. Now do the same for the pair on the right. You'll see the Transform effect is producing the motion, with the Drop Shadow effect again producing the shadow.

In the screen comparison shown here, you can see that the Basic 3D effect has Swivel and Tilt controls, a Distance to Image control for zooming closer and away from the video, and a Show Specular Highlight check box. On the right, the Longitude, Latitude, and Distance controls perform similar functions to Swivel, Tilt, and Distance to Image, with additional Focal Length, Distance, Zoom, and Fill Color controls.

3　Click the top clip on the right, and then in the Effect Controls panel click the Setup icon for the Camera View effect to open the Camera View Settings dialog. Click the Fill Alpha Channel check box, and then click OK to close the dialog. Drag your current-time indicator above the set of clips on the right. Note how Adobe Premiere Pro eliminates the white box behind the PIP.

4　Observe the render bar above both sets of clip. If you have a Mercury Engine–compatible graphics card in your system, you'll note that the render bar is yellow on the left and red on the right.

This tells you that the Basic 3D effect is GPU-accelerated (which makes previewing and rendering more efficient) while the Camera View effect is not.

● **Note:** Not only does Basic 3D provide GPU acceleration, it also can swivel and tilt in both directions, while the Camera View effect's Latitude and Longitude controls work in only one direction. This makes Basic 3D faster and more flexible than Camera View for most applications.

Review questions

1 Which Motion parameter will create a PIP?

2 You start Rotation at its default setting, move the current-time indicator, add a Rotation keyframe with a value of 2x, and then give a value of −2x to the next keyframe. Describe what will happen.

3 You want a clip to appear full-screen for a few seconds and then spin away. How do you make the Motion effect's Rotation feature start within a clip rather than at the beginning?

4 How can you start a PIP rotating slowly and have it stop rotating slowly?

5 If you want to add a drop shadow to a spinning clip, why do you need to use some other motion-related effect besides the Motion fixed effect?

6 One way to apply the same customized effect to multiple clips is to use a preset. How do you make one?

Review answers

1 The Scale parameter will adjust the size of the clip to make it larger or smaller—when a smaller clip is located above another in a sequence, this makes the top clip a PIP.

2 It will spin clockwise twice as it approaches the first keyframe. Then it will spin counterclockwise four times as it moves to the next keyframe. The number of spins equals the difference between two keyframe rotation values. Set the Rotation value back to 0 (zero) to have it spin counterclockwise twice.

3 Position the current-time indicator where you want the Rotation to begin, and click the Add/Remove Keyframe button. Then move to where you want the spinning to end, and change the Rotation parameter; another keyframe will appear.

4 Use the Ease Out and Ease In parameters to change the keyframe interpolation to be gradual rather than sudden.

5 The Motion fixed effect is the last effect applied to a clip. Motion takes whatever effects you apply before it (including Drop Shadow) and spins the entire assemblage as a single unit. To create a realistic drop shadow on a spinning object, use Transform or Basic 3D, and then place Drop Shadow below one of those effects in the Effect Controls panel.

6 Adjust the effect parameters to your liking, click the effect name in the Effect Controls panel to select it, open the Effect Controls panel menu, choose Save Preset, give the preset a name, select one of the three parameters, and click OK.

11 CHANGING TIME

Topics covered in this lesson

- Using slow motion and reverse motion
- Enabling variable time changes with time remapping
- Performing time remapping with speed transitions
- Using time remapping with reverse motion
- Applying Timeline downstream effects for time changes
- Changing the speed of multiple clips simultaneously
- Adjusting the length of multiple stills simultaneously

This lesson will take approximately 30 minutes.

The slow-motion, reverse-motion, and time-remapping features in Adobe Premiere Pro CS5 allow you to vary the speed of a clip with precise control.

Getting started

Slow motion is one of the most often used effects in video production. A simple slow-motion effect applied to a bride walking down the aisle or to an exciting sports clip can create a dramatic look. In this lesson, you will review static speed changes, the time-remapping feature, and some other tools that let you make time changes to multiple clips.

Using slow-motion and reverse-motion techniques

In this exercise, you will start by making a static speed change to a clip. You can speed up or slow down any clip on the Timeline.

1   Open Lesson 11-1.prproj. Notice that the Medieval_Hero_01 clip on the Timeline is six seconds long. It's important to remember that changing the speed of a clip will change its duration.

2   Right-click (Windows) or Control-click (Mac OS) the Medieval_Hero_01 clip, and choose Speed/Duration from the context menu.

3   Change Speed to 50%, and click OK.

4   Play the clip in the Timeline. Render the clip by pressing Enter (Windows) or Return (Mac OS) to see smooth playback.

Notice the clip is now 12 seconds long. This is because you slowed the clip to 50 percent, making it twice its original length.

5   Press Ctrl+Z (Windows) or Command+Z (Mac OS) to undo the speed change.

Sometimes you'll want to change the speed of a clip without changing the duration. This is impossible without trimming the clip as it is slowed down. Adobe Premiere Pro provides a tool that makes this easy to do.

6 Right-click (Windows) or Control-click (Mac OS) the clip, and choose Speed/Duration from the context menu.

7 Click the link icon, which indicates that Speed and Duration are linked, so that the icon shows the settings unlinked (shown here). Then change Speed to 50%. Notice that with Speed and Duration unlinked, the duration remains six seconds.

8 Click OK; then play the clip.

Notice that the clip plays at 50 percent speed, but the last six seconds have automatically been trimmed to keep the clip at its original duration.

Occasionally you will need to reverse time. You can do this in the same Clip Speed/Duration dialog.

9 Right-click (Windows) or Control-click (Mac OS) the clip, and choose Speed/Duration from the context menu.

10 Leave Speed at 50%, but this time also select the Reverse Speed option, and then click OK.

11 Play the clip. Notice it plays in reverse at 50 percent slow motion.

● **Note:** The Clip Speed/Duration dialog shows a Maintain Audio Pitch option if the clip has audio. Selecting this option keeps audio at the original pitch regardless of the speed at which the clip is running. This can be helpful when making small speed adjustments to clips when you want to maintain pitch in the audio.

Speeding up a clip

Although slow motion is the most commonly used time change, speeding up clips is a useful effect as well.

1 Undo your changes until you have the clip at its original speed at six seconds. (As an alternative, you can reopen Lesson 11-1.prproj.)

2 Right-click (Windows) or Control-click (Mac OS) the Medieval_Hero_01 clip, and choose Speed/Duration from the context menu.

3 Set Speed to 300%, click the link icon so Speed and Duration are linked, and then click OK.

4 Play the clip. Notice its new length is two seconds. This is because Speed is set to 300%—or three times its normal speed.

Changing speed with the Rate Stretch tool

Sometimes you'll need to find a clip that's just the right length to fill a gap in your Timeline. You might be able to find the perfect clip, one that's exactly the right length, but most times you will find a clip you want to use that is just a little too short or a little too long. This is where the Rate Stretch tool comes in handy.

1 Open Lesson 11-2.prproj and preview the Timeline.

The situation in this exercise is fairly common. The Timeline is synchronized to music and the clips contain the content you want, but the clips are just too short. You can guess and try to insert just the right Speed percentage in the Clip Speed/Duration dialog, or you can use the Rate Stretch tool to drag the clip to the needed length.

2 Select the Rate Stretch tool in the Tools panel.

3 Move the Rate Stretch tool over the right edge of the first clip, and drag it until it meets the second clip.

Notice that the speed of the first clip changes to fill the space into which you stretched it.

4 Move the Rate Stretch tool over the right edge of the second clip, and drag it until it meets the third clip.

5 Move the Rate Stretch tool over the right edge of the third clip, and drag it until it matches the end of the audio.

6 Play the Timeline to view the speed change made using the Rate Stretch tool.

Enabling variable time changes
with time remapping

Time remapping lets you vary the speed of a clip by using keyframes. This means one portion of the same clip could be in slow motion while another portion of the clip is in fast motion. In addition to giving you this flexibility, variable-speed time remapping enables you to smoothly transition from one speed to another, whether from fast to slow or from forward motion to reverse motion. Hang on—this is really fun.

1   Open Lesson 11-3.prproj if it isn't open already.

2   Open the Practice sequence.

    As you add time adjustments to the clip, it will change length.

3   Adjust the height of the Video 1 track by positioning the Selection tool over the Video 1 label and dragging the edge of the track up.

    Increasing the track height makes adjusting keyframes on the clip much easier.

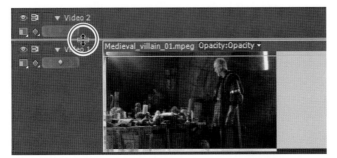

4   Right-click the clip, and choose Show Clip Keyframes > Time Remapping > Speed in the clip's menu. With this option selected, the yellow line across the clip represents the speed.

5   Drag the current-time indicator on the Timeline to the point where the villain turns and starts walking across the room (about 00:00:01:00).

6   Press and hold the Ctrl (Windows) or Command (Mac OS) key, and the pointer will change to a small cross. Then click the yellow line to create the keyframe that will be visible at the top of the clip. You are not yet changing the speed; you are just adding control keyframes.

7   Using the same technique, add another speed keyframe at about 00:00:06:00, just as the villain points to the wall. Notice that by adding two speed keyframes, the clip is now in three "speed sections." You will now set different speeds between keyframes.

8   Leave the first section, between the beginning of the clip and the first keyframe, set as is (the Speed setting is 100%). Position the Selection tool over the yellow line between the first and second keyframes, and drag it down to 30%. Notice the clip has stretched in length to accommodate the speed change of this section.

● **Note:** If you have problems setting the speed keyframes, open the Completed sequence to see the completed process.

9   Play the clip. Notice the speed changes from 100 percent to 30 percent and back to 100 percent at the end. Render the clip for the smoothest playback.

Applying time remapping with speed transitions

Setting variable speed changes on a clip can be a very dramatic effect. In the previous section, you changed from one speed to another instantly. To create a more subtle speed change, it is possible to transition from one speed to another smoothly by using speed keyframe transitions.

1   Open Lesson 11-4.prproj.

2   Select the Practice sequence. You will recognize the clip and speed changes from Lesson 11-3.prproj. You will continue where you left off by creating a gradual speed transition where you changed the speed.

> **Note:** When selecting the Practice sequence, you may need to adjust the height of the Video 1 track by positioning the Selection tool over the Video 1 label and dragging the edge of the track up.

> **Note:** The speed keyframes are actually two icons next to each other. You can drag these two icons apart to create a speed transition.

3   Drag the right half of the first speed keyframe to the right to create a speed transition. Notice the yellow line now ramps down, rather than making a sudden change from 100 percent to 30 percent.

4   Repeat step 3 on the second speed keyframe to create a transition there as well.

5   Render and play the clip to see the effect.

> **Note:** If you have problems creating these speed keyframe transitions, open the Complete sequence to see the completed project.

Using time remapping with reverse motion

Reversing a clip can add comedy or drama to a sequence. Time remapping allows you to easily adjust variable speed remapping and do reverse motion in the same clip.

1   Open Lesson 11-5.prproj.

2   Select the Practice sequence.

    As you add time adjustments to the clip, it will change length.

Note: After the reverse-motion keyframe is created, Adobe Premiere Pro adds a keyframe to the right at the point in the clip where you started the reverse motion.

3 Ctrl-drag (Windows) or Command-drag (Mac OS) the right half of the first speed keyframe to the right about one second, to about 00:00:02:00 on the Timeline. Notice the keyboard modifier creates a reverse speed keyframe; that is, when you drag to the right, you are dragging backward in time.

4 Play the clip to see the effect.

5 To make the reverse portion of the clip move in slow motion, drag the yellow line up to –50% for that section of the clip. (The –50% setting represents 50 percent slow motion in reverse.)

Note: To see how the application of this effect should look, open the Complete sequence.

6 Drag the right half of the first keyframe to the right to make the transition from forward motion to reverse motion gradual.

Time remapping is a powerful feature in Adobe Premiere Pro CS5. The quality of the slow motion is very good. Experiment with slowing down and speeding up time, but always try to make the effect match the mood of your project or the story you are telling.

Recognizing the downstream effects of changing time

You may decide to change the speed at the beginning of the Timeline after assembling many clips in your project. It is important to understand how changing the speed of a clip affects the rest of the clips "downstream."

1 Open Lesson 11-6.prproj. Notice that there are three clips on the Timeline in the Video 1 track, with one title clip, called *drafty*, positioned over the middle clip. In this exercise, you'll change the speed of the first clip and see how the rest of the Timeline is affected.

2 Right-click (Windows) or Control-click (Mac OS) the Medieval_Hero_01 clip, and choose Speed/Duration from the context menu. Change Speed to 50%, and click OK.

Notice that the rest of the Timeline was not affected, but the first clip plays at 50 percent speed. The clip could not expand because it abuts against another clip. The Out point of the clip was adjusted in order to allow it to play at 50 percent speed.

3 Press Ctrl+Z (Windows) or Command+Z (Mac OS) to undo the speed change.

4 Right-click (Windows) or Control-click (Mac OS) the Medieval_Hero_01 clip, and choose Speed/Duration from the context menu. Change Speed to 50%, and also select the Ripple Edit, Shifting Trailing Clips option; then click OK.

● **Note:** Since all the video tracks have Toggle Sync Lock enabled by default, all tracks shift (stay in sync), not just the track with its speed being adjusted.

Notice that now the first clip expands to play at 50 percent and the rest of the Timeline shifts to accommodate it, including the title on the Video 2 track.

Changing the speed of multiple clips simultaneously

Adobe Premiere Pro CS5 has the ability to change the speed of multiple clips at the same time.

1 Continuing where you left off with Lesson 11-6.prproj, press Ctrl+Z (Windows) or Command+Z (Mac OS) to undo any speed changes.

2 Select all three video clips in the Video 1 track by Shift-clicking each one.

3 Right-click (Windows) or Control-click (Mac OS) any of the selected clips, and choose Speed/Duration from the context menu. Change Speed to 50%, and click OK.

All three video clips now play at 50 percent speed, but only the last clip expanded in length. This is because the last clip was not constricted by any other clips.

4   Press Ctrl+Z (Windows) or Command+Z (Mac OS) to undo the speed change.

5   If necessary, select all three video clips again.

6   Right-click (Windows) or Control-click (Mac OS) any of the selected clips, and choose Speed/Duration from the context menu. Change Speed to 50%, and also select the Ripple Edit, Shifting Trailing Clips option; then click OK.

All three clips expand to allow them to play at 50 percent speed.

Changing the length of multiple stills simultaneously

Although a still image does not really have a speed, it does have a duration. Adobe Premiere Pro CS5 allows you to adjust the duration of any group of selected still images.

1   Open Lesson 11-7.prproj. Notice that the Timeline is full of still images of sunsets. The duration of all the images is five seconds, and there is a Cross Dissolve transition between all of them.

2   Press the backslash key (\) to zoom the Timeline so all images are visible.

3   Marquee-select all the images by dragging the pointer around them.

4   Right-click (Windows) or Control-click (Mac OS) any of the selected images, and choose Speed/Duration from the context menu. Change Duration to 10, and then click OK.

You will notice that only the last image on the Timeline (shown here) expanded to ten seconds. This is because the other images are bound by other trailing clips.

5   Press Ctrl+Z (Windows) or Command+Z (Mac OS) to undo the duration change.

6   If necessary, select all the image clips again.

7   Right-click (Windows) or Control-click (Mac OS) any of the selected clips, and choose Speed/Duration from the context menu. Change Duration to 10, and select the Ripple Edit, Shifting Trailing Clips option; then click OK.

All clips expand to ten seconds in duration, and the transitions between the clips remain in place.

Review questions

1 Changing the Speed parameter of a clip to 50% has what effect on the length of the clip?

2 What tool is useful in stretching a clip in time to fill a gap?

3 Where is the Time Remapping command located?

4 Can you make time-remapping changes directly on the Timeline?

5 How do you create a smooth ramp-up from slow motion to normal speed?

6 Explain how you can adjust the duration of several still images after they are already on the Timeline.

Review answers

1 Reducing a clip's speed causes the clip to become longer, unless the Speed and Duration parameters have been unlinked in the Clip Speed/Duration dialog or the clip is bound by another clip.

2 The Rate Stretch tool is useful for the common situation of needing to fill a small amount of time.

3 The time-remapping feature is not found in the Effects folders. It is a common effect available on all clips by default.

4 Time remapping is best done on the Timeline; because it affects time, it is best (and most easily) used and seen within the Timeline sequence.

5 Add a speed keyframe, and split it by dragging away half of the keyframe to create a transition between speeds.

6 Select the clips on the Timeline that you want to change; then adjust the duration, being careful to select the Ripple Edit, Shifting Trailing Clips option.

12 ACQUIRING AND EDITING AUDIO

Topics covered in this lesson

- Connecting microphones to your computer
- Setting up a basic voice-recording area
- Voicing professional narrations
- Using Adobe Premiere Pro audio features
- Examining audio characteristics
- Adjusting audio volume
- Adjusting audio gain
- Adding J-cuts and L-cuts

 This lesson will take approximately 60 minutes.

Audio is critical to good video, and Adobe Premiere Pro CS5 has the tools to take your audio editing to a higher level. It features industry-standard plug-ins, audio conforming, sample-specific editing, and multiple track types.

Getting started

Audio typically takes a backseat to video, but it shouldn't. Clear and well-edited audio is crucial to your projects. The best images lose their impact if the accompanying audio is mediocre. Your first goal is to acquire high-quality audio from the get-go, both in the field and when recording narration.

Adobe Premiere Pro gives video producers and audiophiles all they need to add top-notch aural quality to their productions. The software has a built-in Audio Mixer that rivals the hardware found in production studios. The Audio Mixer lets you edit in mono, stereo, or 5.1 surround sound; has a built-in instrument and vocal recording feature; and offers several ways to mix selected tracks.

You can perform industry-standard edits such as J-cuts and L-cuts on the Timeline, as well as adjust audio volume levels, keyframes, and interpolation.

In addition, Adobe Premiere Pro is in compliance with two audio industry standards—Audio Stream In/Out (ASIO) and Virtual Studio Technology (VST)—which ensures that it works smoothly with a wide range of audio cards and dozens of audio effect plug-ins.

Making the connection

Adobe Premiere Pro lets you record narration directly to your project by using a microphone connected to your computer's sound card. Most sound cards have only a 1/8" (3.5 mm) stereo minijack outlet. Microphones built specifically for personal computers typically cost less than $25. When you visit your local electronics store, you'll have two basic options:

- **Dynamic microphones**: These are headsets or long-necked versions that sit on your desk.

- **Condenser microphones**: Typically lavaliere or clip-on microphones, these offer slightly better voice-over quality and require a battery.

Plug the microphone into the correct sound-card outlet (usually marked Mic or with a microphone icon), not the line-in jack used with amplified devices such as CD players and sound mixers.

Whichever microphone you choose, make sure you also get a good headset—one that covers your ears to block extraneous sound. Use that headset both when shooting your video and when voicing a narration. It's important to hear how the microphone hears you.

Setting up a basic voice-recording area

To create your voice-over narration, you'll need a quiet, sound-absorbing location. The easiest solution is to build a temporary recording area simply by hanging some thick blankets or fiberglass insulation on two adjoining walls. If you can create something like a four-sided blanketed cubicle, so much the better.

If you drape the blankets in a single corner, then you should point the microphone *toward* that corner, place yourself between the microphone and the corner, and speak *away* from the blankets. It seems counterintuitive, but the microphone is sort of like a camera. It "sees" what's in front of it. In this case, it "sees" your face and the hanging, sound-absorbing blankets.

Voicing professional narrations

Review this checklist before recording your voice-over:

- **Practice reading your copy aloud**: Listen to your words. They should sound comfortable, conversational, and even informal.

- **Avoid technical jargon**: Tech-speak demands extra effort from your listeners, and you might lose them.

- **Use short sentences**: If you find yourself stumbling over certain phrases, rewrite them.

- **Stress important words and phrases**: As you review your copy, underline important words. When you record your voice-over, you'll want to give those words extra emphasis with more volume and punch.

- **Mark pauses**: Mark logical breaks in narration with short parallel lines.

- **Avoid overly smooth and constant pacing**: Narration that lacks variation in tone or pacing is characteristic of a scripted delivery. You don't want to remind viewers that this is TV. It should sound conversational, like real life.

- **Punch up your voice**: Do not slip into a dull, monotone voice. Add some zest and enthusiasm to your narration.

- **Practice**: Record a couple of narrations and then listen to them. Most first-time narrators mumble or swallow words. Have you made yourself clear?

- **Don't pop your *p*'s and *t*'s**: As you say *p*- and *t*- words, you project a small blast of wind. Avoid speaking directly into the microphone.

- **Wear a headset**: Hearing yourself helps you avoid popping *p*'s or speaking with too much *sibilance* (an overemphasis on the *s* sound). It also helps minimize room noise and other extraneous sounds.

Creating a high-quality aural experience

Adobe Premiere Pro offers professional-quality audio-editing tools that rival many stand-alone audio-mixing and editing products. For example, it includes the following:

- **Sample-specific edits**: Video typically has between 24 and 30 frames per second. Edits fall between frames at intervals of roughly 1/30 second. Audio typically has thousands of samples per second; for example, CD audio is 44,100 samples per second (44.1 kHz). Adobe Premiere Pro lets you edit between audio samples.

- **Three types of audio tracks**: The three categories of audio tracks are mono, stereo, and 5.1 (six-channel surround). You can have any or all of these track types in a sequence.

- **Submix tracks**: You can assign selected audio tracks to a submix track. That lets you apply one instance of audio and affect the settings of several tracks at once.

- **Channel editing**: You can split out individual audio channels from stereo and 5.1 surround sound files and apply effects only to them. For example, you can select the two rear channels in a 5.1 track and add reverb to them.

- **Recording studio**: Adobe Premiere Pro lets you record any instrument or microphone you can connect to an ASIO-compliant sound card. You can record directly to a track on an existing sequence or to a new sequence.

- **Audio conforming**: Adobe Premiere Pro up-converts audio to match your project's audio settings. It also converts so-called fixed-point (integer) data to 32-bit floating-point data. Floating-point data allows for much more realistic audio effects and transitions.

● **Note:** Floating-point data has no fixed number of digits before and after the decimal point; that is, the decimal point can float. This leads to more accurate calculations.

Camcorder kHz and bit-rate settings

Many DV camcorders give you two audio quality options: 16-bit audio recorded at 48 kHz (16 bits of data per sample at 48,000 samples per second) or lower-quality 12-bit audio recorded at 32 kHz. The latter option lays down two stereo tracks on your DV tape: one with audio recorded by the on-camera microphone, and the other giving you an option to insert narration or some other audio. If you recorded at 32 kHz and set your project to 48 kHz, you shouldn't have a problem. Adobe Premiere Pro CS5 will up-convert your audio during the conforming process.

Examining audio characteristics

Audio editing is similar to video editing. It uses most of the same tools, and you apply transitions and effects in much the same way.

But audio has some characteristics different from video that affect the way you approach editing. In this exercise, you will be introduced to the basics of audio editing. You'll explore more advanced audio-editing topics in Lesson 13.

1 Start Adobe Premiere Pro, and open Lesson 12-1.prproj. Double-click the Completed sequence to open that in the Timeline. This is one of the projects that you worked on in Lesson 5. This project has multiple audio and video files—you'll examine the characteristics of some of them, as well as a 5.1 surround sound file added for analysis purposes.

2 Open the audio bin. Double-click Medieval_Sword Swipe – mono.wav to open it in the Source Monitor.

A waveform appears in the Source Monitor. The peaks and valleys indicate volume levels.

3 Play the audio by clicking the Play button at the bottom of the Source Monitor.

4   Scrub the audio by click-dragging your pointer across the waveform in the Source Monitor.

5   Experiment with zooming in and out on the waveform vertically (the amplitude) by dragging the vertical zoom bar located at the right edge of the Source Monitor. This is helpful for observing more detail in the amplitude of the waveform.

Source Monitor panel menu

Vertical zoom bar

6   Open the Source Monitor panel menu, and choose Show Audio Time Units.

The time ruler switches from the standard video-oriented time increments (seconds: frames) to audio samples.

7   Type **1:0** in the current-time display, and press Enter (Windows) or Return (Mac OS).

Note: Audio units appear with colons (:) versus semicolons (;) for the video frame timecode.

8   Press the left arrow key once, and note that the sample preceding 1:0 is 0:44099.

This sequence has 44,100 audio samples per second (44.1 kHz). Switching to audio units enables you to make sample-specific edits down to (in the case of this project's settings) 1/44,100 of a second. This might seem like splitting hairs, but when cutting audio, this precision will come in handy.

9 Drag the center of the viewing area bar to the left and right to take a closer look at the audio peaks and valleys.

Note: You can drag the right or left handle of the viewing area bar to change the zoom level.

10 Double-click Medieval_JB02 – stereo.aif, and take a look at it in the Source Monitor.

This is how a stereo signal looks. The layout follows the industry standard: The left channel (L) is on the top, and the right (R) channel is on the bottom, as shown here.

11 Choose Edit > Preferences > Audio (Windows) or Premiere Pro > Preferences > Audio (Mac OS), and make sure 5.1 Mixdown Type is set to Front + Rear + LFE. Click OK to close the Preferences window.

You need to use this setting to hear all six channels of the 5.1 clip in the next step.

12 Double-click Music 11 5.1.wav, and take a look at it in the Source Monitor.

This is a 5.1 surround sound clip. It has six channels: right, left, center, right-surround (rear), left-surround (rear), and LFE (low-frequency effects—the subwoofer channel).

13 Click Music 11 5.1 in the Project panel to select it, and then choose Clip > Audio Options > Breakout to Mono.

That creates six links, one for each channel (it does not create six new audio files). Using Breakout to Mono lets you edit individual channels of a stereo or 5.1 clip. For example, you might want to give the LFE channel a bass boost. That does not change the original 5.1 clip. You can link this edited channel to the other 5.1 mono channels and create another 5.1 clip.

Waveforms are immutable

Adding an effect to a clip in Adobe Premiere Pro will not affect the original audio or video clip or the visible audio waveform. If you change a clip's volume or apply audio effects to it, the waveform will always display the clip's original volume levels.

14 In the Project panel, double-click the Practice sequence to open it in the Timeline. Drag Music 11 5.1 to the Timeline, and notice that Adobe Premiere Pro will not let you drop it in the Audio 1 track.

Audio 1 is a stereo track. When you drag an audio clip to a sequence that does not have a track that matches the clip's type, Adobe Premiere Pro automatically creates a new track to suit that clip type. Even though Adobe Premiere Pro appears to move the new clip below the master audio track, the new track will appear above the master audio track once you release the mouse button.

15 Expand the view of the newly added Audio 2 track by clicking its Collapse/Expand Track triangle (shown here) to open its waveform view. Drag the boundary between Video 1 and Audio 1 up the screen, and then drag the bottom of Audio 2 down.

Your sequence should look like the figure shown here. Note the labels for each of the six channels in this 5.1 surround sound clip.

16 At the top of the Source Monitor, click the menu of open clips, and select Source: Medieval_Sword Swipe – mono.wav, which will then open in the Source Monitor.

17 Drag the Drag Audio Only icon to the Timeline to bring the Mono.wav file into the Timeline. Note that Adobe Premiere Pro will not allow you to drop the mono clip in the Audio 1 track, because Audio 1 is a stereo track. Drop it below the master track, and Adobe Premiere Pro CS5 will create a new mono track above the master track.

● **Note:** You can tell the audio track type by its icon: Mono is a single speaker, Stereo is a double speaker, and 5.1 says 5.1. The master audio track is stereo by default. This is set on the Track tab when you create a new sequence.

Adjusting audio volume

You might want to decrease or increase the volume of an entire clip or parts of a clip. For example, you might need to decrease the natural sound on a video clip by half while you narrate, gradually fade up the audio at the start or end of a clip, or fade up an interview just as the narrator completes a segment. The last example is part of a J-cut or L-cut. These will be explained later in the lesson. Let's adjust the volume on a clip:

1   Choose Window > Workspace > Reset Current Workspace to get your workspace back in order. Click Yes in the Reset Workspace dialog.

2   Double-click the Completed sequence to open it in the Timeline.

3   Expand the track view of the Audio 5 track (Medieval_JB02.aif) by clicking the Collapse/Expand Track triangle.

4   Click the Show keyframes button and choose Show Clip Keyframes to ensure you are looking at clip keyframes.

You can now edit a clip's volume in the Timeline rather than using the Volume effect in the Effect Controls panel.

5   On the Audio 5 track, hover your pointer over the volume level graph—the thin, horizontal yellow line between the left and right channels—until it turns into the Vertical Adjustment tool pointer, and then drag that yellow line up and down. This adjustment allows you to increase and decrease the volume of the entire audio track at one time. If you think this track drowns out the dialogue just a bit, drop it to about −5 or −6 dB and see whether it sounds better. Once you're done experimenting, return the volume level to 0 dB for no change in volume.

Note: A dB (decibel) level readout gives you feedback on the volume change (0 dB is the default starting point no matter the actual volume of the original clip). It's not easy to move to an exact setting. You use the Volume effect in the Effect Controls panel to do that.

6   Let's create fade-in and fade-out effects on this audio track. Drag the current-time indicator to about two seconds from the start of the clip. Ctrl-click (Windows) or Command-click (Mac OS) the volume level graph to create a keyframe at that location.

7   Now let's create a key frame at the beginning of the clip. Ctrl-click (Windows) or Command-click (Mac OS) the volume level graph to create a keyframe there, and then drag that keyframe to the bottom of the audio track, essentially muting the audio at that location.

8   Play the beginning of the clip to hear the fade-in. Just for fun, drag the keyframe at the two-second spot closer to and further from the start of the clip. That's how you can easily change the duration of your fade-in.

9   Create two more keyframes on the Audio 5 track at 30:10 and at the end of the clip; then drag the keyframe at the end of the clip down to the bottom of the audio track.

● **Note:** As you can see, you can apply keyframe interpolation in the Timeline. However, selecting one of the Bezier curve options would create a more pronounced curve in the middle. So, stick with Ease In and Ease Out for most audio keyframes.

10 Play the end of the clip to hear the fade-out. Drag the keyframe at 30:10 closer to and further from the end of the clip. That's how you can easily change the duration of your fade-out.

11 Right-click (Windows) or Control-click (Mac OS) the second and third keyframes, and choose Ease In and Ease Out, respectively.

● **Note:** As you slide keyframes around in the clip, you will invariably change their volume settings. Adjusting keyframes on the Timeline is quick and easy. You'll want to use the Volume effect in the Effect Controls panel to fine-tune those keyframe parameters.

Adjusting audio in the Effect Controls panel

The Audio fixed effect works like any other effect in that you can use keyframes to change audio over time. You can also apply an audio transition (which changes audio volume levels over time) and adjust its settings in the Effect Controls panel.

1   Make sure the Medieval_JBO2.aif clip is selected on the Audio 5 track, and open the Effect Controls panel. Click the Volume disclosure triangles to display the parameters and widen the Effect Controls panel so you can see its Timeline.

   If the Timeline is not open, click the Show/Hide Timeline View button. Make note of a few things:

   • **Bypass**: Bypass is something you haven't seen up to this point because only audio effects have this option. For the Volume effect, turning on Bypass at any point in the clip (via keyframes) switches back to the clip's original volume level. You can use Bypass to switch any audio effect off and on any number of times within a clip.

   • **Level**: This is the only adjustable parameter.

   • **Keyframes**: All the keyframes and keyframe interpolation methods (the hourglass icons) you applied to the clip in the Timeline show up in the Effect Controls panel's Timeline.

2   Add several keyframes to the first four seconds of the project, and change the volume level on each one. Play the clip to hear the level adjustments. Click the box next to Bypass, play the clip again, and notice the level adjustments you made are not used.

3   Marquee-select all the keyframes in the Effect Controls panel's Timeline, and press Delete.

4   Now you'll apply a transition to the same clip on the Audio 5 track. Drag the Constant Power audio transition (Audio Transitions > Crossfade) to the beginning of the clip on the Timeline. Release it when you see the start of the clip turn purple.

5   Click the transition rectangle on the clip to select it, and view its parameters in the Effect Controls panel.

6   Change the duration to three seconds.

This gives you a nice fade-in.

7   Click End on your keyboard to move to the end of the Timeline, and then drag another copy of Medieval_JB02.aif to just after the first copy on the Audio 5 track.

8   Drag Constant Power to the edit point between the two clips, and listen to how that works.

9   The intro to the second clip is too abrupt—let's make that side of the transition longer. Hover your pointer over the right edge of the transition until it becomes the grab pointer; then drag the right edge of the transition to the right. Now listen—the intro to the second clip is more gradual.

10 Replace Constant Power with Constant Gain, and listen to it.

Favor constant power

Constant Gain changes audio at a constant rate in and out as it transitions between clips. Sometimes this can sound abrupt. Constant Power creates a smooth, gradual transition, like a video cross-dissolve. It decreases audio for the first clip slowly at first and then quickly falls off at the end of the transition. For the second clip, this audio crossfade increases audio quickly at first and then more slowly as it reaches the end of the transition. Constant Power is the default audio transition. Rely on it for most transitions. But your ears are the best judge.

Adjusting audio gain

Adobe Premiere Pro offers multiple techniques for boosting audio volume. You've just seen the direct volume control; now let's look at the Audio Gain tool. As background, understand that when you boost audio volume manually via the volume graph, you have no way of knowing how the volume compares to other tracks and whether you've increased the volume so high that it will produce distortion. You can listen, but you can't be sure.

In contrast, the Audio Gain tool in Adobe Premiere Pro gives you access to a normalization function that automatically boosts audio volume as loud as it can go without producing distortion. And, if you normalize all your tracks, the volume of all your content should end up more or less the same—a result that's near impossible when you're fussing with the volume graph manually.

Even better, you can set the audio gain over multiple clips simultaneously, speeding your work, and gain adjustments appear in the audio track waveform, so you can gauge the effect of your work. However, you can't keyframe your gain adjustments—it's one setting for the complete clip. Of course, you can split your clips and work on them individually, but that gets time-consuming.

A good working paradigm for choosing when to use the Volume control versus when to use the Audio Gain control is to use Volume for fading in and out or for varying volume over the duration of the clip. In most other instances, use the Audio Gain control.

1 Continuing with the open project, expand the view of the Audio 3 and Audio 4 tracks by clicking their Collapse/Expand Track triangles.

2 On Audio 3, right-click the clip Medieval_dialog_hero.wav, and choose Audio Gain. Notice the four options for adjusting the gain of the clip:

- **Set Gain to**: The default value is 0.0 dB. This option allows you to set the gain to a specific value. This value is always updated to the current gain, even when the radio button is not selected and the value appears dimmed.

- **Adjust Gain by**: The default value is 0.0 dB. This option allows you to adjust the gain by + or - dB. Entering a value other than zero in this field automatically updates the Set Gain to dB value to reflect the actual gain value applied to the clip.

- **Normalize Max Peak to**: The default value is 0.0 dB. You can set this to any value less than 0.0 dB. For example, this clip has a peak amplitude of −3.3 dB (as shown in the next figure). Normalizing this clip to 0 db will raise its gain by an adjustment of 3.3 db. According to the Adobe Premiere Pro Help file, "For a multiple-clip selection, the clip with the maximum peak will be adjusted to the user-specified value, while the other clips will be adjusted by the same amount, preserving their relative gain differences. For example, assume clip one has a peak of −6 dB, and clip two has a peak of −3 dB. Since clip two has the greater peak value, it will be adjusted by +3 dB to boost it to the user-specified gain of 0.0 dB, while clip one also will be adjusted by +3 dB, boosting it to −3 dB, and preserving the gain offset between the two clips in the selection."

- **Normalize All Peaks to**: The default value is 0.0 dB. This is useful when selecting multiple clips at once. This feature will adjust all selected clips to a gain necessary for them all to peak at 0 db. According to the Adobe Premiere Pro Help file, "For a multiple-clip selection, each clip in the selection would have its gain adjusted by amounts necessary to boost them all to 0.0 dB."

3 Set the "Normalize Max Peak to" option to 0 db, and click OK. Notice that the waveform on the Timeline will expand to show the increased gain.

Undo the gain adjustment. Now you'll normalize the gain on Audio 3 and Audio 4.

4 Select both the Audio 3 and Audio 4 tracks. Right-click (Windows) or Control-click (Mac OS), and choose Audio Gain.

5 Set the "Normalize All Peaks to" option to 0 dB, and click OK. Notice that the waveforms on both tracks of the Timeline expand to show the increased gain.

● **Note:** Those are the mechanics of gain adjustment, but here's the karma: Most professional producers tend to maximize volume at about −3 dB rather than 0 dB, leaving "headroom" in case an editor downstream needs to make further adjustments. That's why both of these dialogue clips, which were obviously edited by a pro, have a Peak Amplitude value of −3.3. Wherever you set your peak, remember that consistency is more important than absolute volume. So, work hard to make sure that there's a consistent volume within your clips and, on a multiclip production, among all your clips.

Adding J-cuts and L-cuts

One frequently used technique for transitioning from one clip to another is to play the audio from the second clip before the video shows. This clues in the viewer that a change is coming. Similarly, sometimes you want to cut to the next video visually before the viewer can hear the audio.

The first instance is called a *J-cut*, so named because it looks vaguely like a *J* in the sequence. You hear the second clip and then see it. The second is called an L-cut, where you see the second clip and then hear it.

Although artistically quite powerful, both techniques rely on one simple editing function: the ability to unlink audio and video from the same file so you can adjust them separately. There are two unlinking methods—a context menu and a keyboard modifier.

1   Open Lesson 12-2.prproj, and play the Complete sequence.

  This is how your J- and L-cuts will look and sound by the end of this mini-lesson.

  The cutaway *video* plays over the first few words of the sound-bite *audio*, and then the cutaway *video* dissolves to the interview clip while the cutaway *audio* fades out—a J-cut. That process is reversed for the end of the sound bite—an L-cut.

2   Open the Lesson 12-2 Working sequence.

3   Right-click (Windows) or Control-click (Mac OS) the second clip, and choose Unlink.

4   Complete the unlinking process by clicking outside that clip in the Timeline to deselect it.

  Now when you click either the audio or video portion of that clip, only that portion is selected. You'll relink these clips and then use a keyboard modifier to temporarily unlink them.

5   Shift-click both of those unlinked clips to select them (if one is already highlighted, you don't need to Shift-click it).

6   Right-click (Windows) or Control-click (Mac OS) one of them, and choose Link.

  Now you'll use the keyboard modifier unlinking method.

7   Alt-click (Windows) or Option-click (Mac OS) the audio portion of the second clip to unlink it, and select it.

> **Note:** In this case, the cutaway clips aren't being used as cutaways. They're *B-roll*—basic video used to piece together a project.

8 Drag the unlinked audio portion of the second clip straight down to the Audio 2 track.

9 The audio on the edit director track is very low. Click to select the track, right-click, and choose Audio Gain. In the Audio Gain dialog, select the "Normalize Max Peak to" option, and leave the value at 0. The waveform will expand considerably, and you should be able to hear the director.

10 Click the Rolling Edit tool (⊪) in the Tools panel, or press N on your keyboard. Grab the link between the first and second clips on Video 1, and drag it to the right as far as it will go. When you're done, press V on your keyboard to restore the selection pointer.

● **Note:** As you move the audio portions of your clips in the sequence, take care that you don't slide them left or right when you drag them; otherwise, the audio and video will get out of sync. Adobe Premiere Pro gives you a visual cue to help you line up your clips: If you see a black line with a triangle, your clips are properly lined up. If that black line disappears, you have moved out of sync. In that case, move the clip around a bit until the black line reappears.

11 Apply a fade-out on the first audio clip using the Constant Power transition (you used this transition in the previous exercise) to fade out the explosions gradually as the subject starts to speak. Grab the edge of the transition, and drag it to the left so it starts before the edit director audio clip.

12 Play that J-cut. The explosions should fade as the director begins speaking.

Adding an L-cut

Now that you've unlinked the center clip, adding an L-cut at the end of this segment will take only a few steps:

1   Click the Rolling Edit tool in the Tools panel, or press N on your keyboard. Grab the link between the second and third clips, and drag it to the left about one second. When you're done, click V on your keyboard to restore the selection pointer. You've now created an L-cut.

2   Create a fade-in of the third audio clip to gradually fade in the bike audio over the end of the interview from the second clip.

3   Add a video Cross Dissolve effect between the video portions of all three clips. Make them about four frames long, which is just long enough to soften the cut between the three videos.

4   Play that L-cut.

The hero's dialogue should fade up beneath the director's closing comment.

Review questions

1 When you set up a voice-recording space in the corner of a room, which way do you face to voice the narration, and why?

2 When you videotape indoors, your audio has a "tin can" quality. What's going on?

3 Explain three ways to start your piece by fading up your audio.

4 How is applying the Normalize filter in Adobe Premiere Pro different from just raising the volume?

5 Why use a J-cut or an L-cut?

6 You have a quiet video clip, but in the middle someone honks a car horn. How can you remove that sound and replace it with the original quiet background of the original clip?

Review answers

1   As counterintuitive as it seems, you face away from the sound-absorbing material. The microphone picks up sound from the direction it's facing. The absorbing material minimizes the reflections the microphone picks up.

2   The microphone is probably too far from your subject, and you're in a room with reflective surfaces such as flat walls and an uncarpeted floor.

3   Drag an audio crossfade transition (Constant Power or Constant Gain) to the beginning of the clip. Or use the volume level graph in the Timeline clip display with two keyframes, dragging the first keyframe to the first frame and dragging that keyframe to the bottom of the clip. Or use the Volume audio effect and two keyframes to fade up the audio. Use interpolation controls to smooth what would otherwise be a straight-line fade-in.

4   Raising the gain or volume increases the amplitude of the waveform. Normalizing the audio examines it for peak values and allows you to adjust gain based on the peaks.

5   You use these cuts either to ease into a clip such as a sound bite or to let it fade out. A J-cut starts audio under the preceding video (which also has associated audio or a narration) and then fades up as you transition or cut to the video portion of that clip. An L-cut fades audio under the next clip as a way to ease out of that audio/video clip.

6   Use keyframes to silence that portion of the audio. Then add part of the original audio to another audio track and fade that up to fill the audio gap you created in the original clip.

13 SWEETENING YOUR SOUND AND MIXING AUDIO

Topics covered in this lesson

- Sweetening sound with audio effects

- Trying stereo and 5.1 surround sound effects

- Working with the Audio Mixer

- Outputting tracks to submixes

- Recording voice-overs

- Creating a 5.1 surround sound mix

- Integrating with Soundbooth

- Working with multiple tracks and Adobe Dynamic Link
  in Adobe Soundbooth

 This lesson will take approximately 90 minutes.

Audio effects in Adobe Premiere Pro CS5 can dramatically change the feel of your project. To take your sound to a higher level, leverage the integration and power of Adobe Soundbooth CS5.

Getting started

Adobe Premiere Pro contains more than 20 audio effects that can change pitch, create echoes, add reverb, and remove tape hiss. As you've done with video effects, you can set "keyframeable" audio effect parameters to adjust effects over time.

The Audio Mixer lets you blend and adjust the sounds from all the audio tracks in your project. Using the Audio Mixer, you can combine tracks into single submixes and apply effects, panning, or volume changes to those groups as well as to individual tracks.

Adobe Soundbooth is an audio application that is designed especially for video and Adobe Flash Professional CS5 editors. Adobe Soundbooth provides the tools video editors need to sweeten and repair typical audio challenges. Don't let the easy interface mislead you—Adobe Soundbooth is a powerful tool.

Sweetening sound with audio effects

For most projects, you will probably be happy to use audio in its original, unaltered state, but at some point you might want to start applying effects. If you use music from old cassette tapes, you can use the DeNoiser audio effect to detect and remove tape hiss automatically. If you record musicians or singers in a studio, you can make it sound like they were in an auditorium or a cathedral by adding the Reverb effect. You can also use Delay to add an echo, DeEsser to remove sibilance, and Bass to deepen an announcer's voice.

You'll try a few audio effects in this lesson, but you can expand your knowledge by going beyond that. Experiment. Listen to the possibilities. Test some effects not covered here. Each effect is nondestructive—that is, it does not change the original audio clip. You can add any number of effects to a single clip, change parameters, and then delete those effects and start over.

1 Start Adobe Premiere Pro, and open Lesson 13-1.prproj.

2 Drag Ad Cliches Mono.wav from the Project panel to the Audio 1 track (it's a mono track) of the Practice sequence.

   Play the clip.

3 Open the Audio Effects > Mono folder in the Effects panel.

4   Drag Bass to the Ad Cliches clip, open the Effect Controls panel, and then click
    its two disclosure triangles to expand the parameters.

Note: All mono
effects have the
mono single-speaker
icon (⊲). If you open
the Stereo folder, you'll
see a double-speaker
icon (⊳), and you'll
also recognize the
5.1 icon (5.1).

5   Play the clip, and then move the Bass Boost slider left or right. This increases or
    decreases bass.

6   Delete Bass from the Effect Controls panel, and add Delay.

Note: Listing all the
attributes of all of the
audio effects is beyond
the scope of this book.
To learn more about
audio effect parameters,
search Adobe Premiere
Pro Help.

Try its three parameters:

- **Delay**: This refers to the time before the echo plays (zero to two seconds).

- **Feedback**: This is the percentage of echo added back to audio to create
  echoes of echoes.

- **Mix**: This is the relative loudness of echo.

7 Play the clip, and move the sliders to experiment with the effect.

Lower values are more palatable, even with this over-the-top audio clip.

8 Delete Delay, and add PitchShifter to the Effect Controls panel.

This panel includes three nifty items: knobs, presets, and a Reset button. You can tell an audio effect has presets by the tiny triangle next to what would normally be the Reset button and the addition of a rectangular Reset button (as shown here).

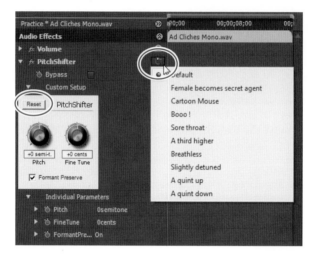

9 Try some of the presets, and note their values below the knobs in the Effect Controls panel.

● **Note:** Formant Preserve is not a misprint. *Formant* is the character, resonance, and phonetic quality of a particular voice, so Formant Preserve attempts to retain those elements even with severe pitch changes.

10 Use the Individual Parameters sliders, and add keyframes at the beginning and end of a few phrases.

Use wildly different Pitch settings from −12 to +12 semitone steps and switch Formant Preserve on and off.

11 Delete Ad Cliches from the sequence, and replace it with Music Mono.wav (you can do that by dragging Music Mono.wav to the beginning of the sequence, on top of Ad Cliches, to do an overlay edit).

12 Drag Treble to that clip, and increase its parameter.

This guitar clip lends itself to a treble boost.

● **Note:** Treble is not simply Bass in reverse. Treble increases or decreases higher frequencies (4,000 Hz and greater), while Bass changes low frequencies (200 Hz and less). The human-audible frequency range is roughly 20 Hz to 20,000 Hz. Apply both Bass and Treble to a clip, and switch between them by clicking their Toggle effect on and off buttons.

13 Delete Treble, drag Reverb to the Effect Controls panel, and open Reverb's Custom Setup.

14 Play the clip, and drag the three white handles in the display to change the character of the reverb.

This is a fun effect that can give some real life to audio recorded in a "dead" room—a room such as a recording studio with minimal reflective surfaces. As shown here, each of the three handles in the graphic control corresponds to a knob below it:

- **Pre Delay**: This is the apparent distance the sound travels to the reflecting walls and back.

- **Absorption**: This assesses how much of the sound is absorbed (not reflected).

- **Mix:** This is the amount of reverb.

These are the additional controls:

- **Size**: This refers to the apparent relative size of the room.

- **Density**: This is the density of the reverb "tail." The higher the Size value, the greater the Density range (from 0% to 100%).

- **Lo Damp**: Adjust this to dampen low frequencies to prevent the reverb from rumbling or sounding muddy.

- **Hi Damp**: This dampens high frequencies. A low Hi Damp setting makes the reverb sound softer.

A treasure trove of VST plug-ins

Reverb's rack of control knobs signals that this is a Virtual Studio Technology (VST) plug-in. These are custom-designed audio effects that adhere to a standard set by Steinberg audio. Invariably, those who create VST audio effect plug-ins want them to have a unique look and offer some very specialized audio effects. Many VST plug-ins are available on the Internet.

Trying stereo and 5.1 surround sound effects

The mono audio effects collection is a subset of the stereo and 5.1 effects. Those multichannel effect groups have additional effects that relate to their extra channels. You'll see here how they work in this exercise:

1   Open Lesson 13-2.prproj.

2   Drag Music Stereo.wav from the Project panel to the Audio 1 track in the sequence. In this project, the Audio 1 track is set up as a stereo track.

3   Attempt to drag any mono audio effect to the Music Stereo clip.

    You'll get a universal "No" symbol—you can't apply a mono effect to a stereo clip.

4   Drag Balance from Effects > Audio Effects > Stereo to the Music Stereo clip.

5   Drag the Balance slider in the Effect Controls panel left and right while you play this clip.

    This clip was mixed with the guitar panned all the way left and the honky-tonk piano panned hard right. If you move the slider all the way to either end, you will hear only one instrument.

6   Add two keyframes, and have the audio pan from left to right. (Using keyframes for audio effects is similar to using them for video effects, as you learned in Lesson 10.)

7 Play the clip.

The sound moves from left to right and, in this case, makes the guitar fade into the piano.

8 Delete Balance, and apply Fill Right.

The Fill effects duplicate the selected channel, place it in the other channel, and discard that other channel's original audio. So, in this example, Fill Right plays the honky-tonk piano in both the left and right channels and discards the guitar (the track in the left channel).

Use the same effect more than once

You've probably seen an equalizer. Many car and home stereos have them. They enable you to punch up or cut a number of preset frequency ranges. The EQ effect in Adobe Premiere Pro fits that bill, but it offers only five frequency ranges. If you want more possibilities, you can use Parametric EQ, which lets you select only one frequency range, but you can use it multiple times and select multiple frequencies. In effect, you can build a full graphic equalizer within the Effect Controls panel.

9 Drag Music 5.1.wav to the sequence, and Adobe Premiere Pro adds a 5.1 audio track to accommodate this new audio clip type.

10 Mute the Audio track containing the Music Stereo clip by clicking the speaker button on the left side of the track label.

11 Drag Channel Volume from the Audio Effects > 5.1 folder to the Music 5.1 clip.

Channel Volume lets you control the volume level for each of the six channels in a 5.1 surround sound clip and both channels of a stereo clip. The default setting for each channel is 0 dB, meaning no change from the original volume.

12 Play the clip, and drag the sliders for each channel to experiment with this effect.

Note: If you don't hear all six channels, it's because you need to change the 5.1 Mixdown setting. Choose Edit > Preferences > Audio (Windows) or Premiere Pro > Preferences > Audio (Mac OS), and change 5.1 Mixdown Type to Front + Rear + LFE.

Looking at one more VST plug-in

Let's check out one more audio effect. This one is guaranteed to make your head spin. Drag MultibandCompressor to the Music 5.1 clip. You'll need to dramatically expand the Effect Controls panel to see its parameters (it might help to put the Effect Controls panel in a floating window).

The MultibandCompressor's purpose is to narrow the dynamic range for up to three sets of frequency ranges, usually to add "punch" to music or speech. This is what sound editors use to make those Saturday car sale advertisements you hear on the radio sound like they were produced by a 6'8" body builder.

Note: Explaining the MultibandCompressor's parameters could take a full lesson (refer to Adobe Premiere Pro Help for parameter details). Instead, note that it offers a collection of presets accessed by clicking the button shown here.

Editing keyframes by using the clip effect menu

You might have noticed that tucked away along the top edge of all clips—audio and video—is a pop-up menu of all the effects applied to a selected clip. You can find it just to the right of the clip name.

You might not be able to see the clip effect menu in all instances. The audio or video track needs to be in its expanded view. To do that, click the disclosure triangle to the left of the track name. If that does not reveal it, the clip is not wide enough. Zoom in on the Timeline to expand the width of the clip and reveal the clip effect menu.

For audio clips, the header is always Volume: Level. For video clips, it's Opacity: Opacity (despite Motion residing on the top of that pop-up menu). Every time you add an effect—video or audio—Adobe Premiere Pro adds that effect (along with a list of its parameters) to the bottom of that clip's effect menu.

1 Delete the MultibandCompressor effect.

2 Open the clip effect menu by clicking Volume: Level > Channel Volume.

3 Select Left.

4 Drag the yellow line, which now represents the left channel volume, up or down to change the left channel's volume.

5 Click the Show keyframes button on the left side of the audio track, and then set it to Show Clip Volume. This causes the track to display the clip's volume, rather than the track's volume.

6 Ctrl-click (Windows) or Command-click (Mac OS) the yellow line to add a couple of keyframes, and adjust them by dragging them left or right along the graph line or dragging them up or down.

The advantages of clip-based effect and keyframe editing are that you can get a better overall view of the entire clip, and if you want to change only one or two parameters, you can easily access them. Some disadvantages are that you can't change the parameters while the clip is playing, setting an exact parameter value is challenging, and changing more than a couple of parameters in the Timeline panel gets tedious.

Working with the Audio Mixer

There is a big difference in how Adobe Premiere Pro handles layered audio tracks and layered video tracks.

Clips in higher-numbered video tracks cover what's below them on the Timeline. You need to do something to those higher video track clips—adjust opacity, create PIPs, or use specialized keying effects—to let clips below them show through.

Clips in audio tracks all play together. If you have ten layered audio tracks loaded up with a variety of audio clips and do nothing to them in terms of adjusting volume levels and stereo panning, they'll all play as one grand symphony (or cacophonous mess).

Although you can adjust volume levels by using each clip's volume graph in the Timeline or Volume effect in the Effect Controls panel, it's much easier to use the Audio Mixer to adjust volume levels and other characteristics for multiple audio tracks.

Using a panel that looks a lot like a production studio's mixing hardware, you move track sliders to change volume, turn knobs to set left/right panning, add effects to entire tracks, and create submixes. Submixes let you direct multiple audio tracks to a single track so you can apply the same effects, volume, and panning to a group of tracks without having to change each of the tracks individually.

In this exercise, you will mix a song recorded by a choir in a studio:

1 Double-click Music Sonoma Stereo Mix, and play it in the Source Monitor. This is how your final mix should sound.

2 Open Lesson 13-3.prproj.

3 Play the Practice sequence, and note that the instruments are way too loud compared to the choir.

4 Choose Window > Workspace > Audio, and adjust the Audio Mixer panel so you can see all five tracks plus the master track.

5 Change the track names along the top row of the Audio Mixer by selecting each one in turn and typing a new name: Left, Right, Clarinet, Flute, and Bass (as shown here).

Those name changes also appear in the audio track headers in the Timeline.

6 Play the sequence, and adjust the sliders in the Audio Mixer to create a mix that you think works well. (A good place to start is setting Left to +4, setting Right to +2, and dropping the Clarinet, Flute, and Bass to −12, −10, and −12, respectively.)

7 Watch the master track VU (volume unit) meter as you make your adjustments.

Little hash marks that float above the volume meters indicate the loudest passages. They remain for a couple of seconds and then move as the music volume changes. These hash marks provide a good way to see how balanced your left and right channels are. You want them to approximately line up most of the time.

Note: You want to avoid setting the volume too high (the VU meter line will turn red). That leads to distortion.

8 Adjust each channel's Left/Right Pan by using the knobs at the top of each track (when completed, your parameters should match those shown here):

- **Left**: All the way left (−100)

- **Right**: All the way right (+100)

- **Clarinet**: Left-center (−20)

- **Flute**: Right-center (+20)

- **Bass**: Centered (0)

9 Click the Show/Hide Effects and Sends button.

Show/Hide Effects and Sends

Effects

Sends

This opens a set of empty panels where you can add effects to entire tracks and assign tracks to submixes.

10 Click the Effect Selection button for the Left track (the little drop-down list to the right of the panel), and choose Reverb from the pop-up menu.

11 Isolate that track by clicking its Solo button (that mutes the rest of the channels).

You can click Solo buttons on more than one track to listen to a group of tracks. You can also click the Mute button to switch off audio playback for one or more tracks. You'll use the Enable track for recording button in the next lesson.

12 Click the Reverb effect pop-up menu at the bottom of the panel, and make changes as desired.

Solo Track

Mute   Enable
Track   Track For
          Recording

● **Note:** It's easier to apply effect parameters in the Effect Controls panel, but you can edit only clips there—not audio or video tracks. In this case, you could apply this effect to the clip instead of the track because there is only one clip on the track, but it's good to see how track-based effects work.

Play the clip to listen to your changes as you make them.

13 Undo your settings by removing the Reverb effect. To do that, click the Effect Selection button and select None.

Keep tabs on Mute and Solo settings

After working in the Audio Mixer for a while and then returning to the Timeline, you might not hear anything. Audio Mixer Mute and Solo settings do not show up in the Timeline but are still in effect when you play a clip in the Timeline, even if the Audio Mixer is closed. So, check those Mute and Solo settings before shutting down the Audio Mixer.

Automating changes in audio tracks

In the previous section, you set volume and panning values for entire tracks while listening to the audio. Adobe Premiere Pro also lets you apply volume and panning values that change over time, and you can apply them as you play your sequence.

To do so, use automation modes, accessed via pop-up menus at the top of each track in the Audio Mixer. Using one of the automation modes creates a series of track (as opposed to clip) keyframes for volume and panning, saving you from adding them one at a time.

Briefly, here's what each setting means (you can read more about this in Adobe Premiere Pro Help):

- **Off**: This setting ignores any changes you apply and thus lets you test some adjustments without recording them.
- **Read**: Adjusting a track option (such as volume) affects the entire track uniformly. This is the default setting you used when setting the mix volume in step 6 of the previous exercise.
- **Latch**: This works like Write (see below) but won't apply changes until you move the volume slider or panning knob. The initial property settings are from the previous adjustment.
- **Touch**: This works like Latch except that when you stop adjusting a property, its option settings return to their previous states before the current automated changes were recorded.
- **Write**: This setting records adjustments you make as you listen to a sequence.

Outputting tracks to submixes

You place your audio clips into audio tracks on the Timeline. You can apply effects and set volume and panning on a clip-by-clip basis. Or you can use the Audio Mixer to apply volume, panning, and effects to entire tracks. In either case, by default Adobe Premiere Pro sends audio from those clips and tracks to the master track.

But sometimes you might want to route tracks to submix tracks before sending them on to the master track.

The purpose of submix tracks is to save you steps and ensure some consistency in how you apply effects, volume, and panning. In the case of the Sonoma recording, you can apply Reverb with one set of parameters to the two choir tracks, and you can apply Reverb with different parameters to the three instruments. The submix can then send the processed signal to the master track, or it can route the signal to another submix.

1 Open Lesson 13-4.prproj. This project picks up where you left off with the Sonoma Choir.

2 Right-click (Windows) or Control-click (Mac OS) an audio track header in the Timeline, and using the figure shown here as a guide, choose Add Tracks. Set the Add values for Video Tracks and Audio Tracks to 0, set the Add value for Audio Submix Tracks to 2, and set Track Type for Audio Submix Tracks to Stereo; then click OK.

That adds two submix tracks to the Timeline and two tracks to the Audio Mixer (they have a darker hue), and it adds those submix track names (Submix 1 and Submix 2) to the pop-up menus at the bottom of the Audio Mixer.

3 Click the Left track's Track Output Assignment pop-up menu (at the bottom of the Audio Mixer), and select Submix 1.

4 Do the same for the Right track.

Now both the Left and Right tracks have been sent to Submix 1. Their individual characteristics—panning and volume—will not change.

5 Send the three instrument tracks to Submix 2.

6 Apply Reverb to the Submix 1 track by clicking the Show/Hide Effects triangle and adding Reverb as an effect. Click its Solo Track button, play the audio, and adjust the Reverb parameters to make it sound like the choir is singing in a large auditorium (setting Size to about 60 is a good place to start).

7 Apply Reverb to the Submix 2 track, click its Solo Track button, switch off the Submix 1 Solo button (remember you can solo more than one track, but in this case you want to solo only Submix 2), play its audio, and set its parameters to create a sound a bit less dramatic than the voices.

8 Click the Solo button on Submix 1, and listen to these two submixes as a single mix to see how they sound.

Feel free to tweak the Volume and Reverb settings.

Recording voice-overs

The Audio Mixer in Adobe Premiere Pro is also a basic recording studio. It can record anything you can connect to your sound card. In this case, you'll use your computer's microphone to do a voice recording.

1 Remove any audio files from the Timeline, and set the current-time indicator at the beginning.

2 Make sure your computer's microphone is plugged in to the Mic input on your sound card, and make sure your audio setup is set to recognize and record from the microphone and that it is not muted. Check your computer's documentation if you are not sure how to set up a microphone to record.

3 Choose Edit > Preferences > Audio Hardware (Windows) or Premiere Pro > Preferences > Audio Hardware (Mac OS), and ensure that your default device is the hardware to which you have connected your microphone.

4 In the Audio Mixer, click the Enable track for recording button (the microphone) at the top of the audio track to which you want to record.

Enable track for recording

You can enable as many tracks as you like, but you can't record to the master track or a submix track. If you have more than one microphone enabled on your system, choose the microphone you want to use in the pop-up menu that appears above the microphone button.

● **Note:** Selecting Default will work in most circumstances. However, if you have a higher-end audio card, you should select it, refer to its product manual, and make any needed changes to its ASIO settings.

5 Click the red Record button at the bottom of the Audio Mixer. The button starts blinking.

Note: If you choose to locate the current-time indicator in the music, you'll hear the music as you record your voice. Being able to hear your sequence's audio as you narrate can be a big help. Laying down video clips and then recording a narration is a workflow some editors follow.

6 Move the current-time indicator to where you want this narration to begin (it'll cover up any audio on the selected track at that location).

7 Click the Play button in the Audio Mixer, and start your narration.

8 When you finish recording, click the Stop button.

An audio clip appears on the selected audio track and in the Project panel. Adobe Premiere Pro automatically names that clip based on the audio track number or name and adds that audio file to the project file folder on your hard drive.

What about feedback?

If you record audio and you have not taken steps to mute the output, you might get feedback—that lovely screeching noise that happens when a microphone gets too close to a loudspeaker. You can deal with that in several ways: You can click the Mute button for the track, turn down your speakers (use headphones to listen to yourself), or choose Edit > Preferences > Audio (Windows) or Premiere Pro > Preferences > Audio (Mac OS) and then select "Mute input during timeline recording."

Creating a 5.1 surround sound mix

Adobe Premiere Pro lets you create a full, digital, 5.1 surround sound mix. You can use 5.1 surround sound in two places: audio on a DVD or Blu-ray Disc or an audio file for playback on a computer with 5.1 surround sound speakers.

5.1 digital audio has six discrete channels: left front, front center, right front, right rear or surround, left rear or surround, and the low-frequency effects (LFE) channel designated for a subwoofer.

If you have a 5.1 surround sound setup on your computer, this section will be a lot of fun and lead to much experimentation. If you don't have a six-speaker setup, this at least will give you a feel for how to add 5.1 surround to a DVD.

Here are the basic steps to follow:

1 Open Lesson 13-5.prproj. This project has seven mono tracks and a 5.1 audio master track.

2 Drag the music clips to the Timeline as shown here. Note that Sonoma-Left and Sonoma-Right appear on the Timeline twice.

3 In the Audio Mixer, drag each track's 5.1 Panner puck to the proper location (shown here).

● **Note:** Each square in the figure is your 5.1 speaker configuration. The puck (circled) dictates where the sound is panned.

Panner puck   LFE volume knob

4 Set volume levels for tracks 1–5 that are similar to those you set for the stereo mix. For Audio 5 (the bass), adjust the volume using the LFE volume knob, and place its puck in the center. Set volume levels for tracks 6 and 7 (left-rear and right-rear) to 0 and –2, respectively.

Now you have some options:

• You can move the clips on Audio 6 and Audio 7 about a tenth of a second (three frames) into the Timeline (causing them to play a little after the rest of the clips) to make it sound like they're coming from the back of the room. To do that, select each clip in turn, press the plus sign (+) on the numeric keypad, type 3 on the numeric keypad, and press Enter on the numeric keypad.

• You can add a Reverb with a Size parameter a bit higher than what you set for the front channels. You might find that you don't need to have as much reverb for the front channels when you work in 5.1 surround sound.

Fixing, sweetening, and creating soundtracks in Adobe Soundbooth

● **Note:** Adobe Soundbooth is not included with Adobe Premiere Pro. You must purchase Soundbooth separately or as part of Adobe Creative Suite CS5. The basics of Adobe Soundbooth are included in this book to demonstrate its integration and easy workflow with Adobe Premiere Pro.

Adobe Soundbooth is audio software designed especially for video and Flash editors. Adobe Soundbooth can be run as a stand-alone audio tool, or it can be launched from Adobe Premiere Pro. Although many audio tools are built into Adobe Premiere Pro, Adobe Soundbooth is designed to deal with specific audio challenges that video editors face every day. You will find Adobe Soundbooth easy to use yet very powerful.

Rather than give you a series of full-blown lessons on Adobe Soundbooth, we will review the most common uses you will run into: adding effects and cleaning up noisy audio.

Cleaning up noisy audio

Of course, it's always best to record perfect audio at the source. However, sometimes you cannot control the origin of the audio, and it's impossible to re-record it, so you are stuck needing to repair a bad audio clip. To that end, the sample you will work on is a real-world nightmare—a voice-over narration with a horrible 60 Hz hum and a cell phone ringing in the background—but don't pull your hair out, because Adobe Soundbooth is up to the task.

1   Open Lesson 13-6.prproj.

● **Note:** A 60 Hz or 50 Hz hum can be caused by many electrical problems, cable problems, or equipment noise.

2   Double-click audio problem.wav to open it in the Source Monitor. Play the clip, and notice the 60 Hz hum throughout and the cell phone ringing near the end.

3   Open audio problems fixed.wav in the Source Monitor, and listen to it. Adobe Soundbooth was used to remove the hum and the cell phone without noticeably affecting the voice.

4   Drag audio problems.wav to the Audio 1 track on the Timeline.

● **Note:** You can also choose to edit the source file if you don't need to keep the original file. The Render and Replace command does not affect the original file. Rather, it renders a new copy of the file and replaces it automatically on the Timeline, so the original file is not changed.

5   Right-click (Windows) or Control-click (Mac OS) the audio problem clip on the Timeline, and choose Edit in Adobe Soundbooth > Render and Replace from the context menu. Soundbooth starts and displays the clip.

6 Soundbooth displays two views of your audio file: the common waveform view showing audio amplitudes near the top of the screen and a colorful spectral display view showing audio frequencies near the bottom of the screen. If you can't see both views, drag the horizontal divider between the panels up or down so they are both visible. Give the frequency display more room.

Note: The spectral display shows frequencies over time rather than amplitudes over time. In this display, colors represent amplitude—dark blue for low amplitude and bright yellow for high amplitude.

7 Play the file again to hear the problems, the hum, and the cell phone ringing. You can drag the current-time indicator, much as you would in Adobe Premiere Pro, and use the playback controls at the bottom of the screen.

8 To remove the 60 Hz hum, click the Effects tab in the left-center panel. Click the Stereo Rack Preset pop-up menu, and choose Fix: Remove 60 Cycle Hum.

9 Play the file again, and hear the amazing difference.

10 The effect is not permanently applied to the file yet. To permanently apply this change, click the Apply to File button at the bottom of the Effects Rack.

11 To remove the cell phone sound, you need to use the spectral display. The ringing cell phone is not visible as a change in amplitude, so you can't use the waveform display to locate this problem. However, if you zoom out so the whole file is visible, the cell phone rings are quite obvious in the spectral display as short horizontal dashes between 2 kHz and 3 kHz.

12 Position the current-time indicator over the first cell phone ring, and zoom in by pressing the equal sign key (=) on the keyboard or the plus sign (+) on the numeric keypad.

13 Select the Rectangular Marquee tool, and then select the cell phone ring. Make the marquee selection just slightly bigger than the visible ring. Be as precise as possible. When you're finished, the selection appears as an opaque box around the cell phone ring with a dB adjustment tool floating above it.

● **Note:** A common mistake is to reduce noise selections to the maximum (–96 dB) to remove them completely. However, this creates a complete void in that frequency spectrum for your selection, which is often noticeable. Most noises are soft enough that –34 dB is enough to eliminate them without removing the frequency space completely. Experiment by removing the least amount possible to keep your audio sounding natural.

14 Adjust the selection to –34 dB. This reduces the frequencies you selected with the Marquee tool by –34 dB.

15 Zoom out, and play the clip. Even though it appears that some of the ring tone is still there, notice it is dark blue, which means very low volume.

16 Save the changes to the clip by choosing File > Save. Switch back to Adobe Premiere Pro, and notice that the audio file on the Timeline has been updated with the changes.

Adding audio effects in Adobe Soundbooth

You will use the same audio file to add a few effects in Adobe Soundbooth. Continue where you left off in Adobe Soundbooth with the audio problem.wav file.

1   Another way to add an effect to the Effects panel is to click the "Add an effect to the rack" icon (⚡) in the lower-right corner of the panel. Choose Vocal Enhancer from the Effects menu. In the Effects panel, choose Male as the effect preset for the Vocal Enhancer effect.

2   Play the file to hear the effect.

3   Choose Analog Delay from the Add an effect to the rack icon, and experiment with the many presets available.

You can add multiple effects to the Effects Rack at the same time. When you get a combination of effects you like, you can save them as a Rack preset. There are many preloaded Rack presets you can choose from and experiment with.

4   Try one of the Rack presets—Choose Voice: Old Time Radio—and play the effect.

5   If you want to get more advanced and tweak some of the settings yourself, click the Settings link to the right of each effect name. This gives you access to the detailed settings of each effect.

Review questions

1 There are at least four ways to make audio move from the right channel to the left and back. What are they?

2 You are playing a 5.1 surround sound clip but can't hear all the channels. What's a possible cause?

3 What's the difference between the Delay and Reverb effects?

4 Can you record a voice-over while other audio is playing on the Timeline?

5 How do you apply the same audio effect with the same parameters to three audio tracks?

6 Describe the difference between the Edit Source File and Render and Replace commands when editing a file from Adobe Premiere Pro in Adobe Soundbooth.

Review answers

1 Balance adjusts the overall balance, left or right. Channel Volume enables you to adjust the volume of each channel individually. You can also use the Audio Mixer's Left/Right Pan knob or use clip or track keyframes on the Timeline.

2 Check the audio preferences, and make sure the 5.1 Mixdown setting includes all channels.

3 Delay creates a distinct, single echo that can repeat and gradually fade. Reverb creates a mix of echoes to simulate a room. It has multiple parameters that take the hard edge off the echo you hear in the Delay effect.

4 Yes. When you start recording the voice-over, any other audio tracks on the Timeline will be heard as you record.

5 The easiest way to create a submix track is to assign those three tracks to that submix track and apply the effect to the submix.

6 Edit Source File changes the original source audio file. Render and Replace creates a new copy of the audio file and changes the copy rather than the original.

14
ANALYZING CONTENT

Topics covered in this lesson

- Converting speech to text
- Enhancing the accuracy of speech analysis
- Searching a transcription for keywords
- Setting In and Out points using speech analysis text
- Modifying an audio file's metadata
- Detecting faces in a sequence or digital picture

 This lesson will take approximately 30 minutes.

Adobe Premiere Pro CS5 can convert an audio file containing speech to a text transcription file. Then you can search the audio file for keywords, mark the In and Out points of your clips, and even locate a specific video frame using a text search tool. New is the ability to detect faces in your clips so you can more quickly find clips with faces in the Project panel.

Getting started

Although it may not be obvious from the small sample files used in this lesson, speech transcription can be a huge time-saver, allowing you to do text searches to find precisely the video frame in which a specific word is spoken. You can easily add markers or edit points after using this feature to locate keywords. Without this feature, you would need to scrub or play the audio of the file to listen for keywords.

You'll notice that it takes some time for Adobe Premiere Pro CS5 to transcribe an audio file to text. But this process can run in batch mode in the background while you do other work. It's also worth noting that once the transcription occurs, the transcribed text becomes part of the audio file's metadata. Even if you export the file, the transcription will remain with the file.

Transcribing speech to text

The first step in transcribing audio to text is to change your workspace to the Metalogging workspace and make the metadata associated with your files visible in the Adobe Premiere Pro interface.

● **Note:** XMP metadata is text information about a source file that is stored with the source file. The text transcription you are about to do will store the words transcribed from the audio file as metadata. Transcriptions are special in that the metadata is associated with time as well, so the transcribed text is in sync with the audio file.

1   Open Lesson 14-1.prproj.

2   Click Window > Workspace > Metalogging to change the workspace layout to Metalogging.

   This workspace is designed to make it easy for you to see the metadata associated your audio and video files.

3   Double-click the Hero-analysis.mpeg clip in the Project panel to load it into the Source Monitor.

4   Click the Play button in the Source Monitor to play the clip.

   The words spoken by the actors are what you want to convert to a text transcript.

5   On the right side of the workspace is the Metadata panel with three fields: Clip, File, and Speech Analysis. Click the Speech Analysis triangle to open that field, and then click the Analyze button (highlighted here) to start the transcription process. Note that if you're working in a restricted screen space, you may have to expand the Metadata window to see the Analyze button.

The Analyze Content dialog appears.

6   In the Analyze Content dialog, choose the options shown in this figure, and click OK.

● **Note:** Select the Identify Speakers option if you want the transcription process to attempt to tag the text with different speaker tags. This function works best if each speaker has a unique voice.

This will launch Adobe Media Encoder, which is a stand-alone application that handles some batch-processing tasks for Adobe Premiere Pro, including exporting media (which we will cover in detail in Chapter 20) and speech transcription. Since it is a stand-alone application, it can process these tasks while you continue to work on other things in Adobe Premiere Pro CS5 or other applications.

7 You will see the file you want to transcribe loaded into Adobe Media Encoder, and the program should start transcribing immediately. If not, click the Start Queue button that appears instead of the highlighted Stop Queue button.

Adobe Media Encoder processes and transcribes the file.

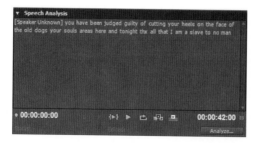

8 Switch back to Adobe Premiere Pro, and note that there is a progress indicator at the bottom of the Metadata panel.

When the encoding and transcription process is complete, the text transcription will appear in the window.

Your transcription should look similar to what is shown here. The time it takes to complete the transcription depends on the length of the source file and the speed of your system.

9 Click the Play button to play the clip. Notice that the words in the transcription are highlighted as they are spoken.

Enhancing the accuracy of speech analysis

The accuracy of the speech analysis in Adobe Premiere Pro depends upon the quality of the audio, with the best results achieved when shooting on a set or sound studio. In most movie productions, the final audio will be re-recorded in a sound studio, so the audio captured with the video is for synchronization, not for use in the project. For this reason, audio quality is usually only fair, and transcription quality may suffer.

In a scripted production, however, you can improve the quality of the speech analysis by importing an Adobe Story script into Adobe Premiere Pro. For the purposes of this lesson, you'll use a script already saved to disk.

1 In the Metadata panel, click the Analyze button again.

2 In the Analyze Content dialog, click the Reference Script drop-down list, and choose Add. In the Open dialog that appears, navigate to Lessons > Assets, choose Paladin_Script_Hero.astx, and click Open.

3 In the Import Script dialog, select the Script Text Matches Recorded Dialogue check box, and click OK.

4 In the Analyze Content dialog, click OK. This will open Adobe Media Encoder again, and the program should start transcribing immediately. If not, click the Start Queue button that appears instead of the highlighted Stop Queue button.

When the encoding and transcription process is complete, the text transcription will update in the Speech Analysis field in the Metadata panel.

Searching transcription for keywords

Now that you have the transcription, what can you do with it? One of the most useful applications for transcribed text is to search for a keyword in order to find a specific frame of video.

1 Continue working with the transcribed file you just created. In the search bar at the top of the Metadata panel, type **slave**, and note that "slave" is highlighted in the transcribed text.

2 Click "slave."

The playhead in the Source Monitor moves to the corresponding frame of video. The timecode is also displayed at the bottom left of the Metadata panel (00:00:40:06).

3 Click multiple words in the transcription, and notice that the playhead moves to match each corresponding location in the Source Monitor.

Setting In and Out points using speech analysis text

You can also set In and Out points using the text found in the speech analysis text, which is very useful when you have multiple shots and want to include only a short segment from the clip in your production. For example, in this close-up, say you want to include the segment where the hero says, "I am a slave to no man." Here's the procedure:

1 Choose Window > Workspace > Editing to return to the Editing workspace. Click the Hero-analysis.mpeg clip in the Project Panel to select it.

2 Click the Metadata panel. If it's not currently open, choose Window > Metadata to open the panel. Click the Hero-analysis.mpeg clip.

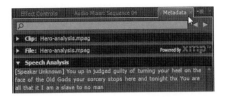

3 In the Metadata panel, click the word "I" on the third line of the text and then the Set In Point icon. Then click the word "man" and the Set Out Point icon.

4 On the bottom of the Metadata panel, click the Insert icon to insert the marked video clip in the sequence.

5 Click Play in the Program Monitor to play the video clip Adobe Premiere Pro just inserted into the Timeline (is that cool or what?).

Modifying the metadata

You'll notice that a couple of words in the transcription are not perfect. You can edit the transcribed text by adding, modifying, or deleting words, and the transcribed audio will not go out of sync with the corresponding clip.

1 If necessary, clear the Metadata panel's search bar so that no words are highlighted in the transcribed text.

2 Double-click the word "up" in the transcribed text (first line, second word). This will allow you to edit that word. Change it to **are**, because this is what the actor actually said.

3 Right-click the word "thx" (second line, eighth word), and choose Delete Word from the context menu. Note the other options that you can use to correct your transcription.

This metadata is saved with the source file, so if you use this file in another project, the transcription will already be there.

Note: You can copy the transcribed text to your clipboard by right-clicking any word and choosing Copy All. Then you can paste the text into other applications as normal.

This feature can be a huge time-saver for applications such as long interviews where you could spend a long time trying to find a specific frame by listening for the keywords. Again, the accuracy of the transcription is dependent on the quality and clarity of the source file. For example, background noise behind speech will make transcription difficult.

Detecting faces in a sequence

Adobe Premiere Pro can now analyze one or more clips to determine which ones contain faces. After this analysis, you can filter the Project panel for clips that contain faces. Note that you can run this analysis on all supported media, including still images.

1 In the Project panel, choose the four clips in the Project panel: Hero-analysis. mpeg, Sunset_14.JPG, Sunset_15.JPG, and Medieval_villain_01.mpeg. Note that the two video clips contain faces, while the JPEGs do not. Right-click the selected clips, and choose Analyze Content.

2 In the Analyze Content dialog, select the Face Detection check box. In the Quality drop-down list, choose High (slower). Make sure that the Speech check box is not selected. Click OK to start analyzing.

3 Adobe Media Encoder opens and analyzes the selected clips. When Adobe Media Encoder is finished, return to Adobe Premiere Pro.

● **Note:** To make the rest of your content re-appear after finding clips with faces, click the X in the Filter Bin Content drop-down list to clear the [Find Faces] entry.

4 In the Project panel, click the Filter Bin Content drop-down list, and choose [Find Faces]. Only the video clips should remain in the Project panel.

Review questions

1 What is the main benefit of the speech analysis feature in Adobe Premiere Pro CS5?

2 Transcription can take a long time with a long file. Can you continue to work while the transcription is running?

3 Can you close Adobe Premiere Pro CS5 while the transcription process is running or open a different project?

4 If you edit or add words manually to a transcription, will it mess up the timing of the existing words?

5 If you use the same source file that is already transcribed in a new project, will you have to run the transcription process again?

6 What is the main benefit of face detection?

Review answers

1 The main benefits are the ability to use text searches to locate a specific keyword or frame of video and also to mark the In and Out Points of clips for insertion into the Timeline.

2 You may continue to work in Premiere Pro CS5 or any other application while Adobe Media Encoder processes the file.

3 You may close Adobe Premiere Pro or open a new project file while Adobe Media Encoder is processing the file.

4 The timing will remain in sync even if you add or delete words.

5 The transcribed text is added as metadata to the source file, so it is not necessary to transcribe the file again.

6 It lets you identify clips that contain faces in the Project panel so you can quickly find clips to include in your project.

15 EXPLORING COMPOSITING TECHNIQUES

Topics covered in this lesson

- Incorporating compositing into your projects
- Working with the Opacity effect
- Using blend modes
- Working with alpha-channel transparencies
- Color keying a green-screen shot with Ultra Key
- Blurring a moving object with a track matte

 This lesson will take approximately 50 minutes.

An important feature of Adobe Premiere Pro CS5 is its ability to composite (or layer) any number of video clips, graphics, and still images. Compositing will become a significant part of your video productions.

Getting started

Adobe Premiere Pro and other Timeline-based, multitrack nonlinear editors have a general operating practice: Clips placed in higher video tracks cover up whatever is below them. However, the object isn't to use clips in these higher tracks to obliterate what's beneath them. It's to combine the content from the various tracks using a technique called *compositing*.

In fact, you've already used compositing, back in Chapter 7, when you inserted a title over your video. As you'll learn in this chapter, Adobe Premiere Pro gives you many ways to composite videos, graphics, and images for best effect.

You use compositing techniques on clips so the clips below them on the Timeline can show through. The five basic compositing methods are as follows:

- Reducing the opacity of an entire clip
- Combining layers based on a blend mode
- Using alpha-channel transparencies in clips and effects
- Color keying a green-screen shot
- Using matte keying effects

In this lesson, you will try all of these compositing methods and use different techniques with a few you've already tried. Once you see all the possibilities, you'll start to plan and shoot your projects with layered videos, graphics, and images in mind.

Making compositing part of your projects

You see compositing when you watch a TV meteorologist standing in front of a map or some other graphic background. As shown in the photos here, most times the person is standing in front of a green or blue wall. The technical director uses a *keying* effect to make that wall transparent and then inserts a weather graphic. You can do the same thing in your video projects by using an Adobe Premiere Pro video keying effect.

Matt Zaffino, chief meteorologist—KGW-TV, Portland, Oregon

Many movies, as well as most computer games with live actors, use compositing. *Green-screen* studios enable game developers and film directors to place actors in science fiction and other artificial settings created with 3D computer graphics. Such sets make it possible for actors to work in relative safety while the finished product shows them dangling from a skyscraper, hundreds of feet in the air.

Shooting videos with compositing in mind

Making keying effects work well takes some extra effort. Proper backdrop colors, lighting, and keying techniques all come into play. You need to consider which keying effect will work best for your project.

Some keys use textures or graphics, so you don't need to do a whole lot of planning, but most keying effects take some extra thought and work:

- High-contrast scenes lend themselves to making either the dark or the light portions transparent. The same holds true for shooting light objects against a dark background, or vice versa.

- Solid-color backgrounds are fairly easy to make transparent. Take care that the subjects you *don't* want to key out aren't wearing clothing with colors that match the background.

- For most keying shots, you need to use a tripod and lock down your camera. Bouncing keyed objects creates viewer disconnects. There are exceptions to this rule: Typically, if you're keying in wild, animated backgrounds, then camera movement will not be a problem.

- Most times you want your background (or the other images you'll insert in the transparent areas you create with keying effects) to match those keyed shots. If you're working with outdoor scenes, try to shoot the keyed shots outside or use lights balanced for daylight.

Working with the Opacity effect

One easy way to see compositing at work is to place a video or graphic on a super-imposing track and then make it partially transparent—turn down its opacity—to let videos on lower tracks show through. You can accomplish this using the Opacity effect. Though it can be very useful, you'll discover in this exercise that the Opacity effect's blanket approach to compositing is not always effective. In certain circumstances, you might want to use some other similar Adobe Premiere Pro tools.

In this exercise, you'll reduce the opacity of several items. Later you'll learn ways to achieve more effective results using some of the same clips.

1   Open Lesson 15-1.prproj.

2   Play the clip in the Video 1 track.

3 Drag the clip entitled brown matte to the Video 2 track directly above the video clip in the Video 1 track. Stretch the brown matte clip so it's the same length as the video clip in the Video 1 track.

The matte completely covers the video. If you play the clip in the Program Monitor, you'll notice that you cannot see any of the video on Video 1 track because the brown matte clip in the Video 2 track is covering it.

4 Select the brown matte clip, and expand Opacity in the Effect Controls panel.

5 Use keyframes to set an Opacity effect of 100% (opaque) at the beginning of the clip and an Opacity effect of 0% (completely transparent) at the end.

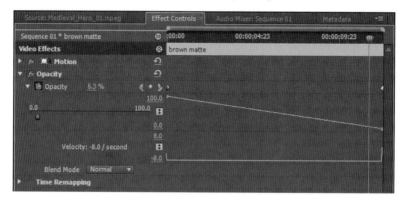

6 Play the clip.

The brown gradually becomes less opaque and more like a tint. Finally, it disappears altogether.

7 Right-click (Windows) or Control-click (Mac OS) the brown matte clip, and then choose Copy.

You'll paste the Opacity parameters on another clip to save a few steps.

8 Right-click (Windows) or Control-click (Mac OS) the brown matte clip, and choose Clear to remove the clip from the Video 2 track.

9 Drag the gradient circle to Video 2 track, and stretch the gradient circle clip to the same length as the video clip in Video 1.

10 Right-click (Windows) or Control-click (Mac OS) the gradient circle clip, and choose Paste Attributes.

This applies the Opacity parameters with the keyframes you set for the brown matte clip to the Gradient clip.

Copy a clip and paste its attributes

Adobe Premiere Pro allows you to copy a clip and paste it somewhere else in any sequence. Or you can merely paste its attributes—any effects applied to it along with their parameters and keyframes—onto another clip. That latter feature is a great way to achieve consistent results. If you do PIPs, you can set a clip size and then apply that to all the clips in the PIP, changing only their screen locations.

11 Play the composited clips.

This gradient was set up using the Titler. It's simply a rectangle with a radial gradient fill applied. You can double-click the gradient circle clip in the Project panel to open the Titler and change the characteristics of the gradient.

It is fairly effective to use the Opacity effect to composite a scene with another clip that has a bright object with a dark background. But sometimes shots composited using the Opacity effect have a washed-out look; later you'll see ways to avoid that undesirable effect.

Combine layers based on a blend mode

If you have used Adobe Photoshop CS5, you may already be familiar with blend modes. Adobe Premiere Pro CS5 uses blend modes in a similar way.

1 Open Lesson 15-2.prproj. Notice the same gradient circle is in Video 2.

2 Select the gradient circle clip in the Video 2 track.

3 Expand the Opacity effect in the Effect Controls panel, and make sure it is set to 100%.

4 Change the blend mode to Multiply, and then play the sequence to see the effect.

Rather than making portions of the clip transparent by changing the opacity, the blend modes actually blend the clip with the clip below it based on the blend mode selected.

5 Try a few other blend modes to observe their effect.

6 Delete the gradient circle clip from the Video 2 track, and drag the blend title to where it was. Stretch the title to the same length as the video clip in the Video 1 track.

7 Change the blend mode on the Blend title menu to Color Dodge, and then play the clip. Notice how the color of the video clip now interacts with the colors in the title.

Working with alpha-channel transparencies

Many graphics, some of the Adobe Premiere Pro transitions, and some video clips have what are called *alpha channels*—portions of the clips or gaps in the transitions that can be made transparent, revealing what's below those clips and transitions on a sequence. You'll work with both in this exercise:

1 Delete the gradient circle clip from Video 2 track, and drag the logo.psd image where it was. Stretch the clip to the same length as the video clip in the Video 1 track.

2 Click the logo.psd clip, open the Effect Controls panel, and adjust the position parameters to 1075 and 550. This moves the logo to the lower-right corner where logos (or bugs) are commonly displayed.

This is a Photoshop graphic with an alpha channel. By default, Adobe Premiere Pro makes the graphic opaque and its alpha channel transparent, allowing whatever is below the alpha channel on the sequence to show through. You can use the Alpha Adjust effect to see the alpha channel.

3 Choose Video Effects > Keying > Alpha Adjust to apply Alpha Adjust to Logo.psd.

Alpha Adjust is the clip-based version of the Opacity fixed effect. As with the Transform effect's connection to Motion, you can use Alpha Adjust to apply Opacity at some other point in the effect chain, instead of second-to-last, where it would occur if you were to use the Opacity fixed effect. Alpha Adjust has a few extra parameters in addition to Opacity.

- **Ignore Alpha**: This makes the alpha channel opaque, covering up the clip below it.

- **Invert Alpha**: This makes the graphic transparent and the alpha channel opaque.

- **Mask Only**: This converts the graphic to a white silhouette.

4 Select Ignore Alpha to see the alpha channel as opaque rather than transparent.

5 Select Alpha Adjust in the Effect Controls panel, and press Delete.

Using video effects that work with graphic-file alpha channels

Four video effects work well with graphic-file alpha channels: Alpha Glow, Bevel Alpha, Channel Blur, and Drop Shadow. You've already seen Drop Shadow, so here you'll use the other three:

1 Choose Video Effects > Stylize > Alpha Glow to apply an Alpha Glow effect to the graphic in Video 2; then open its Settings dialog box, and experiment with its settings.

The Start Color and End Color parameters set the colors of the glow.

2   Delete Alpha Glow from the Effect Controls panel, choose Video Effects > Perspective > Bevel Alpha, and then drag the Bevel Alpha effect into its place.

Give this graphic a 3D beveled feel by adjusting the effect's parameters.

3   Choose Video Effects > Perspective, and add a Drop Shadow effect below the Bevel Alpha effect in the Effect Controls panel. Set Shadow Opacity to 70%, Direction to –220, Distance to 15, and Softness to 30, as shown on the left.

Some video formats may also contain alpha channels. DV cannot, but the QuickTime.mov and uncompressed .avi formats are examples of formats that can contain alpha channels.

4   Drag the scratches.mov clip to the Video 3 track over the logo clip in Video 2 to overlay it. Click to select scratches.mov, and then in the Effect Controls panel, increase the Scale to 151 so that scratches.mov covers the clips beneath it. This .mov clip contains moving scratches and flicker to simulate an old movie. It contains an alpha channel that makes the areas where there are no scratches transparent, so the content under it can be seen. Play the sequence to observe the effect.

5   To enhance the old movie look, drag the brown matte clip to Video 4, and set its Opacity parameter to 20%. Press Enter (Windows) or Return (Mac OS) to render and play the sequence.

Color keying a green-screen shot with Ultra Key

Keying effects use various methods to make portions of a clip transparent. To get a quick overview, choose Video Effects > Keying in the Effects panel. You'll see many effects. With the exception of Alpha Adjust (the clip-based Opacity video effect), they fall into three basic categories:

- **Color/chroma**: Blue Screen (Windows only), Chroma (Windows only), Color, Non-Red, RGB Difference (Windows only), and Ultra Key

- **Luminance**: Luma, Multiply (Windows only), and Screen (Windows only)

- **Matte**: Difference, Garbage, Image, Remove, and Track

Color keys and chroma keys all work in basically the same way: You select a color for them to make transparent and then apply a few other parameters (basically adjusting the width of that color selection). Luminance keys look for dark or light areas in a clip and make them transparent or opaque.

Rather than relying on color or brightness to exclude areas, mattes allow you to manually exclude regions in the frame by dragging a box around them, like the Garbage matte, or by using a graphic. We'll spend more time on matte keys later in the lesson.

Using the Ultra Key effect

Now you'll use the Ultra Key effect, which is a powerful new feature in CS5.

1   Load Lesson 15-3.prproj.

2   Scrub the Timeline to see the background you are using for the green-screen clip.

3   Drag greenscreen.mp4 to Video 2. Play the Timeline now to see the hero talking in front of a green screen that obscures the clip on Video 1. Don't adjust your speakers as this track has no audio.

4   In the Program Monitor, choose Fit for the zoom magnification level. It's important to be able to see the entire frame, because most problems with keying occur around the edges.

5   In the Effects panel, choose Video Effects > Keying, and then drag the Ultra Key effect to the clip in Video 2.

6   In the Effect Controls window, click the triangle next to the Ultra Key effect to expose its controls. Click the eyedropper icon next to the Key Color chip, and click the green background just over the hero's left shoulder to choose the key color. Drag the current-time indicator to preview the Timeline. Most of the green is gone, but patches of white residue remain on the lower right and upper left.

Get an average color value to improve keying

The eyedropper selects a color from a single pixel. Frequently that single pixel does not represent the average color of the region you want to key out, leading to keying results that are less than satisfactory. When using the eyedropper to get a color sample for a key, Ctrl-click (Windows) or Command-click (Mac OS) to get a subsample—a 5x5-pixel area.

7 In the Ultra Key Setting drop-down list, choose Aggressive. Drag though the Timeline again—the key is nearly perfect.

8 In the Ultra Key Output drop-down list, choose Alpha Channel to display this view, where the black represents the alpha channel being removed and the white the region that remains. You should see little black dots in the middle of the white, representing regions on the body that may become transparent. Let's remove the dots.

9 In the Ultra Key effect, twirl the triangle next to Matte Cleanup to open those options. Increase the Contrast value to 40, which should remove the black dots.

10 The edge around the hero is a bit pixelated, especially at 100% zoom magnification. Fix that by increasing the Soften value to 40.

Note: Adobe Premiere Pro Help contains an excellent description of the Ultra Key's controls, so if you find yourself needing to customize your own keys to produce a good result, search for *Ultra* in Adobe Premiere Pro Help.

11 In the Ultra Key Output drop-down list, Choose Composite to return to that view. Drag the current-time indicator to view the finished key, which should be close to perfect.

If you produce a lot of videos with green- or blue-screen videos, you'll find the Ultra Key effect to be a huge improvement over the Color Key and other older Adobe Premiere Pro effects. Even better, it's GPU-accelerated, so if you have the right NVIDIA card, you can preview without rendering and quickly render your finished work.

Tips for effective color or chroma key shots

Chroma key video shoots don't always go smoothly. For the key effects to work effectively, you should follow these tips:

- Use flat lighting (two lights at 45° angles to the screen) to avoid creating hot spots. Don't overdo the lighting. Simply make it even.

- The actor's lighting does not have to be flat. Controlled spotlights or lights with "barn doors" work well.

- If you're going to key in an outdoor background, use daylight-balanced blue gels over your lights to re-create outdoor lighting, or shoot your chroma key shots outdoors. If you're working with live actors, use a fan to blow their hair around to enhance the illusion.

- Avoid chroma key spill—keep actors at least 4 feet away from the backdrop to avoid picking up its reflected color. A backlight on the actors minimizes spill.

- The tighter the shot, the more realistic the finished look will be.

- Fast-paced action is harder to key right to the edges of your subjects.

- Use a wide-open iris on your camcorder to limit the depth of field and to throw the blue screen or green screen a bit out of focus, making it easier to key out.

- Chroma key fabric and paper cost about $8 a square yard, and paint costs about $60 a gallon. You can find many dealers online.

- Which color should you use? With chroma key green, you have a reasonable assurance that no one will have clothing that matches it, and therefore it will key out. Chroma key blue works well because it's complementary to most skin tones.

- Consumer and prosumer camcorders do not key as well as professional camcorders because they record less color information. However, because they give more weight to green colors to correspond to the color sensitivity of human eyes, green screens key more cleanly than blue.

Using matte keys

Matte keys cut "holes" in one clip to allow portions of another to show through or to create something like cutout figures you can place on top of other clips.

The nomenclature can be confusing. Matte keys are not the same as color mattes, such as the brown matte you used earlier in this lesson. However, matte keys generally use matte graphics that you create to define the areas you want to make transparent or opaque.

Two basic types of matte keys exist:

- **Garbage**: Garbage mattes are four-, eight-, or sixteen-sided polygons. They're named *garbage* because you typically use them to remove something you don't want in the video. You move their vertices to define the outline of an area you want to display.

- **Graphic**: Graphic mattes are shapes that you create for keying out or keying in another graphic or a clip. Types of graphic mattes include Difference Matte Key, Image Matte Key, Remove Matte Key, and Track Matte Key.

In this exercise, you'll work with the Four-Point Garbage Matte Key effect and the Track Matte Key effect.

1 Load Lesson 15-4.prproj.

2 Drag the Medieval.psd clip to Video 3, and stretch it to be the same length as the video clip.

Your goal is to cut out a box around the hero's face and make it an overlay on the upper right of the video.

3 Drag the Four-Point Garbage Matte Key effect from the Keying folder to the Medieval.psd clip.

4   Click the Medieval.psd clip in the Timeline to select it; then open the Effect Controls panel and click the Four-Point Garbage Matte title. This will activate the four control points in the garbage matte. Use your mouse to drag the four control points in the Program Monitor to create a box around the hero's face in the image. Zoom the Program Monitor to make finer adjustments.

5   Set the zoom of the Program Monitor back to Fit when you are done adjusting the Four-Point Garbage Matte control points.

6   Expand the Motion field, and adjust the Size, Position, and Rotation fields so that the face appears in the upper-right corner, as shown here on the right. Consider adding a Bevel Alpha effect to make the image stand out from the background.

Creating a split-screen effect

You can use garbage mattes to create split-screen effects. The most frequent application is simply to layer two clips, apply the Four-Point Garbage Matte effect to each, and move the vertices to create two side-by-side rectangles. You can also layer more clips and use the Eight- and Sixteen-Point Garbage Matte effects to create all sorts of shapes.

The one little gotcha is that the garbage matte effects reveal part of a clip—they don't shrink the clip to fit it in the borders of the garbage matte, as happens when you use Motion to make PIPs. So, plan your shots accordingly. If you want to put more of the scene within the garbage matte's borders, use Motion or some other effect to accomplish that.

You can achieve a cool effect by locking down your camcorder on a tripod (ensuring the lighting, focus, and exposure settings don't change for the duration of the shoot) and having an actor do a scene on one side of a set and then play another role on the other side of the set. You can use a garbage matte on one of the scenes to have the actor appear on both sides of the set at once.

This takes some planning. The actor shouldn't cross the line that divides the set in two (though you can keyframe the garbage matte box edges to accommodate some overlap), and there can't be any movement in the vicinity of the scene's dividing line.

Using mattes that use graphics or other clips

Four keying effects fall into the matte category. You'll work with the Track Matte Key effect, because it's the most useful and works the best. Here's a quick rundown on the others:

- **Difference Matte Key**: Making this effect work smoothly is very difficult. In theory, you use it to place in a single set multiple actors, animals, or objects that could not all be in a scene at the same time ordinarily. You have to create the various shots with the same lighting and camera angle, and you need to work with high-end video to have a chance of making it work. It's best to stick with green/blue screens.

- **Image Matte Key**: This matte works like the image mask used in the Gradient Wide transition. You apply it and open a graphic or still image, and the effect makes dark areas transparent and makes light areas opaque. This is a static effect with limited usability.

- **Remove Matte Key**: The Remove Matte effect is designed specifically for graphics that, when used in keyed shots, have something akin to a thin halo around their edges. Apply the effect to remove it.

Using Track Matte Key

Track Matte Key works like Image Matte Key, but it has several advantages and one obvious difference. What makes it different is that you place the matte—a still image, graphic, or something you created in the Titler—in a video track rather than applying it directly to the clip.

Track Matte Key uses the clip in a separate track to define areas of transparency in the selected clip and reveal whatever is below it on a sequence. Its huge advantage is that you can animate the matte. For example, you can use Motion's Scale parameter to gradually reveal the matte or move it in the clip to follow some action. The latter application of Track Matte Key is called a *traveling matte*.

Making a traveling matte

You will use this effect time and again. It's a great way to follow action or hide an object. In this case, you will use Track Matte Key to blur the moving face of the hero moving around in this scene.

1 Open Lesson 15-5.prproj, and open the Practice sequence. Notice that the same video clip is on Video 1 and Video 2.

2 Drag the face matte to Video 3. Stretch the face matte clip to the same length as the other clips. If you play this sequence, you will notice the face matte just stays in the middle of the frame. You need to animate the face matte so it follows the hero's face.

3 Select the face matte clip, and then expand the Motion effect in the Effect Controls panel. Click the Show/Hide Timeline View to open the Timeline in the Effect Controls panel if it isn't already visible.

4 Set the current-time indicator at the start of the clip, and then set a Position keyframe at the beginning of the clip by clicking the Toggle Animation button to the left of Position. Using the Position controls, position the white circle over the hero's face, even if it is offscreen.

5 Scrub the Timeline to about the halfway point of the clip, and adjust the matte to be over the hero's face. Move halfway across the remainder of the clip; then do the same thing again. Continue setting keyframes until you can scrub the clip and have the matte over the face at all times.

Note: Keyframing motion can be a tedious task, but you don't have to set a keyframe at every frame. A good technique is to set a keyframe at the beginning, then the end, and then in the middle. The in-between times will be smoothly calculated. If the motion is constant and there is no camera movement, you will not need to set many in-between keyframes. If you need to add more keyframes, keep dividing the space between keyframes in half until the animation is correct.

6 In the Effects panel, choose Video Effects > Stylize, and drag the Mosaic effect to the Video 2 clip (and not on the face matte clip you just added). Set the horizontal and vertical blocks' values to 50. This makes the clip in Video 2 a mosaic. Now you need to use the Track Matte Key effect to make the mosaic appear over only the face as it moves.

7 Locate the Track Matte Key effect in Video Effects > Keying, and apply it to the clip in Video 2. This is the same clip to which you applied the Mosaic effect.

● **Note:** You can also use this technique to highlight, rather than obscure, a person or object in motion. To highlight with a track matte, simply change the effect on the matted clip from Mosaic to a tinted color, a brighter color, or even black and white.

8 Set Matte to Video 3 and Composite Using to Matte Alpha.

9 Play the sequence.

The Mosaic effect is now on the hero's face only.

Review questions

1   Explain how to copy all the effects from one clip to another.

2   How do you create a logo with beveled edges and a glow that grows and then shrinks?

3   What's the preferred effect for compositing blue- or green-screen videos?

4   Why is it helpful to light a green screen evenly when shooting a scene?

5   How is using the blend modes different from just adjusting the Opacity setting's percentage?

6   Describe what a track matte is.

Review answers

1   Select the clip from which you want to copy the attributes, and choose Edit > Copy. Then select the clip or clips to which you want to copy the attributes, and choose Edit > Paste Attributes.

2   Apply Bevel Alpha and Alpha Glow. Use keyframes in Alpha Glow to animate the size of the glow.

3   Ultra Key provides the best quality for both simple and complex color key–related compositing tasks and is GPU-accelerated with the Adobe Mercury Engine.

4   If a green screen is not lit evenly, it will be more difficult to key out. Multiple key filters may be necessary to select the various shades of green in a poorly lit green screen.

5   The Opacity setting adjusts the amount of transparency of all the pixels in the frame evenly. Blend modes allow you to blend the clip with the clip below it based on the blend mode selected.

6   A matte allows you to make a portion of the video frame transparent. A track matte can be static, or it may be animated to follow motion in the video.

16 WORKING WITH COLOR, NESTED SEQUENCES, AND SHORTCUTS

Topics covered in this lesson

- Exploring color-oriented effects
- Adjusting and enhancing color
- Using nested sequences
- Applying recommended keyboard shortcuts

 This lesson will take approximately 60 minutes.

Adobe Premiere Pro CS5 offers a dozen video effects for enhancing or adjusting colors. In this lesson, you'll explore some specialized editing techniques, including nesting clips and sequences, and you'll learn some keyboard shortcuts to speed up your editing.

Getting started

Most feature films are color-corrected. The purpose of *color correction* is less to fix a shot gone bad than it is to give the film a look that matches its mood or genre: from warm reds for landscapes and sepia tones for historic shots to cold blues for hard-edged films or a gritty look for urban dramas. Color correction (also known as *color enhancing* or *color grading*) is big business, and Adobe Premiere Pro has a full suite of professional color-enhancing effects.

These color-oriented effects offer more than just color correction. You can select a color and change it, convert a clip to grayscale (with the exception of a single color), or remove all colors outside a specific color range. You'll see samples of some of these techniques in this lesson.

You'll also learn about the power of nested sequences as you change the look of a complex effect by changing one nested clip.

The default keyboard shortcuts in Adobe Premiere Pro are too numerous to use all of them, much less memorize them, but you will come to rely on several. In this lesson, you'll also learn how to customize keyboard commands to suit your editing style.

An overview of color-oriented effects

Adobe Premiere Pro has many video effects that adjust or enhance color. Some have narrow functionality, while others are professional-level tools that take a lot of trial and error to gain some level of expertise. Entire books are devoted to color correction, and a good number of video editors specialize in that field.

Adobe Premiere Pro offers a wide range of "colorful" possibilities—more than enough to spark some ideas for your upcoming video projects.

To see what Adobe Premiere Pro has to offer in the color effects department, click the Effects tab and type **color** in the Contains text box. However, that's just a start. Adobe Premiere Pro has several more effects that have to do with color.

Here, the color-oriented effects have been grouped into four categories and are listed within those groups more or less from simplest to most complex. (This taxonomy is one example of why you might want to create and organize some custom effects bins.) The following sections offer a brief overview of the color effects.

Coloring effects

These are the coloring effects:

- **Tint**: This is a simple way to apply an overall color cast to a clip.
- **Change Color**: Like Tint, Change Color applies a color cast but adds more control, and it allows you to change a wider range of colors.
- **Ramp**: This creates a linear or radial color gradient that blends with the original image colors.
- **4-Color Gradient**: This gradient is like the Titler's eponymous feature, but it has more options, and it allows you to keyframe the parameters for some wild results.
- **Paint Bucket**: This effect paints areas of a scene with a solid color.
- **Brush Strokes**: This effect applies a painted look to a clip.
- **Channel Blur**: This creates a glow by blurring red, green, and blue channels separately and in user-specified directions.

Color removal or replacement

These are the color removal or replacement effects:

- **Color Pass**: This Windows-only effect converts an entire clip to grayscale, with the exception of one user-specified color.
- **Color Replace**: This Windows-only effect changes a user-selected color in a scene to a different user-specified color.
- **Leave Color**: Though similar to Color Pass, Leave Color offers much more control.
- **Change to Color**: This effect is like Color Replace, but it has more options and control.

Color correction

These are the color-correction effects:

- **Color Balance, Color Balance (HLS), and Color Balance (RGB)**: Color Balance offers the most control over the red, green, and blue values in midtones, shadows, and highlights. Color Balance (HLS) controls only the overall hue, lightness, and saturation; Color Balance (RGB) controls only the red, green, and blue color values.
- **Auto Color**: This effect is a simple generic color balance.
- **RGB Color Corrector and RGB Curves**: Offering even more control than Color Balance, these effects include controls over the tonal range of shadows and highlights, as well as controls for midtones values (*gamma*), brightness (*pedestal*), and contrast (*gain*).

- **Luma Color and Luma Curve**: These filters adjust brightness and contrast in the highlights, midtones, and shadows of a clip. They also correct the hue, saturation, and luma in a selected color range.

- **Fast Color Corrector**: This effect lets you make instant color changes that you can preview in a split-screen view within the Program Monitor. This is a tool you are likely to use frequently.

- **Three-Way Color Corrector**: This tool enables you to make more subtle corrections by letting you adjust hue, saturation, and luminance for highlights, midtones, and shadows.

Technical color effects

These are the technical color effects:

- **Broadcast Colors**: The Broadcast Colors effect conforms video to display properly on TV sets. It corrects problems created by overly bright colors and geometric patterns due to some effects or added graphics.

- **Video Limiter**: Like Broadcast Colors but with much more precise control, Video Limiter enables you to preserve the original video quality of your clip while conforming to broadcast TV standards.

Adjusting and enhancing color

In this exercise, you will work with five color-oriented effects: Leave Color, Change to Color, Color Balance (RGB), Auto Color, and Fast Color Corrector.

The Leave Color effect

You'll begin with the Leave Color effect.

1   Open Lesson 16-1.prproj.

2   Note the office.avi clip is on Video 1, with a good view of the blue desk lamp.

3   In the Effects panel, open the Video Effects folder and then the Color Correction subfolder, and drag the Leave Color effect to the clip.

4   Expand Leave Color in the Effect Controls panel. Using the eyedropper next to Color To Leave, click the blue lamp to select the color to retain.

5   Set Amount to Decolor to 100%. This converts everything but the selected color to grayscale.

6 Set Tolerance to about 24%. You might need to adjust this figure to include the entire lamp without adding color back to other regions in the clip. Experiment with the Edge Softness control as well, to get familiar with its effect.

7 Play the clip. Only the blue lamp is in color.

The Change to Color effect

Next let's work with the Change to Color effect.

1 Delete the Leave Color effect, and in the Color Correction subfolder in the Effects panel, apply the Change to Color effect to the clip on the Video 1 track.

2 Expand the Change to Color effect in the Effect Controls panel.

3 Move the current-time indicator over the clip so you can see the blue lamp clearly in the Program Monitor.

4 Use the eyedropper next to From to sample the blue color from the lamp.

5 Click the To color swatch, and select a red color in the Color Picker. Click OK to close the Color Picker.

The lamp should change from a blue hue to a red hue.

● **Note:** The Leave Color and Change to Color effects work best in clips that have distinct objects with unique colors, like the lamp in this video.

Color correction

Depending on how you define *color correction*, Adobe Premiere Pro offers several color-correction effects. They run the gamut from basic color balance (like an automatic white balance on a camcorder) to the richly detailed and complex Three-Way Color Corrector effect. In this lesson, you'll devote the most attention to the middle ground: Fast Color Corrector.

● **Note:** The Three-Way Color Corrector effect lets you make separate adjustments, using individual wheels, to adjust tonal ranges for shadows, midtones, and highlights.

The Fast Color Corrector and Three-Way Color Corrector effects offer what are called the Hue Balance and Angle color wheels. You use them to balance the red, green, and blue colors to produce the desired white and neutral grays in the image.

Depending on the desired effect, you might not want the color balance in a clip to be completely neutral. That's where color enhancement comes in. For example, you can give your videos a warm orange color or a cool blue color.

Before tackling the Fast Color Corrector effect, you'll learn briefly about two other color-correction effects.

The Color Balance (RGB) effect

Let's begin with Color Balance (RGB), which is probably the most intuitive color-correction effect.

1 Load Lesson 16-2.prproj. The clip on the Timeline (Behind_the_Scenes_SD) looks a bit yellowish; let's try to fix that.

2 Drag the Color Balance (RGB) effect from the Image Control subfolder in the Effects panel to the clip on the Timeline.

Color Balance (RGB) has a Settings window where you can manually adjust the red, green, and blue levels. The starting point for all clips is 100 no matter what the actual color levels in the clip are.

3 Change the Red, Green, and Blue settings to give this scene a cooler appearance (more blue). Try 104% for Red, 95% for Green, and 106% for Blue.

4 This is a pretty subtle effect, so toggle it on and off by clicking the "on or off" icon. The color looks better with the effect applied, but let's try another approach.

The Auto Color effect

The next color-correction effect you'll learn is Auto Color, which, according to Adobe Premiere Pro Help, "adjusts contrast and color by neutralizing the midtones and clipping the white and black pixels."

1 Delete Color Balance (RGB) from the clip, open the Adjust subfolder in the Effects panel, and drag the Auto Color effect onto the Behind_the_Scenes_SD clip.

2 Try some parameters.

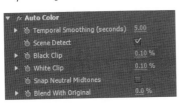

Auto Color is a good tool for quick-and-dirty edits, but most of the time, you'll get a better result using the Fast Color Corrector effect, discussed next. If you do use the Auto Color effect, enable Temporal Smoothing and Scene Detection. Otherwise, the videos tend to flicker a bit, since the color correction is applied on a frame-by-frame basis, rather than over a group of clips. About five seconds is a good value for the Temporal Smoothing setting, but be aware that it can dramatically increase rendering times. Higher Black Clip and White Clip values increase contrast.

The Fast Color Corrector effect

Fast Color Corrector is the workhorse of color-correction filters in Adobe Premiere Pro. It is extremely useful when correcting the color or lighting of a clip.

1   Delete the Auto Color effect from the clip, open the Color Correction subfolder in the Effects panel, and drag the Fast Color Corrector effect onto the Behind_the_Scenes_SD clip.

2   Click the clip on the Timeline, and open the Effect Controls panel. Twirl the triangle next to the Fast Color Corrector effect to expose all parameters. Holy cow, that's a lot of parameters! That's OK, because it will all make sense in a moment or two.

● **Note:** If there's an object that you know is white in the video frame, you can click the eyedropper next to the White Balance color chip and click that object in the Program monitor. Adobe Premiere Pro will choose the Balance Magnitude and Angle values for you. Unfortunately, this clip didn't have any objects that we knew were white, so we had to use the manual approach.

3   Click the Balance Magnitude control point in the middle of the color wheel, and drag it a little away from the yellow, toward the lower right (east-southeast if you're a geography buff or right around 3:30 on a single-handed clock).

4   Click the Show Split View check box beneath the Output parameter to see the difference between the corrected portion of the clip and the original. Note that you can split the view either vertically or horizontally via the Layout drop-down list, and you can control the Split View Percent. If the split view isn't noticeable right away, increase the Balance Magnitude setting to 100, and it will quickly become obvious.

If the effect is too subtle to be apparent in the split-screen view, toggle the effect on and off by clicking the "on or off" icon.

5   Take a look at the color wheel. Here are its parameters:

*   **Hue Angle**: Move the outer ring clockwise to shift the overall color toward red; move it counterclockwise to shift it toward green.

*   **Balance Magnitude**: Move the circle out from the center to increase the magnitude (intensity) of the color introduced into the video.

*   **Balance Gain**: Set the relative coarseness or fineness of the Balance Magnitude and Balance Angle adjustments. Moving the handle toward the outer ring makes the adjustment very obvious. Keeping the perpendicular handle of this control close to the center of the wheel makes the adjustment very subtle.

*   **Balance Angle**: Shift the video color toward a target color.

6 Change the Saturation parameter (below the color wheel) to about 120 to make the colors a bit less intense.

7 Slide the midtone input level to about 1.6 to lighten the midtones. This is the same as adjusting the Gamma values of the clip, which you could also do using the Gamma effect in Adobe Premiere Pro.

8 Deselect the Show Split View option. Note that if you don't deselect this view, Adobe Premiere Pro will render the split view into your final video. Once you've done that once or twice, you tend not to forget to deselect Split View.

9 Choose Window > Workspace > Color Correction.

Note that you have a new video panel: the Reference Monitor.

10 Click the Reference Monitor panel menu, and choose All Scopes.

These are three Waveform Monitors and a Vectorscope (in the upper-right corner). For decades, broadcast TV engineers have used these to ensure that TV signals meet standards (that is, they don't get too bright or have too much contrast).

As you ramp up your color-enhancing skills, you might want to use them for that reason as well as to adjust color. To learn more about them, choose Help > Adobe Premiere Pro Help, and then open Applying Effects > Vectorscope and Waveform Monitors.

Using nested sequences

A *nested* sequence is a sequence in a sequence. You can break your project up into more manageable chunks by creating a project segment in one sequence and dragging that sequence—with all its clips, graphics, layers, multiple audio/video tracks, and effects—into another sequence. There it will look and behave like a single audio/video clip.

One great way to take advantage of a nested sequence is to apply color correction to a long sequence with multiple edits. Instead of applying that effect to each clip in turn, you simply place—*nest*—that sequence in another sequence and apply a single instance of that effect to it. If you want to change the effect parameters, you can then do it on one nested sequence clip, rather than changing each clip in that original sequence.

Multiple uses for nested sequences

Nested sequences have many other uses:

- They allow you to apply an effect or effects to a group of layered clips. That saves having to apply effects to each layer, one at a time.

- They simplify editing by creating complex sequences separately. This helps you avoid running into conflicts and inadvertently shifting clips on a track that is far from your current work area.

- They let you reuse sequences, as well as use the same sequence but give it a different look each time.

- They organize your work in the same way you might create subfolders in the Project panel or in Windows Explorer. This avoids confusion and shortens editing time.

- They allow you to apply more than one transition between clips.

- They make it possible to build multiple picture-in-picture effects.

Nesting a video in a newspaper

In this exercise, you will learn to create the classic newspaper spinning onto the screen—except you will use a nested sequence to add a motion video as a "picture" on this spinning newspaper. Using nested sequences will make it very easy.

1 Open Lesson 16-3.prproj.

2 Select the completed sequence, and play it to see the effect you will create.

The spinning newspaper is the last set of clips in the sequence.

3 Open the nested practice sequence. Initially, it is empty.

4   Drag the Medieval_Hero_02 clip to the Video 1 track of the nested practice
    sequence. Press backslash (\) to zoom in the Timeline.

5   Right-click (Windows) or Control-click (Mac OS) the clip, and choose Scale to
    Frame Size to scale the clip to match the sequence resolution.

6   Drag newspaper.psd to the Video 2 track, directly above the Medieval_Hero_02
    clip. Adjust the length of the newspaper clip to match the movie clip.

    The newspaper clip has a square transparent area where the movie clip
    underneath shows through.

7   Select the Medieval_Hero_02 clip in Video 1, and using the Scale and Position
    parameters of the Motion effect, adjust the video to fit in the window of the
    newspaper. Set Scale to 59 and Position to 360, 322, which should work well.

8   Delete the audio of the Medieval_Hero_02 clip by Alt-clicking (Windows) or
    Option-clicking (Mac OS) the audio track and pressing Delete.

    That's all you need to do with the nested sequence. You'll animate the newspaper
    and video together by animating the sequence, not the individual clips.

9   Click the practice sequence to make it active.

10 Drag the Medieval_wide_01 clip to the Video 1 track of the practice sequence.

11 Right-click (Windows) or Control-click (Mac OS) the clip, and choose Scale to
    Frame Size to scale the clip to match the sequence resolution.

12 Drag the nested practice sequence to the Video 2 track, directly above the
    interview clip. Make the clip in Video 1 the same length as the nested practice
    sequence in Video 2.

13 With the nested practice sequence clip selected, add a Scale keyframe in the Motion effect at about three seconds from the beginning of clip. Set its value to 80. Set another Scale keyframe at the beginning of the clip, and set its value to 0.

14 Set a keyframe for the Rotation parameter in the Motion effect at the beginning of the clip. Set its value to –4x0.0. Set another Rotation keyframe at the same point in the Effect Controls Timeline as the second Scale keyframe. The keyframes snap to each other to make this easy. Set the value of this Rotation keyframe to 0.0.

15 As a nice touch, you can right-click (Windows) or Control-click (Mac OS) the last Rotation keyframe you set and set it to Ease In.

This will make it gradually stop rotating, rather than stop suddenly.

16 Play the clip.

The power of nesting allows you to apply effects to multiple clips at once by nesting clips in a sequence. You can also nest sequences in sequences.

Nesting clips

In the previous exercise, you nested an entire sequence in another sequence. It's also possible to select a group of clips and nest them in a sequence. It does not have to be all the clips in a sequence. This can be useful for collapsing a complex set of clips into a single nested sequence.

1 Open Lesson 16-4.prproj, and double-click the completed sequence to open it in the Timeline. Play the Timeline.

We will create a Cube Spin transition at the edit point of the Medieval_wide_01 clip and Medieval_villain_02. Since there are two other clips composited over the Medieval_wide_01 clip, inserting a Cube Spin transition that correctly impacts the first three clips is difficult—but not if you collapse the first segment to a single nested clip.

2 Shift-click the three clips that make up the first segment—Title 01, nested complete, and Medieval_wide_01—to select them.

3 Right-click (Windows) or Control-click (Mac OS) the selected clips, and choose Nest.

The three clips are collapsed to a single nested clip. Play the clip to see that the nest contains the three clips.

4   In the Effects panel, click the Video Transitions folder to open it, and then click the 3D Motion subfolder. Drag the Cube Spin transition to the edit point between the two clips.

● **Note:** To edit a nested set of clips, double-click the nested sequence in the Timeline. The nested sequence becomes the active sequence, which you can edit.

Getting to know the recommended keyboard shortcuts

Adobe Premiere Pro has more than 100 keyboard shortcuts. You won't use all of them, but about 25 should become part of your repertoire. You can customize them and create additional ones to suit your needs.

To get an idea of just how vast the shortcut opportunities are, choose Edit > Keyboard Customization. Not surprisingly, that opens the Keyboard Customization dialog, shown here.

Note that the Adobe Premiere Pro Factory Defaults list includes the main menu headings: File, Edit, Project, and so on. You can open each of those lists and find commands that match virtually everything available in the menus.

Many mimic standard system-level shortcuts:

FUNCTION	WINDOWS	MAC OS
Save	Ctrl+S	Command+S
Copy	Ctrl+C	Command+C
Undo	Ctrl+Z	Command+Z

Adobe Premiere Pro has three sets of keyboard shortcuts: the factory defaults and sets for two competing products, Avid Xpress DV 3.5 and Final Cut Pro 4.0. The latter two facilitate migration from those products to Adobe Premiere Pro.

Changing a shortcut

You can create a fourth, custom set of shortcuts. The more you work with Adobe Premiere Pro, the more you'll want to do that. Here's how:

1   Choose Edit > Keyboard Customization if the dialog isn't already open.

2   Open the Edit list, and click Redo.

    You'll see that the keyboard shortcut to redo something you've undone is Ctrl+Shift+Z (Windows) or Shift+Command+Z (Mac OS). That shortcut is valid in various Adobe products. Your experience with other products might be to use Ctrl+Y (Windows) or Command+Y (Mac OS).

3   Click the Redo shortcut in the Shortcut column (not the word *Redo*), and then press Ctrl+Y (Windows) or Command+Y (Mac OS).

    [Custom] appears in the Set menu. You'll name and save this as a custom set in a moment, but first check out what happens when you try to change a keyboard shortcut to one that's already in use.

4   Click Copy to highlight it in the list, and then click its shortcut—Ctrl+C (Windows) or Command+C (Mac OS)—to clear that entry.

5   Press Ctrl+Y (Windows) or Command+Y (Mac OS).

A small warning (shown here) appears, noting that you are about to redefine an existing shortcut. Click anywhere in the dialog to make that change.

6   Click Undo to undo that change.

If you were to click OK, the dialog would close, and the [Custom] set would have the new shortcut for Redo and would be the currently selected set of keyboard shortcuts. If you click Save As instead, you can give that [Custom] collection a more descriptive name.

7   Click Save As, give your customized keyboard shortcut collection a name, and then click Save.

Most frequently used shortcuts

About 25 shortcuts seem to be the most frequently used (including system-level "imitations" such as Ctrl+C/Command+C). In no time at all, the following shortcuts will become second nature to you:

- **Tools**: Each tool has a single-letter keyboard shortcut. To remind yourself of those shortcuts, open Keyboard Customization and choose the Tools menu under the Set menu.

  You'll use these frequently. At the very least, Selection (V), Ripple Edit (B), Rolling Edit (N), and Razor (C) should be ingrained in your brain. In case you need reinforcement, roll your pointer over each icon in the Tools panel to see a tool tip with the tool's keyboard shortcut.

● **Note:** Pressing the backslash key twice will return you to the previous zoom level. This is a great time-saver.

- **Backslash (\)**: This resizes the Timeline to display your entire project. It's a great way to get a handle on where you are in the workflow.

- **J and L**: These are playback controls. J is reverse; L is forward. Press one of these keys two or three times to increase speed incrementally.

- **K**: This is a multifunction playback modifier key. Press K to stop playback. Hold down K while either pressing or holding down the J or L key to change playback speeds.

  - Hold down K while pressing J to play in reverse one frame at a time.

  - Hold down K while pressing L to play forward one frame at a time.

  - Press and hold down K+J to play in reverse slowly (8 fps).

  - Press and hold down K+L to play forward slowly (8 fps).

- **Plus sign (+) or minus sign (−) and a number**: You'll need a numeric keypad for this one. Use this keystroke combination to move a clip by a specified number of frames. Select the clip, and then press + or − on the numeric keypad (not Shift+= or the hyphen key) followed by the number of frames (you also need to use the numeric keypad). Press Enter (Windows) or Return (Mac OS) to move the clip.

- **Home and End**: Use these to move to the beginning or end of a sequence if the Timeline is active or to the first or last clip in the Project panel if it's active.

- **Page Up and Page Down**: Use these to move to the beginning or end of the selected clip or next edit point in the Timeline or to the top or bottom clip currently displayed in the Project panel.

- **Asterisk (*)**: This adds a marker. The asterisk key on the numeric keypad (not Shift+8) adds a marker to the Timeline. (Markers will be covered in more detail in Lesson 21.)

- **S**: Pressing S turns on or turns off the Snap feature (the little two-pronged icon in the upper-left corner of the Timeline). You can toggle Snap on or off even while dragging or trimming a clip.

- **Alt/Option**: This shortcut temporarily unlinks audio and video. Press the Alt (Windows) or Option (Mac OS) key as you click the video or audio portion of a linked audio/video clip to unlink that portion, enabling you to trim or move that portion of the clip without affecting the other portion.

- **Alt+[and Alt+] (Windows) or Option+[and Option+] (Mac OS)**: This shortcut sets the work area bar's end points (shown here). If you want to render or export part of your project, you need to set the beginning and end of that section. Pressing Alt+[(Windows) or Option+[(Mac OS) sets the beginning to wherever the current-time indicator edit line is. Pressing Alt+] (Windows) or Option+] (Mac OS) sets the end. You can simply drag the ends of the bar to those points as well. The work area bar end points will snap to the clip edit points.

- **Ctrl+T/Command+T**: Pressing Ctrl+T (Windows) or Command+T (Mac OS) opens the Titler.

Note: When viewing the Timeline panel in audio units, the clip will move by the specified number of audio samples.

Note: The current-time indicator does not snap to items—items snap to it. If the current-time indicator did snap to edit points, moving the current-time indicator through the sequence would become a jumpy mess.

Note: Double-clicking the center of the work area bar sets the bar's ends to the visible area of the sequence or to the full length of the sequence if it's visible in its entirety in the Timeline.

- **Marquee-select**: Drag a marquee to select a group of clips in the Timeline or Project panel. This should be a routine part of your workflow. Marquee-selecting clips in the Timeline lets you move a whole group of clips, and marquee-selecting clips in the Project panel lets you add all those clips at once to a sequence.

- **Import folders**: Instead of importing a file or collection of files, you can import an entire folder. Right-click in the Project panel and select Import, and click the Import Folder button on the bottom of the Import dialog. That creates a bin in the Project panel with the exact folder name and imports the associated files.

Review questions

1 What's the difference between the Leave Color effect and the Change to Color effect?

2 What is the purpose of the split-screen option in the Fast Color Corrector effect?

3 What are the basic settings you apply with the color wheel in the Fast Color Corrector effect?

4 How can you edit a nested sequence once you nest selected clips on a Timeline?

5 What keyboard shortcuts enable you to rewind, stop, and play your project?

Review answers

1 Leave Color turns everything in a scene gray with the exception of objects that have a user-selected color. Change to Color replaces a user-specified color with another color.

2 The split-screen function allows you to instantly preview the effect of your color corrections and compare it to the original.

3 The settings are Balance Angle (the color added to the clip) and Balance Gain (the intensity of that color). You can also adjust the overall Hue Angle parameter to move all colors in a clip toward a selected color.

4 Double-click the nested sequence, and the original sequence will become active.

5 The shortcuts are J, K, and L. Pressing J or L more than once speeds up the reverse and forward speeds. K stops playback.

17
MANAGING YOUR PROJECTS

Topics covered in this lesson

- Working in the Project menu
- Using the Project Manager
- Importing projects or sequences

 This lesson will take approximately 30 minutes.

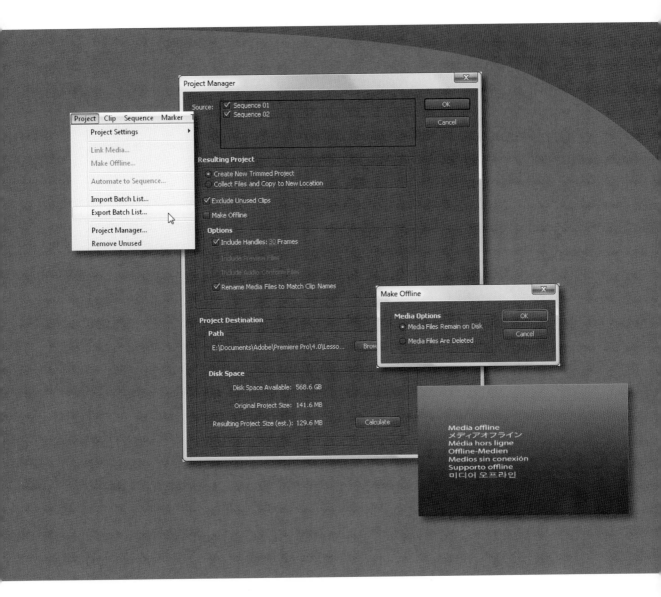

Managing assets and backing up projects are
critically important to professional video producers.
The Project Manager lets you easily consolidate a
project for archival purposes.

Getting started

If you are a one-person band, tracking projects is probably a snap for you. However, once you start bringing others into the production mix, you need to find ways to manage your assets. Adobe Premiere Pro CS5 has a slick project-management tool, called the Project Manager, that reduces a project's storage size and consolidates the files associated with a project.

The Project Manager allows you to save or consolidate your project for easy archiving, and its import features allow you to share complete projects or portions of projects.

You can also save time editing various projects by importing sequences from older saved projects. You have the ability to import the entire project or selective sequences from that project.

Project menu overview

Project management starts in the Project menu. It presents several options that let you track projects and reuse assets. In particular, it offers two ways to export your project:

- **Batch list**: A Batch list is a text file of audio/video asset names and timecodes. It contains no information about your project such as edits, transitions, or graphics.

- **Project Manager**: The Project Manager creates a trimmed version of your project by saving only the portions of the assets you used in your sequences or consolidates the project by storing all its assets in a single file folder. If you choose to create a trimmed project, you can use only offline filenames that you later recapture. Whether you trim or consolidate your project, the Project Manager also stores a copy of your original Adobe Premiere Pro project file with all its information about edits, transitions, effects, and Titler-created text and graphics.

In the following exercise, you will briefly run through the Project menu commands and then focus on the menu's most important feature—project management.

1 Load Lesson 17-1.prproj.

2 Click in the Project panel to select it, but don't select any of the clips (otherwise several options in the Project menu will be unavailable).

● **Note:** If you select a clip, that will be the sole entry in the Batch list you will make in step 4.

3 Open the Project menu in the menu bar.

You'll see the following options:

- **Project Settings**: You worked with project settings in Lesson 2.

- **Link Media**: Use this to link offline filenames to their actual files or videotapes.

● **Note:** Some of these options will be dimmed depending on what files or panel you have selected.

- **Make Offline**: This allows you to convert an online file to offline.

- **Automate to Sequence**: Use this to move selected files to a sequence, as you did in Lesson 5.

- **Import/Export Batch List**: Use this to create or import a list of filenames.

- **Project Manager**: You'll work with the Project Manager in this lesson.

- **Remove Unused**: This is a quick and easy way to clean up your project. Choose it to remove any assets from the Project panel that you are not using in your project.

4 Choose Export Batch List, accept the default name and location (the current project folder), and click Save.

That creates a comma-delimited or comma-separated value (CSV) file that you can read with most text editors. The content is simply the filenames, timecodes, and original source tape names (if any). The Batch list stores only audio and video filenames, not graphics or images.

5 Choose Import Batch List from the Project menu, and double-click Adobe Premiere Pro Batch List.csv (the file you just created in step 4).

The Batch List Settings dialog opens.

6 Accept the defaults, which should be the same as your sequence settings, as shown here. Click OK.

This adds a new bin to the Project panel.

7 Open the Adobe Premiere Pro Batch List bin.

The status of each clip is Offline, which is evident because of the icon next to each clip.

Clips offline

● **Note:** The Import Batch List feature has a limitation in functionality. It can link to audio/video files only. If you attempt to link to audio-only or video-only files, you will get an error message.

8 Click bike low shot.mov in the Adobe Premiere Pro Batch bin.

9 Choose Project > Link Media.

10 In the Link Media dialog, navigate to the Lesson 17 folder, and double-click bike low shot.mov.

● **Note:** If you select more than one offline file, the Link Media dialog appears in turn for each file you select. Pay attention to the offline filename in the title bar of the dialog so that you relink the correct source file to each offline file.

Making a clip offline

It's possible to purposely make clips offline and still work with them in the Timeline. This can be useful for saving disk space while working in the early stages of a project or for relinking to a clip that is being reshot.

1   Delete the Adobe Premiere Pro Batch bin you just imported.

2   Click the bike cable shot1.mov clip in the Project panel to select it.

3   Choose Project > Make Offline.

4   In the Make Offline dialog, select Media Files Remain on Disk, and click OK.

The file becomes offline in the project but remains on the hard drive. Selecting Media Files Are Deleted takes the file offline and removes it from the hard drive. If you select that option and you want to use that file in a project, you'll need to recapture it (or, in this case, copy it from the DVD).

5   Move the current-time indicator over the first clip in the Timeline.

Note these two things:

- The clip remains in the project with all its effects applied. (The first clip has scaled motion and a transition at the end.)

- The Program Monitor displays a "Media offline" placeholder graphic for that clip.

This is useful if you work with massive files and want to speed up editing. The drawback is that you can't see the video if you want to make frame-specific edits.

Note: If you're using the clip in another project, it will still be online there.

Using the Project Manager

Typically the Project Manager comes into play after you complete a project.

You can use it to create a separate file folder that consolidates into one spot all the assets used in your sequences. This is a great way to archive a project and make it easier to access later. Once consolidated, you can remove all the original assets if you choose.

You can conserve hard-drive space by saving only those assets you used in the project, trimming them to the portions you used in your sequences, and then saving them (or offline references to them) in a single file folder.

To see your options, choose Project > Project Manager.

You can choose to save all sequences (the default) or only specific sequences.

You have two basic choices that determine how the project will be saved, each with its own set of options (shown here):

• Create New Trimmed Project

• Collect Files and Copy to New Location

Working with a trimmed project

In the trimmed project, the resulting files (or offline file references) refer only to the portions of the clips you used in the project sequences. You have some options, as shown in the previous figure:

- **Exclude Unused Clips**: This almost goes without saying when you are making a trimmed version of your project.

- **Make Offline**: Instead of storing the clips as files, create a list of file data so that you can capture the clips from videotape.

- **Include Handles**: This works the same as video capture in that you retain some extra head and tail frames to allow for smooth transitions or slight editing changes later.

- **Rename Media Files to Match Clip Names**: If you changed the clip names to make them more descriptive, you can use the new names in the trimmed project.

Note: If you select Make Offline, the Project Manager checks all the video files to see whether they have source tape names associated with them. If not, because they can't be recaptured, the Project Manager will copy those files into the newly created project rather than just list them as offline.

Collecting files and copying them to a new location

The Collect Files and Copy to New Location option in the Project Manager menu will store all the media assets from the current project to a single location. You might use it to prepare a project for sharing or archiving. This feature is useful if you have media assets stored in many different folders or many different drives. It will organize all your files into one location.

This selection shares two options with the trimmed project selection: Exclude Unused Clips and Rename Media Files to Match Clip Names. In addition, it has two other choices:

- **Include Preview Files**: These are files created when you render effects. Using this approach saves you time later but takes up more disk space.

- **Include Audio Conform Files**: This is only a minor time-saver. Audio conforming runs in the background when you import files with audio into a project. There is generally no need to include audio conform files.

Note: Because the video files in all the lessons in this book do not have source tape names associated with them, clicking Calculate with Make Offline selected or unselected will yield the same results. By default, even if you select Make Offline, the Project Manager copies all video files that don't have source tape names associated with them to the new project to ensure you don't delete them accidentally.

Final project management steps

Click Calculate (at the bottom of the Project Manager), and Adobe Premiere Pro will determine the size of the files in the current project and the resulting trimmed project's estimated size. You can use this to check what difference it will make to select Make Offline or to include preview files, audio conform files, or handles.

Finally, select (or create) a file folder for the trimmed or consolidated project, and click OK.

Importing projects or sequences

It is helpful to be able to use one Adobe Premiere Pro CS5 project in another. You can save hours of time by importing a project, or a portion of a project, into a new project.

1   Load Lesson 17-2.prproj.

    You want to import the twirling newspaper sequence you created in Lesson 16 and add it to this project.

2   Choose File > Import, navigate to the Lesson 16 folder, and select Lesson 16-3. prproj. Click Open.

    The Import Project dialog opens.

3   Selecting the Import Entire Project option will do as it suggests. In this case, you just want the twirling newspaper sequence, not the entire project, so select Import Selected Sequences and click OK.

    The Import Premiere Pro Sequence dialog opens, displaying all the sequences available in the imported project.

4   Choose the "completed" sequence, and click OK.

    A new bin appears in the Project panel with the name of the imported project. Expand this bin, and you will notice it has the completed sequence and associated clips you requested, but it also imported the nested complete sequence, which you did not request. Adobe Premiere Pro analyzed the request and determined that the nested complete sequence was also required because it was nested inside the complete sequence.

5   Drag the completed sequence to the Timeline and play it to see that the imported sequence plays as expected.

Review questions

1 What are the basic differences between Batch lists and Project Manager-trimmed projects?

2 Explain the two principal uses of the Project Manager.

3 Why does selecting Make Offline in the Project Manager have no effect on clips with no source tape name associated with them?

4 When you import a project into a project, must you import the entire project?

Review answers

1 Batch lists are simply text files consisting of audio/video filenames, timecodes, and their source tape names. Project Manager–trimmed projects have full project information, plus trimmed original clips or offline filename references.

2 You use the Project Manager either to create a trimmed version of your project or to consolidate the original, untrimmed project files in one folder. In either case, you can store all your assets in one easily accessible spot to simplify collaboration and archiving.

3 Adobe Premiere Pro has a built-in fail-safe mechanism. If it sees that a video clip has no source tape associated with it, it won't allow the Project Manager to make that an offline clip, since you might not be able to recapture it.

4 No. Adobe Premiere Pro allows you to import an entire project or one or more sequences.

18 EXPLORING ADOBE ONLOCATION CS5

Topics covered in this lesson

- Connecting your camcorder to Adobe OnLocation CS5
- Calibrating your camera with the Camera Setup Assistant
- Recording live video
- Recording video to a shot list
- Analyzing video with Adobe OnLocation
- Analyzing audio with Adobe OnLocation
- Importing clips not captured with Adobe OnLocation
- Importing OnLocation clips with the Adobe Premiere Pro Media Browser

 This lesson will take approximately 40 minutes.

Adobe OnLocation allows you to bypass the time-consuming step of capturing video and also provides tools for ensuring your camera and lighting are set up perfectly, before you ever record a frame of video.

Getting started

When working with cameras connected to your computer via an IEEE 1394 connection, Adobe OnLocation can record video directly to disk, bypassing the slow process of recording to tape and then capturing. Adobe OnLocation also provides professional monitoring tools and scopes, which can dramatically improve the quality of the video that you shoot.

In addition, Adobe OnLocation provides great organizational functionality by allowing you to set up your shot lists beforehand, either manually or by importing a script from Adobe Story. It also lets you name and add metadata to shots in real time as you shoot. This functionality works with both tape-based devices, such as DV and HDV camcorders, and also camcorders capturing in SD cards or hard drives, such as Digital SLRs and high-end MPEG2-based camcorders from a number of vendors, including Canon, JVC, Panasonic, and Sony.

Specifically, with Adobe OnLocation CS5, you can create timestamped placeholders for video shot with such nontape devices and then link the actual clips to these timestamped placeholders after the shoot. Finally, you can import these clips, and the associated metadata, directly into Adobe Premiere Pro.

Setting up Adobe OnLocation

Adobe OnLocation communicates with camcorders and other OHCI-compliant devices using the IEEE 1394 standard. You can connect your camera to your desktop or notebook computer, as described in Chapter 4, via an IEEE 1394 cable, just as you would to capture video that you've already recorded to tape. However, instead of capturing video to Adobe Premiere Pro, you will be recording live video directly to your computer. This requires your computer to be "on location" with your camcorder. These are the basic steps to follow:

1 Connect the camcorder to your computer.

2 Turn on your camcorder, and set it to camera mode.

3 In Windows XP, if the Digital Video Device message pops up, click Take No Action, select the Always Perform The Selected Action option, and click OK. (The next time you fire up your camcorder, you should not see this connection query.) In Windows Vista, an AutoPlay dialog may appear. Click "Set AutoPlay defaults in Control Panel." In Mac OS, if iMovie or another application starts, see that application's Help for information about which application to open when a camera is connected.

4 Start Adobe OnLocation.

5 Click New Project.

6 Name the project *First_Project*, and save it to a folder of your choice.

7 Choose Window > Workspace > Calibration to change to the Calibration workspace.

8 Click the Camera Setup Assistant tab near the bottom of the window.

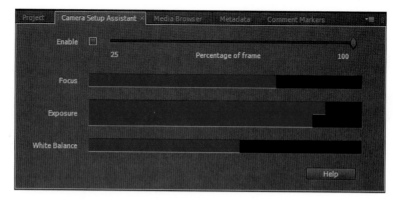

Calibrating your camera with Camera Setup Assistant

You can dramatically improve your videos by fine-tuning your camera setup before recording a single frame of video. The Camera Setup Assistant in Adobe OnLocation is an excellent tool to help you calibrate your camera's focus, exposure, and white balance. To fine-tune your camera setup effectively, it will be helpful to set your camcorder to manual focus, manual exposure, and manual white balance so you have complete control over these attributes.

Setting up your frame

To set up your frame, follow these steps:

1 Point your camera at your subject, and place the Camera Setup Assistant Focus and Exposure chart (which is included in the box with Adobe OnLocation) next to the subject.

2 Zoom in with your camera lens so the Focus and Exposure chart takes up most of the frame.

3 If necessary, enable the slider and adjust the percentage of frame value on the Camera Setup Assistant panel to crop the frame to include just the Focus and Exposure chart.

Setting your focus

To set up your focus, adjust the focus on your camcorder until the focus indicator in the Camera Setup Assistant component grows as large as possible. You will also notice the focus fine-tuning in the monitor window.

Setting your iris/exposure

To set up your iris/exposure, adjust the exposure on your camera so that the exposure meter in the Camera Setup Assistant panel grows as far to the right as possible but remains even. Achieving this exposure gives you the maximum range of darks to whites without overexposing the video. Note that the top exposure line indicates darks, and the bottom exposure line indicates lights.

About exposure

Exposure is determined by multiple factors: lighting, iris/aperture, shutter speed, and gain.

- Adjust the physical lighting of your scene (ambient or created) to achieve the best exposure.

- Adjust the aperture of your camera to let more or less light into the camera. (The wider your iris, the shallower your depth of field.) Try to achieve optimal exposure via the aperture, since boosting brightness via gain can inject noise into the video and lower quality.

- Adjust the shutter speed to allow light into the camera for shorter or longer periods of time. (Shutter speeds of 1/60 second are typical for shoots not involving very fast action.)

- Adjust the gain to set the level of electronic lighting enhancement. Boosting gain to achieve the desired exposure should be considered a last resort after adjusting lighting, aperture, and even shutter speed, since gain injects noise into the video.

Setting your white balance

White balancing your shot is important to help ensure that the camera records the correct colors. When properly white balanced, the recorded images will accurately reflect the real colors in the scene. By following these steps, you can ensure that your camera will record an optimally exposed and focused video.

● **Note:** If you've worked through the previous steps in this chapter, the white balance card should fill your frame; if not, zoom in until it does.

1 Flip over the Camera Setup Assistant Focus and Exposure chart to reveal a blank white card.

2 Adjust the white balance on your camera until the white balance meter in the Camera Setup Assistant panel is maximized to the right. When properly set, the white card in the field monitor component will appear white rather than gray or a different hue.

White balance controls on camcorders

The white balance controls on most camcorders include manual settings, presets, and custom presets:

- **Manual**: Some camcorders allow you to manually dial any color temperature. This is the most flexible method.

- **Presets**: Some camcorders have white balance presets such as Indoors, Outdoors, and so on. Scroll through them to see which one best matches your scene.

- **Custom presets**: Some camcorders can "learn" custom white balance settings by pointing the camera at a white card and pressing a button on the camcorder to "learn" the color temperature.

Review the documentation for your camcorder to learn how to set the white balance properly on your camera.

Recording live video

Recording live video from your camera to your computer can save you hours of time in capturing and logging tapes. Recording directly to your computer's hard drive happens in real time, and the clips recorded are available immediately for editing. You simply need to import them into Adobe Premiere Pro.

Now that your camera is set up and calibrated, record some video directly to your hard drive.

1 Choose Window > Workspace > Production to change to the Production workspace.

2 If your camera is on, you should see the live video displayed in the monitor.

3 Click the red Record button at the bottom of the monitor panel. Notice that a clip appears in the Shot List panel to indicate the recording activity. Press Stop when you are finished recording.

Adobe OnLocation recording features

The digital recorder will actually start recording video five seconds before you click the Record button. This helps ensure you never miss a good scene. You can adjust the amount of time this *preroll* is buffered in Edit > Preferences > Device Control (Windows) or OnLocation > Preferences > Recording and Playback (Mac OS). Then you can set the Pre-Roll Buffer to a number of seconds.

If you want to break up a scene into multiple clips, clicking the Record button while already recording will start a new clip.

You can record directly to your hard drive and to tape with Adobe OnLocation. Simply follow the instructions for recording directly to disk and also put a tape in your camcorder. The tape can become a backup or archive as needed.

Recording video to a shot list

Planning a video shoot well can save you hours of time. Adobe OnLocation allows you to create a shot list in advance of the shoot to help you plan and organize your shots. In this exercise, you will create a shot list of three shots.

1 Use the project that is already open.

2 Click the "Add shot placeholder" icon three times to create three new shots for the shot list.

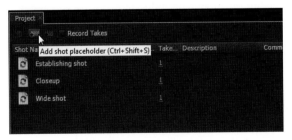

3 The shot placeholders will be named based on your project name. Rename them as shown in the figure.

4 Make sure your camera is connected and powered on in camera mode.

5 Select the "Establishing shot" clip in the shot list.

6   Click the Record button near the bottom of the Monitor panel. Notice the video is being recorded into the "Establishing shot" placeholder clip. Click the Stop button when you are done recording.

7   Repeat this recording for the wide-shot and close-up placeholder clips.

Retakes

It is common to encounter problems when shooting a scene, so it is often necessary to record multiple takes of the same shot. If a second or third take is required when recording to a shot list, click the Add Shot Placeholder icon while the main shot is selected, and Adobe OnLocation will create a new take for the same shot.

Analyzing video with Adobe OnLocation

Earlier in this lesson, you calibrated your camera to ensure that focus, exposure, and white balance are correct. This is an important step, and the Camera Setup Assistant is a very helpful tool in accomplishing that. But changing conditions in the scene can alter color or exposure, so it's important to monitor your shoot continuously. Adobe OnLocation provides a powerful set of tools to help you monitor video.

1   Open a new Adobe OnLocation project by choosing File > Open Project.

2   Navigate to the Lesson 18 folder, and open the project called Lesson 18.olproj.

Notice that three clips were captured in this project. These clips have some metadata in the Comments fields to help the editor choose the best clips. These clips are of the same scene but recorded with different exposure and audio settings on the camera.

Working with the Waveform Monitor

● **Note:** The IRE scale stands for Institute of Radio Engineers.

The Waveform Monitor represents luminance (or brightness) in a graphical form in real time as the video plays, using the IRE scale with brightness values from below 0 to over 100. The brightness value of each pixel in the video frame is represented by the waveform graph. The higher the graph, the brighter the pixel.

A well-exposed scene has brightness values across the entire scale. It is easy to see that pixels that are all dark would make a dark video or that pixels that are all bright would make a bright video. But it is also important to understand that having brightness values across the entire scale gives a feeling of depth to the image. Having brightness values across the entire scale is called *range*. Let's take a look at some examples of good range and bad range using the Waveform Monitor as a tool.

1   Select the clip named normal.mov. Play it by clicking the Play icon near the
    bottom of the monitor.

2   Observe the Waveform Monitor.

The luminance or brightness values have a nice range, from just below 7.5 (the
normal low range for black) to about 100 (the normal high range for white), with
the brightest pixels in the face around 70–75, which is good exposure for a moody
shot like this one. This clip is an example of a scene that is properly exposed.

3   Select the clip named dark_loud.mov. When you play this clip, notice that
    the pixels that correspond to the face are all below 60 and that most of the
    brightness values are clumped at the bottom, including lots of pixels below 7.5.
    This means that detail in the darker pixels is likely lost for good and that the
    video will look "dark" when played. When you see a waveform like this, you
    should consider adjusting the exposure on the camera or changing the lighting
    to provide a greater range of luminance. Observing the Waveform Monitor
    while you make lighting changes is a good way to know when you have it right.

4   Select the clip named light_quiet.mov. When you play this clip, notice that the waveform is pushed to the top, with lots of pixels above 100 IRE and none near 7.5 IRE. This means that the detail in the brightest pixels will be lost and that

the video will appear faded. This is another case where adjusting the lighting or camera exposure would make a much nicer image.

Analyzing color with the Vectorscope

Although the Waveform Monitor is helpful for analyzing brightness, the Vectorscope is useful for analyzing color. The Vectorscope is a round graph with "no color" represented in the center and a high value of color represented on the outer edge. The color wheel is represented in quadrants around the circle of the Vectorscope. Starting at 11 o'clock and going clockwise are Red, Magenta, Blue, Cyan, Green, and Yellow. The farther the graph extends to the edge, the higher the saturation of that color.

In addition, the line between red and yellow represents flesh tones, and the positioning of the pixels along that line tells us that the face tones, which comprise the bulk of the saturated pixels in this shot, are accurately white balanced.

Looking at the waveform, you can tell that there aren't a lot of saturated colors in the frame (it is shot in a medieval tower, after all) but that facial colors appear accurate.

Analyzing audio with Adobe OnLocation

So far we have been focusing on Adobe OnLocation's video capabilities. But audio is half of any good production, so let's take a look at one of the audio tools included with Adobe OnLocation: the Audio Meter.

1 Play the clip named normal.mov, and observe the levels represented by the green/yellow lines in the meter. Since this is a stereo clip, you can see the left and right channels represented as it plays. Notice that there are good levels across most of the frequency range, indicated by green and some yellow high points in the audio. This is an example of a good audio file. The meter did not peak (turn red) as you played this file. The overall volume is good and it's not too loud.

2 Play the clip named dark_loud.mov. Notice this clip peaks, or *clips*, on the meter, as shown indicated by the red bars. This audio is too loud at some points, which causes clipping and makes the loud sections sound very flat. In this case, you should turn down the audio to the camera or reposition the microphone.

3 Play the clip named light_quiet.mov. Notice the overall level or volume is too low. This is represented visually by displaying only green levels, never peaking into yellow. This would be difficult to correct in postproduction. It is much easier to fix the problem at the scene when detected with the Audio Meter.

Volume good   Volume too loud   Volume too low

Using these video- and audio-monitoring tools can save you hours in postproduction trying to correct problems. Adobe OnLocation can be a real time-saver in preventing problems and helping you produce high-quality video and audio.

Importing clips not captured with Adobe OnLocation

Many producers shoot with cameras not tethered to the computer via IEEE 1394 connections. Although you can't capture video from these devices directly to disk, you can create shot lists with placeholders for each shot and capture metadata about the clips to these placeholders before, during, and after the shoot. Then you can link the actual video files to the placeholders. Linking can be either manual or automatic; here's the workflow for automatically linking placeholders with clips:

1 Create your shot list as you would normally, and bring the computer with the Adobe OnLocation project to the shoot.

2 While capturing each shot with your camcorder, click the shot placeholder, and then click "Create timestamped placeholder" or press Ctrl+T (Windows) or Command+T (Mac OS). This adds a timestamp to the placeholder.

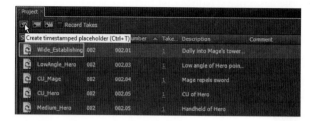

3 Either at the shoot or while importing the clips (preferably at the shoot), synchronize the time and date of your computer to that of your camera by choosing Edit > Camera Date Time in Adobe OnLocation and entering the camera's date and time into OnLocation. This synchronizes the computer and camera so that when you create your timestamped placeholders in Adobe OnLocation, the times and dates should match the clips shot by the camera.

4 Copy the clips from the camera to your computer as normal.

5 In the Media Browser, navigate to the content, and choose the correct format in the "View as" drop-down list.

6   If you've previously imported clips from this folder, select the Hide Media in Project check box to avoid importing the same clips twice.

7   Click to select the content files to import, and then click the "Import and auto-match to existing items" icon.

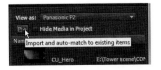

8   If you didn't synchronize your camera and computer at the shoot, click the Change Time button and synchronize the camera and computer. Otherwise, click OK.

Adobe OnLocation will compare all the selected clips against all timestamped placeholders in the project. Before synchronizing the matching pairs, Adobe OnLocation will display a dialog summarizing the results. Adobe OnLocation will replace the placeholder icon with a thumbnail icon for all matched placeholders, and you can double-click the icon to load and play it in Adobe OnLocation.

9   If matching errors occur, either follow the suggestions in the error message that Adobe OnLocation displays, or watch this video for help in diagnosing and fixing any problems: *http://tv.adobe.com/watch/adobe-story/matching-metadata-to-shots-in-onlocation/*.

10 If all else fails (or if you didn't timestamp any placeholders at the shoot), you can link the shots to the clips manually by dragging and dropping the clips onto the shot placeholders.

Working with multiple cameras

With multiple-camera shoots, take the following steps to promote accurate automatching:

1   Synchronize the time and date of all cameras as closely as possible.

2   Assign a camera to all clips in the project in the Camera Label field.

3   When importing the clips, click the Limit Auto-Match to Single Camera check box, and import footage from each camera separately.

Importing OnLocation clips with the Adobe Premiere Pro Media Browser

With the CS5 release, there is also a more streamlined way to import files into Adobe Premiere Pro from Adobe OnLocation projects. Here's the procedure:

1   In Adobe Premiere Pro, open the Media Browser, and navigate to the folder that contains the OnLocation project file.

2   Choose the correct format in the "View as" drop-down list. The Media Browser displays thumbnails of the clips and associated metadata.

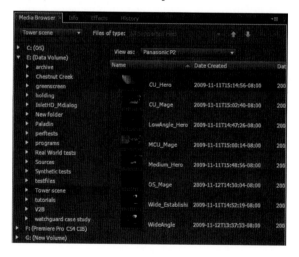

3   To preview any clip, double-click it. The clip will load the clip in the Source Monitor. You can also view its metadata in the Metadata panel.

4   To import the clip or clips, drag them into the Project panel, or right-click and choose Import, and then import as normal. Adobe Premiere Pro imports the selected file(s) into the project.

Review questions

1 Why should you take the time to white balance your camera?

2 What is the value of recording directly to disk?

3 Which does the Waveform Monitor indicate: color or brightness?

4 How is a shot list helpful?

5 What does it mean when the audio meters peak at red?

6 Why is it important to synchronize your camera with your computer at the shoot?

Review answers

1 You white balance your camera to make sure the color hue you are recording is accurate. It takes much longer to fix poorly white-balanced video in postproduction than it does to correct it during a shoot.

2 Recording directly to disk saves a lot of time because you don't have to capture clips, which is a serial process.

3 The Waveform Monitor indicates luminance (or brightness).

4 The shot list lets you organize your shots prior to shooting a scene. This can save a lot of time during the actual shoot.

5 When the Audio Meter illuminates red at the high end of the scale, it's an indication that the volume of the audio is too loud. Red on the Audio Meter causes clipping in those sections of the audio.

6 To use the new automatch feature that matches placeholders and the associated metadata with the actual clip.

19 USING PHOTOSHOP AND AFTER EFFECTS TO ENHANCE YOUR VIDEO PROJECTS

Topics covered in this lesson

- Working with Adobe Creative Suite 5 Production Premium
- Importing Photoshop files as sequences
- Using Adobe Dynamic Link with After Effects
- Replacing a clip with an After Effects composition

 This lesson will take approximately 50 minutes.

Adobe Photoshop CS5 and Adobe After Effects CS5 can play valuable roles in your video production workflow. You can animate Photoshop layered graphics in Adobe Premiere Pro CS5, and you can use After Effects to dynamically link text and graphic animations with Adobe Premiere Pro.

Getting started

Adobe Premiere Pro is a powerful tool on its own, but it is also part of Adobe Creative Suite 5 Production Premium. You can purchase Adobe Premiere Pro by itself and use all its built-in features, or you can purchase it as part of Adobe Creative Suite 5 Production Premium, where it becomes one piece of a powerful combination of integrated components.

Anyone who works with print graphics or does photo retouching has probably used Adobe Photoshop. It is the workhorse of the graphic design industry. Adobe Photoshop is a powerful tool with great depth and versatility, and it is becoming an increasingly important part of the video production world. In this lesson, you will explore how to use the integration features between Adobe Photoshop and Adobe Premiere Pro.

Adobe After Effects is the *de facto* standard in the video production industry for text animation and motion graphics. In this lesson, you will explore the unique integration between Adobe Premiere Pro and After Effects for powerful and time-saving techniques.

Exploring Adobe Creative Suite 5 Production Premium

Adobe Creative Suite 5 Production Premium is not just a collection of software bundled together in a box. This suite of components is designed to work together through common interface elements and tight integration to provide you with the tools you need to move from vision to output on virtually any platform.

Adobe Premiere Pro by itself is a powerful tool for acquiring, editing, and outputting video projects. As part of Adobe Creative Suite 5 Production Premium, however, it becomes even stronger. If you purchased Adobe Premiere Pro by itself, you may not be able to follow along with all the examples in this lesson, but please read through them to understand how Adobe Premiere Pro fits into the larger picture of this suite of products. If you purchased Adobe Premiere Pro as part of Adobe Creative Suite Production Premium, read on to experience the impressive integration and timesaving techniques engineered into the product.

Adobe Creative Suite Production Premium combines Adobe Bridge CS5, Dynamic Link, and Adobe Device Central CS5, and it includes the following components:

● **Note:** For more information on any of these products, please visit www.adobe.com/products.

- Adobe Premiere Pro CS5
- Adobe After Effects CS5
- Adobe Photoshop CS5 Extended
- Adobe Flash Professional CS5

- Adobe Illustrator CS5
- Adobe Soundbooth CS5
- Adobe Encore CS5
- Adobe OnLocation CS5

You have already taken a look at capturing with Adobe OnLocation, importing Photoshop and Illustrator files, and sweetening and mixing audio with Soundbooth.

In this lesson, you'll focus on the integration among Adobe Premiere Pro, After Effects, and Photoshop.

Importing Adobe Photoshop files as sequences

Making the move to Photoshop means joining forces with just about every image-editing professional on the planet. It's that ubiquitous. Photoshop is *the* professional image-editing standard.

Photoshop has some strong ties to Adobe Premiere Pro and the entire DV production process:

Note: In this exercise, you will animate a Photoshop PSD file in Adobe Premiere Pro. The PSD file is provided on the DVD, so it is not necessary to have Adobe Photoshop to complete this lesson.

- **Editing in Adobe Photoshop**: Right-click (Windows) or Control-click (Mac OS) any Adobe Photoshop graphic in Adobe Premiere Pro—in either the Timeline or the Project panel—and choose Edit in Adobe Photoshop (or Edit Original). This launches Adobe Photoshop and lets you immediately edit the graphic. Once saved within Adobe Photoshop, the new version of the graphic appears in Adobe Premiere Pro.

- **Exporting a filmstrip**: This feature is specifically designed to export a sequential collection of video frames for editing in Adobe Photoshop. You open the filmstrip in Adobe Photoshop and paint directly on the clips—a process called *rotoscoping*.

- **Creating mattes**: Export a video frame to Adobe Photoshop to create a matte that will mask or highlight certain areas of that clip or other clips.

- **Cutting objects out of a scene**: Adobe Photoshop has several tools that work like a cookie cutter. You can remove an object and use it as an icon, make it into a button in a DVD menu, or animate it over a clip.

- **Importing PSD files**: You can natively import Adobe Photoshop PSD files with video, blend modes, and layers.

You looked briefly at importing Adobe Photoshop CS5 files as footage in Lesson 3. In this exercise, you will take a closer look at importing a layered Photoshop file into Adobe Premiere Pro as a sequence.

1 Open Lesson 19-1.prproj. Notice there is a bin in the Project panel named Finished. Expand the Finished bin, and open the Finished sequence if it's not already open.

2 Play the Finished sequence, and notice that the title at the bottom of the screen is animated in layers.

Titles appearing at the bottom of the frame like this are often referred to as *lower thirds*. The lower-third graphic is a nested sequence called *finished lower third*. In the following steps, you are going to open that sequence to see how it was made and then re-create it.

3   Inside the Finished bin is another bin named Finished Lower Third. From that bin, open the "finished lower third" sequence.

This sequence is built from a Photoshop image that has three layers.

4   Move the current-time indicator to about two seconds into the sequence. Toggle the track output off for each video track (click the eye icon), and then toggle them back on to see the contents of each track. Examine the Motion settings of each clip, and notice that the Motion effect was used to animate each clip to achieve an interesting appearance.

You will now re-create this lower third by importing the Photoshop graphic into a new sequence.

5   Collapse the Finished bin in the Project panel so you are back at the root level of the bins.

6   Import lower third.psd from the Lesson 19 folder. When prompted, choose to import as a sequence rather than as layers, and click OK.

7   Expand the new "lower third" bin that has been added to the Project panel. This bin contains three clips that constitute the three-layered Photoshop file. It also contains a "lower third" sequence that has the three layers assembled in the same layered order as they were in Photoshop.

8   Open the lower third sequence by double-clicking it in the Project panel, and
    press the backslash (\) key to expand the view in the Timeline.

Re-creating the lower-third animation

The next step is to re-create the lower third animation. Here's how:

1   Select the Lower Third bg/lower third clip, and open the Effect Controls panel.

2   Expand the Motion fixed effect, and then position the current-time indicator at
    about one second into the clip.

3   Enable keyframes for the Position parameter by clicking the stopwatch. This
    places a keyframe at the position of the current-time indicator. Change the
    Position value to –360, 240. This adds a keyframe at this position. Next, move the
    current-time indicator ten frames, and change the Position value to 360, 240.

4   Play the sequence to verify that the lower third background slides from the left
    side to the center over the first second of the clip. Right-click (Windows) or
    Control-click (Mac OS) the second keyframe, and set Temporal Interpolation
    to Ease In. Play the sequence again, and notice what a nice touch the Ease In
    setting has on the animation.

5   Expand the Opacity effect, and notice that Opacity is set to 70%. This Opacity
    value was set in Photoshop and is imported correctly in Adobe Premiere Pro.

● **Note:** In this case, the blend modes in the imported Photoshop layers are set to Normal. But if
you import Photoshop layers with other blend modes, Adobe Premiere Pro will import and use the
blend modes as they were set in Photoshop.

6 Select the film reel/lower third clip, and expand the Motion fixed effect in the Effect Controls panel. Set a Position keyframe just after one second, at about 00;00;01;10. Change the Position value to –360, 240. Set another keyframe at 00;00;01;20 by changing the value of this position keyframe to 360, 240. This will animate the logo off the left side of the frame at the beginning of the clip.

7 Play the sequence. You can adjust the speed the logo travels by moving the second keyframe farther from or closer to the first keyframe. Experiment with this until you have the speed you desire. Also set the Ease In option on the second keyframe as you did on the background clip motion.

8 The text of the lower third should follow the logo so you can copy the logo's animation and paste it in the text clip. Select the Logo/lower-third clip, click Motion, and choose Edit > Copy.

9 Select the Behind the Scene/lower third clip, click a blank area inside the Video Effects panel, and choose Edit > Paste.

The animation of the sequence is complete. The only step left is to superimpose this lower third over the interview clip.

10 Create a new DV – NTSC Widescreen 48 kHz sequence by choosing File > New Sequence. Name it Practice.

11 Drag the Behind_the_Scenes_SD.avi clip to the Video 1 track of the Timeline, and press the backslash (\) key to expand the view in the Timeline.

12 Drag the lower third sequence you just animated to the Video 2 track above the writers 1 clip. Adjust the position of the lower third so it starts about one second after the interview clip starts.

13 To polish it all off, drop a Cross Dissolve transition on the end of the lower third sequence clip.

The lower third animation sequence references the original Photoshop file. So if you change the original Photoshop file, the changes will ripple through any instances where it was used in Adobe Premiere Pro. For example, you might open the lower third.psd file in Photoshop and change the background or text color. When you save the Photoshop file, the changes will immediately be reflected wherever that file was used in Adobe Premiere Pro.

Using Dynamic Link with After Effects

Adobe After Effects is the tool of choice for editors who want to produce exciting and innovative motion graphics, visual effects, and animated text for film, video, DVD, and the Web.

Adobe After Effects users tend to fall into two distinct camps: motion-graphics artists and animated-text artists. Some production houses specialize in one or the other. After Effects can do so much that it will be hard to wrap your brain around all of it. You are likely to use only a subset of its creative prospects.

● **Note:** Adobe Dynamic Link requires Adobe Creative Suite Production Premium. Purchasing Adobe Premiere Pro and Adobe After Effects separately will not allow Adobe Dynamic Link to work. Adobe Dynamic Link is a suite-based feature.

Surveying After Effects features

After Effects has numerous options:

- **Text creation and animation tools**: Create animated text with unprecedented ease. After Effects offers dozens of groundbreaking text animation presets. Simply drag them to your text to see them in action.

- **Leading-edge visual effects**: More than 150 effects and compositing features enhance your images well beyond the capabilities of Adobe Premiere Pro.

- **Vector paint tools**: Use built-in vector paint tools based on Adobe Photoshop technology to perform touch-up and rotoscoping tasks.

- **Comprehensive masking tools**: Easily design, edit, and work with masks using flexible autotracing options.

- **Tight Adobe integration**: Copy and paste assets, compositions, or sequences between Adobe Premiere Pro and Adobe After Effects. Preserve layers and other attributes when you import Adobe Photoshop and Adobe Illustrator files. The Adobe Dynamic Link feature (remember, available only in Adobe Creative Suite Production Premium) means you will not need to render an Adobe After Effects composition before moving it between Adobe After Effects and Adobe Premiere Pro or Encore.

- **Motion Tracker**: This option accurately, quickly, and automatically maps the motion of an element and lets you add an effect to follow that action.

Looking at the Adobe After Effects workspace

In this exercise, you will animate the same lower third graphic that you did at the beginning of this lesson. You will import the same Photoshop file into Adobe After Effects, use After Effects tools to animate the three layers of the graphic, and then use Adobe Dynamic Link to link the After Effects animation into the Adobe Premiere Pro Timeline.

1 In Adobe Premiere Pro, open Lesson 19-2.prproj.

2 Launch Adobe After Effects.

3 In After Effects, open the finished.aep file by choosing File > Open Project and selecting finished.aep from the Lesson 19 folder.

Notice the many similarities to the Adobe Premiere Pro user interface.

As with Adobe Premiere Pro, Adobe After Effects has a Project panel, but the icons and terminology are a bit different. For instance, Adobe Premiere Pro sequences become *compositions* in After Effects.

Double-clicking a composition (as shown here) opens it in the Timeline panel. Instead of tracks, you work with *layers* in Adobe After Effects.

4 Scrub the Adobe After Effects Timeline to see the final animation you will create.

5 After Effects may not be able to play back the animation in real time, depending on your computer speed. However, After Effects can do a RAM preview when you press the 0 (zero) key on the numeric keypad or click the RAM preview button in the playback controls. This renders the Timeline to RAM and then plays it back smoothly in real time.

6 Close finished.aep by choosing File > Close Project.

Animating the lower third

In this exercise, you will start a new project in After Effects and create the animation you just saw in the finished example.

1   With After Effects still open, import the lower third.psd file by choosing File > Import File and selecting lower third.psd from the Lesson 19 folder. Change the Import As parameter from Footage to Composition, and click Open.

2   A dialog will open where you can specify the kind of composition import. Accept the default, as shown here, and click OK.

3   Double-click the lower third composition icon in the Project panel to open the composition in the Timeline.

4   Notice the Adobe Photoshop CS5 layers are intact and in the correct order in the Timeline. Scrub the Timeline, and you will see this is a static graphic. No animation has been applied yet. Return the current-time indicator to the beginning of the clip.

5   Locate the Effects & Presets panel on the right, and expand the * Animation Presets folder. Within that folder, expand the Transitions – Movement folder. Drag the "Zoom – 3D tumble" preset to the Lower Third bg layer of the Timeline.

6   Do a RAM preview of this effect by pressing the 0 (zero) key on the numeric keypad.

Next you will animate the logo.

7   Position the current-time indicator at the one-second mark, just as the lower third background animation is finishing.

8   Drag the Slide – Swoop preset (located in the Transitions – Movement folder) to the Film Reel layer. RAM preview the Timeline.

After Effects has some dazzling animation presets designed especially for text. These animations are aware of individual characters, words, or lines of text. You'll use one of these text effects on the text layer. However, because you didn't create the text in Adobe After Effects, After Effects doesn't know the layer is text. You need to tell After Effects that the top layer (Behind the Scenes) is text.

9   Select layer 2 (the Behind the Scenes text layer), and choose Layer > Convert to Editable Text. Now Adobe After Effects will treat this layer as text that can be edited and animated with special text effects or presets. After Effects indicates this is a text layer by showing a T icon to the left of the layer name.

10 Position the current-time indicator at the one-second mark on the Timeline.

11 In the Effects & Presets panel, expand the Text folder within the *Animation Presets folder. Within the Text folder, expand the Animate In folder, and drag the Raining Characters In preset to the Behind the Scenes text layer in layer 2.

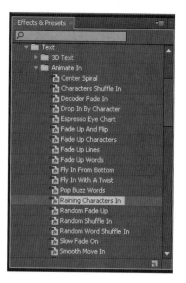

12 Do a RAM preview.

13 Save the project by choosing File > Save. Save the project in the Lesson 19 folder, and name it ae practice.aep.

Importing a project from Adobe After Effects to Adobe Premiere Pro using Adobe Dynamic Link

With the animation complete, it's time to use it in your Adobe Premiere Pro project, superimposed over the behind-the-scenes clip. In the past, this would have involved rendering the animation out to a movie, importing the movie into Adobe Premiere Pro, and then placing it in the Timeline. If you ever wanted to change the animation, you would have to edit the movie in Adobe After Effects, rerender it, and re-export it, which would be very time-consuming. With Dynamic Link, the process is much simpler.

1   Leave Adobe After Effects open, and open or switch back to Adobe Premiere Pro.

It is not necessary to leave After Effects open for Adobe Dynamic Link to work, but you will be editing the animation again, so to save time here, you will leave it open.

2   In Adobe Premiere Pro, open Lesson 19-2.prproj, and then open the Lower Third sequence.

3   Drag Behind_The_Scenes_SD.avi from the bin to the Video 1 track.

4   Import the After Effects composition you just made via Dynamic Link by choosing File > Adobe Dynamic Link > Import After Effects Composition.

5   On the left side of the Import Composition dialog, navigate to the Lesson 19 folder, select ae practice.aep, select the ae_practice composition in the right window, and click OK.

6   This adds the lower third/ae practice composition to the Adobe Premiere Pro Project panel. Drag it to the Video track above the Behind the Scenes clip.

Position it about one second after the start of the interview. Trim the end of the ae_practice composition so it is about seven seconds long.

7   As a nice finish, add a Cross Dissolve transition to the end of the lower third Dynamic Link clip so it dissolves away.

8   Render and play the sequence in Adobe Premiere Pro.

You now have an After Effects animation playing in Adobe Premiere Pro—and you didn't need to render or export the animation in After Effects. This is a real timesaving feature. The power of this feature becomes more obvious when you need to edit or tweak your animation.

Editing an existing dynamically linked animation

In this exercise, you will make an adjustment to the animation in After Effects to show the dynamic nature of this feature:

1   Leave the project open in Adobe Premiere Pro, and switch to After Effects, which should still be open, with the lower third composition open.

2   Set the current-time indicator position to the beginning of the After Effects Timeline.

3   In the Effects & Presets panel, expand the Backgrounds folder, which is inside the * Animation Presets folder.

4   Drag the Silk preset to the Lower Third bg layer. Do a RAM preview to see this effect.

5   Without saving the After Effects project, switch back to Adobe Premiere Pro.

6   Play the sequence in Adobe Premiere Pro. Without saving the After Effects project, the changes you made in Adobe After Effects are already updated in Adobe Premiere Pro. That's why they call it Dynamic Link!

Replacing a clip with an After Effects composition

There are times when you're editing an Adobe Premiere Pro project and you want to apply some special effects that are available in After Effects. You could create a new After Effects composition and import it into Adobe Premiere Pro with Adobe Dynamic link, but there is an even faster way to do it. You can convert a clip or clips on an Adobe Premiere Pro sequence to an Adobe After Effects composition right from the Timeline. Let's give it a try:

1   Open Lesson 19-3.prproj. This project already has the After Effects title sequence linked via Dynamic Link in the Video 2 track.

    You want to apply a special effect to the Behind_The_Scenes_SD.avi clip to make it look like bad TV reception. After Effects has this effect as a preset.

2   Right-click the Behind_The_Scenes_SD.avi clip in the Practice sequence, and choose Replace With After Effects Composition.

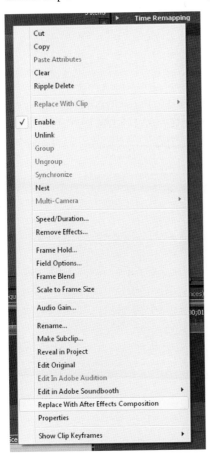

3 You will be prompted to name the new After Effects project. Name it writers bad tv.aep in the Lesson 19 folder, and click Save.

4 Locate the Bad TV 2 – old effect in *Animation Presets > Image – Special Effects, and drag it to the Behind_the_Scenes_SD.avi clip.

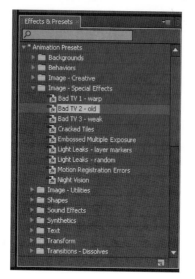

Without saving the After Effects composition, switch back to Adobe Premiere Pro, and notice the Bad TV 2 effect is applied to the writers clip. You may need to render the sequence in Adobe Premiere Pro to see it play back smoothly. This is a fast way to apply special Adobe After Effects effects to a clip in Adobe Premiere Pro.

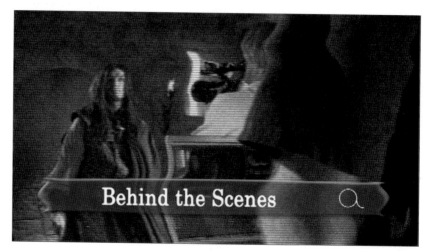

Review questions

1 What is the difference between importing a Photoshop file into Adobe Premiere Pro as footage and importing it as a sequence?

2 If you set the Opacity value of a layer to something less than 100% in Adobe Photoshop, what will be the Opacity setting for the clip when imported into Adobe Premiere Pro?

3 Can Adobe Premiere Pro import blend modes set in Photoshop layers?

4 In some ways, Adobe Premiere Pro and Adobe After Effects have similar functionality. Only the terms are different. Give a couple of examples.

5 Once a dynamic link is established between an After Effects composition and an Adobe Premiere Pro project, must the After Effects composition be rendered after making changes?

Review answers

1 Importing Photoshop files as layers brings them in as a single clip, with either all the layers collapsed or a single layer selected. Importing as a sequence brings all the Photoshop layers into Adobe Premiere Pro in the same stacking order as in the Photoshop file. An Adobe Premiere Pro sequence is created to nest them all together.

2 Adobe Premiere Pro imports the opacity as set in Adobe Photoshop.

3 Yes. Adobe Premiere Pro respects the blend modes set in Adobe Photoshop.

4 Adobe Premiere Pro has sequences and tracks. Adobe After Effects has compositions and layers.

5 No. Once a dynamic link is established, changes made in After Effects are immediately available in Adobe Premiere Pro.

20 EXPORTING FRAMES, CLIPS, AND SEQUENCES

Topics covered in this lesson

- Choosing export options
- Recording to tape
- Making single frames
- Creating movie, image sequence, and audio files
- Using Adobe Media Encoder
- Exporting to mobile devices
- Exporting to Final Cut Pro
- Working with edit decision lists

 This lesson will take approximately 60 minutes.

Exporting your project is the final step in the video production process. Adobe Media Encoder offers multiple high-level output formats: Windows Media, QuickTime, RealMedia, Adobe Flash, and MPEG. Within those formats you have dozens of options and can also export in batches.

Getting started

Adobe Premiere Pro CS5 offers a full array of export options—methods of recording your projects to tape, converting them to files, or burning them to DVDs.

Recording to tape is straightforward, while file creation has many more options. For example, you can record only the audio portion of your project; convert a video segment or entire project into one of many standard file formats; or export still frames, sequences of still frames, or animation files.

Of greater relevance are the higher-level video encoding formats available in Adobe Media Encoder. You'll use that powerful tool to create projects for posting on a web site, for burning to multimedia CDs, or for exporting to mobile devices using the new Adobe Device Central CS5 software. If you need to create Flash Video for web sites, you can export Flash Video with web markers. Adobe Media Encoder is a stand-alone application that handles exports in batches, so you can export in several formats simultaneously and process in the background while you work on other applications, including Adobe Premiere Pro.

● **Note:** Note that Adobe Premiere Pro can export clips selected in the Project panel, as well as sequences or work areas within sequences. The content that's selected when you choose File > Export is what Adobe Premiere Pro will export. In most instances, that's your sequence, but of course, Adobe Premiere Pro doesn't know that. So, get in the habit of clicking your sequence to select it before starting your export workflow, lest you waste precious time rendering content from the Project panel rather than your sequence.

Overview of export options

When you complete a project, you have a number of export choices:

- You can select a single frame, a series of frames, a clip, or an entire sequence.
- You can choose audio-only, video-only, or full audio/video output.
- You can export directly to videotape; create a file for viewing on a computer or the Internet; or put your project on a DVD with or without a complete set of menus, buttons, and other DVD features.

Beyond the actual export formats, you can set several other parameters as well:

- Any files you choose to create can be at the same visual quality and data rate as your original media, or they can be compressed.
- You need to specify the frame size, frame rate, data rate, and audio and video compression techniques.

You can use exported files for further editing, in presentations, as streaming media for Internet and other networks, or as sequences of images to create animations.

Checking out export options

The first step in exploring export options, naturally, is opening a project with some content to export.

1. Start Adobe Premiere Pro, and open Lesson 20-1.prproj.

2. Click somewhere in the Sequence 01 Timeline to select the sequence.

3. Choose File > Export.

Adobe Premiere Pro offers seven export options (some options might be dimmed because of the particulars of the content you're exporting):

- **Media**: Selecting this option opens the Export Settings dialog, which allows you to export to all popular media formats.

- **Title**: Since Adobe Premiere Pro stores Titler-created objects in the project file, the only way to use the same title in more than one project is to export it as a file. To use this option, you need to select a title in the Project panel.

- **Tape**: This option transfers your project to tape.

- **EDL**: Use this to create an edit decision list (EDL) to take your project to a production studio for further editing.

- **OMF**: This option exports active audio tracks from an Adobe Premiere Pro sequence to an Open Media Format (OMF) file that programs such as DigiDesign Pro Tools can import if the DigiTranslator feature is licensed.

- **AAF**: This option exports to an Advanced Authoring Format (AAF) file that allows you to exchange digital media and metadata between platforms, systems, and applications, such as the Avid Media Composer.

- **Final Cut Pro XML**: This option exports an XML file that you can import into Apple Final Cut Pro for further editing.

Recording to tape

If you captured your original video from DV or HDV tape, you may want to write the finished project back to tape for safekeeping. If so, follow the steps listed here.

You can use an analog tape recorder without video control, but doing so takes some extra effort. That will be explained later in this lesson.

1 Connect your DV or HDV camcorder to your computer, just as you did when you captured the video.

2 Turn it on, and set it to VCR or VTR (not to Camera, as you might expect).

3 Cue the tape to where you want to start recording.

● **Note:** When using the standard DV device control tape export method, you can export only an entire sequence, as opposed to a selected segment. To export a segment, follow the analog tape recording instructions later in this exercise.

Bars and tone or black video

If you're going to have a postproduction studio duplicate your tapes, add 30 seconds of bars and tone to the beginning so the studio can set up its gear. Otherwise, give your project a little breathing room on your DV tape by adding black video to its beginning. To do either one, click the New Item button at the bottom of the Project panel, and select Bars and Tone or Black Video. The default duration is five seconds. Right-click (Windows) or Control-click (Mac OS) the clip in the Project panel, choose Speed/Duration, and change the time to suit your needs. Then drag that clip from the Project panel to the start of your project by holding down Ctrl (Windows) or Command (Mac OS) to insert it and by sliding all other clips to the right.

4 Select the sequence you want to record.

5 Choose File > Export > Tape.

If you're working with a DV camcorder, you'll see the Export to Tape dialog shown here.

Here's a rundown of options:

- **Activate Recording Device**: When you select this option, Adobe Premiere Pro will control your DV device. Deselect it if you want to record to a device that you'll control manually.

- **Assemble at timecode**: Select this option to pick an In point on the tape where you want recording to begin. When this option is not selected, recording will begin at the current tape location.

- **Delay movie start by _x_ frames**: This is for the few DV recording devices that need a brief period of time between receiving the video signal and recording it. Check your device's manual to see what the manufacturer recommends.

- **Preroll _x_ frames**: Most decks need little or no time to get to the proper tape recording speed. To be on the safe side, select 150 frames (5 seconds), or add black video to the start of your project (see the previous "Bars and tone or black video" tip).

The remaining options are self-explanatory.

6 Click Record (or Cancel if you don't want to make a recording).

If you haven't rendered your project (by pressing Enter for playback instead of the spacebar), Adobe Premiere Pro does that now. When rendering is complete, Adobe Premiere Pro starts your camcorder and records your project to it.

Recording to an analog recorder without device control

To record to an analog machine without device control, set up your camcorder for recording.

1 Render the sequence or portion you want to record by pressing Enter.

2 Play the sequence to make sure you see it displayed on your external recording device.

3　Cue your tape to where you want recording to begin, position the Timeline current-time indicator to where you want playback from your sequence to begin, press the Record button on your device, and play the sequence.

4　When the sequence or segment finishes, click the Stop button in the Program Monitor and then stop the tape on the device.

Exporting single frames

Oftentimes, you'll want to export single or multiple frames from your video projects. Adobe Premiere Pro CS5 has a new simplified workflow for still-image export, as well as the tried-and-true multiple-frame export via Adobe Media Encoder. Let's look at the new Export Frame function.

Exporting a single frame via the Export Frame function

Adobe Premiere Pro CS5 has a new, simplified workflow for exporting single frames. Note that you can use the Export Frame function both in the Source panel, with content selected from the Project panel, and in the Program Monitor, with a frame selected from the active sequence. When using the Export Frame function from the Source panel, Adobe Premiere Pro will create a still image that matches the resolution of the source video file. When using the Export Frame function from the Timeline, Adobe Premiere Pro will create a still image that matches the resolution of the selected video sequence.

1　In the Program Monitor, click the Export Frame button on the lower right.

2 In the Export Frame dialog, choose the desired filename, still-image format, and path, clicking the Browse button to open the Browse for Folder dialog.

● **Note:** In Windows, you can export to the BMP, DPX, GIF, JPEG, PNG, TGA, and TIFF formats. On the Mac, you can export to the DPX, JPG, PNG, TGA, and TIFF formats.

3 Click OK to export the frame.

Using the Export Settings dialog

Whenever you choose File > Export > Media, Adobe Premiere Pro CS5 opens the Export Settings dialog, which is where you create all stand-alone still-image, audio, and video files.

1 If necessary, open Lesson 20-1.prproj.

2 Choose File > Export Media.

Let's spend a few minutes looking over this important dialog, with a particular focus on new, modified, or particularly important features and options.

It's best to work through the Export Settings dialog from the top down, first choosing your format and presets, then the output, and finally deciding whether you'd like to export audio, video, or both.

3 Choose the FLV|F4V format and the F4V-Web Large, NTSC Source preset. This doesn't match our sequence setting precisely but will expose some of the issues that you'll face when working with the Export Settings dialog and Adobe Media Encoder.

4 Note that the tabs presented on the bottom right of the Export Settings dialog will vary by format. Most of the critical options are contained on the Format, Video, and Audio tabs, and the options here will vary by format as well. Here's an overview of the various tabs:

- **Filters**: The filter available for encoded output is Gaussian Blur. Enabling this filter reduces the video noise introduced by slightly blurring the video. Export the project without this filter to see whether noise is a problem. If it is, increase noise reduction in small amounts. Increasing noise reduction too much will make the video blurry.

- **Format**: This determines the type of stream to which the video and audio are multiplexed.

- **Video**: The Video tab allows you to adjust the frame size, frame rate, field order, and profile. The default values are based on the preset you chose. Note that in this case, if you were outputting the video for actual deployment, you would want to change your Frame Height setting to 360 to eliminate the letterboxes shown in the figure, or choose a wide-screen preset. You would also want to change the Frame Rate setting to 23.976 to match your sequence setting and source footage.

- **Audio**: The Audio tab allows you to adjust the bit rate of the audio and, for some formats, the codec. The default values are based on the preset you chose.

- **FTP**: This tab primarily allows you to specify an FTP server for uploading the exported video when it is finished encoding. Fill in the appropriate FTP values supplied by your FTP host if you want to enable this feature.

5 Moving to the left side of the Export Settings dialog, look over the Source Settings drop-down list, where you can choose to export the work area bar selected in the sequence, a region selected using the handles directly above the drop-down list, or the entire sequence. This is useful when you want to export selected regions on the Timeline rather than the entire sequence.

6 Also on the left, note the Source/Output tabs, the latter of which shows a preview of the video to be encoded. It's useful to view the video on the Output tab to catch errors like the letterboxing shown in the previous figure.

In terms of new or modified features, here are some highlights:

- **Match Sequence Settings check box**: This is a no-muss, no-fuss way to export the edited sequence using the settings selected for the sequence. For example, let's say you shot your video in DVCPROHD 1080p24 and chose that format/resolution for your sequence preset. If you wanted to render video out in that format, just click the Match Sequence Settings check box, and Adobe Premiere Pro will output in that format.

- **Use Maximum Render Quality**: This option was available in Adobe Premiere Pro CS4, but only via the Export Settings wing menu. Consider enabling this setting whenever scaling from larger to smaller formats during rendering, but note that this option requires more RAM than normal rendering and can slow rendering by a factor of four or five.

- **Use Previews**: This option, also available only in the wing menu in Adobe Premiere Pro CS4, uses previews created while producing your project as the starting point for the final rendered file, rather than rendering all video and effects from scratch. This can speed encoding time but can also degrade quality when rendering to a format different from your sequence preset. For example, if you used HDV as your sequence preset and were outputting to Flash in H.264 format, basing the H.264 encoding on HDV-encoded preview files may degrade the quality slightly. (If you were rendering from scratch, Adobe Premiere Pro would send uncompressed frames to Adobe Media Encoder rather than HDV-encoded video.)

- **Use Frame Blending**: Enable this option to smooth motion whenever you change the speed of a source clip in your project or render to a different frame rate than your sequence setting.

- **Metadata**: Click this button to open the Metadata panel.

- **Export**: Select this option to export directly from the Export Settings dialog rather than rendering via Adobe Media Encoder. This is a simpler workflow, but you won't be able to edit in Adobe Premiere Pro until the rendering is complete.

- **Queue**: Click the Queue button to send the file to the Adobe Media Encoder, which should open automatically.

Working with Adobe Media Encoder

Adobe Media Encoder is a stand-alone application that can be run by itself or can be launched from Adobe Premiere Pro. Working from within Adobe Premiere Pro, after you choose your export settings and click OK, Adobe Media Encoder adds your export to its queue.

In addition to sequences loaded from Adobe Premiere Pro (like the second file in the batch shown in the previous figure), Adobe Media Encoder can also encode from several sources.

For example, it can encode stand-alone files of multiple formats added to the batch by choosing File > Add. The final file in the batch shown in the previous figure was added via this technique.

You can also import and encode compositions from Adobe After Effects by choosing File > Add After Effects Composition, and you can import sequences from Adobe Premiere Pro by choosing File > Add Premiere Pro Sequence. The third file in the previously shown batch is an Adobe Premiere Pro sequence loaded from Lesson 15-5.prproj.

You can also create watch folders by choosing File > Create Watch Folder and then assigning a preset to that watch folder. Source files dragged into the folder later will be automatically encoded to the format specified in the preset.

You choose a Format/Preset separately with each approach, and once the encoding tasks are loaded into Adobe Media Encoder, administration is straightforward. To change any encoding setting, you click the target task and then the Settings button on the right.

You can add, duplicate, or remove any tasks by using the like-named buttons and drag any tasks that haven't yet started encoding to any place in the queue. If you haven't set the queue to start automatically, click the Start Queue button to start encoding. Adobe Media Encoder encodes files serially, rather than in parallel, and if you add any files to the queue after starting encoding, they'll be encoded as well.

Speaking of setting the queue to start automatically, this is a critical new feature to the Adobe Media Encoder CS5 that you control in the Preferences dialog by choosing Edit > Preferences (Windows) or Premiere Pro > Preferences (Mac OS). Specifically, check the "Start queue automatically when idle for: *x* minutes" box, dial in the desired delay time, and Adobe Media Encoder will start encoding automatically after the specified time expires. This is a critical enhancement to watch folder functionality. In previous versions, you had to click Start Queue to begin encoding, which prevented unattended operation. Now, if you have access to a designated shared folder on a network, you can encode files immediately without any action on your part—a very significant enhancement.

You can also preview while encoding via the "Preview while encoding" check box, which is a nice option that lets you check for errors during encoding and supplements the encoding progress bar to let you know how your encoding is progressing. You can also use the Preferences dialog to select a default output folder and many other options.

Format overview

Adobe Premiere Pro CS5 can export in a number of formats; let's run through them quickly to identify when you should use them.

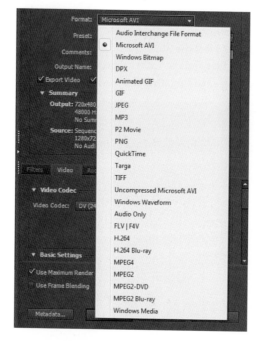

- **Audio Interchange File Format**: This is an audio-only file format popular on the Mac.

- **Microsoft AVI**: This "container format," available only in the Windows version of Premiere Pro, can store files using multiple compression technologies, or *codecs*. It's useful for storing SD files in DV format, but it's no longer used as a distribution format and is rarely used by HD producers.

- **Windows Bitmap**: This is an uncompressed, rarely used still-image format with a .bmp extension. It's available only on the Windows version of Premiere Pro.

- **DPX**: DPX stands for Digital Picture Exchange and is a high-end still-image format for digital intermediate and special-effects work.

- **Animated GIF and GIF**: These compressed still-image and animated formats are used primarily on the web. Available only on the Windows version of Premiere Pro.

- **JPEG**: This is the most popular compressed still-image format for the Internet and other uses.

- **MP3**: This compressed audio format is very popular on the Internet.

- **P2 Movie**: This output option is used for rendering sequences back to P2 cards.

- **PNG**: This is a lossless but efficient still-image format for Internet use.

- **QuickTime**: This container format can store files using multiple codecs. All QuickTime files use the .mov extension and it is the preferred format for use on Macintosh computers.

- **Targa**: This is a rarely used uncompressed still-image file format.

- **TIFF**: This popular high-quality still-image format offers both lossy and lossless compression options.

- **Uncompressed Microsoft AVI**: This is a very high-bit-rate intermediate format that is not widely used and is available only on the Windows version of Premiere Pro.

- **Windows Waveform (.wav files)**: This uncompressed audio file format is popular on Windows computers.

- **Audio Only**: With this option, you can produce files in the Advanced Audio Coding format (the audio codec used with most H.264 encoding).

- **FLV|F4V**: This is the only option for producing Flash output to be played back with Flash Player. It includes two options: F4V files that use the H.264 video codec/AAC audio codec and FLV files that use the VP6 video codec/MP3 audio codec.

- **H.264**: This is the most flexible and widely used format today, with options for devices such as the iPod/iPhone and Apple TV, TiVo Series3 SD and HD, and services such as YouTube and Vimeo. H.264 files produced via this option can also be transmitted to smartphones, such as Android, Blackberry, and Palm devices, or used as high-quality, high-bit-rate intermediate files for working in other video editors. It's also popular for encoding files for uploading to online video providers such as Brightcove and other user-generated content sites like Blip.tv. H.264 encoding produces files with the standard .mp4 extension.

- **H.264 Blu-ray**: This option produces files for including on Blu-ray Discs.

- **MPEG4**: Selecting this codec produces lower-quality H.263 3GP files for distribution to older cell phones.

- **MPEG2**: This older file format is primarily used for DVD and Blu-ray Discs. Presets in this group allow you to produce files that can be distributed for playback on your own or other computers, but H.264 generally produces better quality at a smaller file size.

- **MPEG2-DVD and MPEG2 Blu-ray**: These formats are to be used when producing files for burning onto an optical disc.

- **Windows Media**: This option produces MWV files for playback using the Windows Media Player and on some devices like the Zune (Windows only).

That's only a brief overview of the formats, but it should provide some useful direction when it's time to produce your videos.

Using the formats

Let's reverse this approach and take a user-centric view, identifying the use of the video and then pointing toward a format and preset. There are few absolutes, but these should get you in the ballpark. Just to state the blindingly obvious, try whatever option you choose with a short file first to test the workflow, before going live with it.

- **Uploading to a web site for Flash deployment**: When you choose the FLV|F4V format, choose an FLV preset for producing the file with the older On2 VP6 codec, and choose F4V for the newer, higher-quality H.264 format. If you don't know which format to use, go with F4V. In terms of resolution, the 720p Source, Half Size presets in both F4V and FLV formats encode your video at 740x360 (for HD source), which is a nice conservative resolution that should look quite good. Check with your web administrator for the format, resolution, data rate, and other details.

- **Encoding for DVD/Blu-ray**: Use MPEG2 for both, namely, MPEG2-DVD for DVD and MPEG2 Blu-ray for Blu-ray Discs. MPEG2 looks indistinguishable from H.264 in these high-bit-rate applications and will encode much, much faster. Better yet, input your sequence without rendering in Encore (choose File > Adobe Dynamic Link > Import Adobe Premiere Pro Sequence).

- **Encoding for devices**: Use the H.264 format for current devices (Apple iPod/iPhone, Apple TV, and TiVo), as well as some generic 3GPP presets; use MPEG4 for older MPEG4-based devices, and use Windows Media for Zune. When encoding for smartphones, find the manufacturer's specifications, and make sure the files that you produce don't exceed these specs. As you'll see, Adobe Device Central can help in this regard.

- **Encoding for uploading to user-generated video sites**: H.264 has presets for YouTube and Vimeo in wide-screen, SD, and HD. Use these presets as a starting point for your service, being careful to observe resolution, file size, and duration limits.

- **Encoding for online video platforms (OVPs) such as Brightcove and Kaltura**: Typically, H.264 is the highest-quality format. Check the recommendations and requirements of your service provider, and check the YouTube and Vimeo presets as a guide.

- **Encoding for editing in other applications**: Export to Final Cut Pro XML (File > Export > Final Cut Pro XML) for Final Cut Pro, and try the AAF format (File > Export > AAF) for Avid Media Composer. If these options don't work, use either QuickTime or Microsoft AVI format for SD files, using the DV codec. For HD formats, try creating a file by selecting the Match Sequence Settings check box, which will render in your acquisition format (if that's what you used for the sequence). If that option isn't available, encode in high-resolution, high-data-rate H.264, using the QuickTime format for Final Cut Pro; however, there are no presets, so you'll be on your own when it comes to choosing encoding parameters. For other applications, use the H.264 format, which most editors now support.

- **Windows Media or Silverlight deployment**: The Windows Media format is your safest option, though more recent versions of Silverlight can play H.264 files. If producing H.264 for Silverlight, follow the Flash rules provided earlier, since Silverlight should play any file produced for Flash.

In general, the Adobe Premiere Pro presets are proven and will work for your intended purpose. Don't adjust parameters when encoding for devices or optical discs, because changes that seem subtle can render the files unplayable. Even with other presets, resist the urge to tinker unless you know what you're doing from an encoding perspective. Most Adobe Premiere Pro presets are conservative and will deliver very good quality using the default values, so you probably won't improve the output by tinkering, and you could even degrade it considerably.

Now let's work through a specific example of producing a file for a mobile device.

Exporting to mobile devices

With the array of mobile devices that support video, it would be nice if there were a way to see what a video project would look like on various mobile devices. That is exactly what Adobe Device Central is designed to provide. In this exercise, you will export your project to Adobe Device Central and see how your video looks on various mobile devices.

Most mobile devices, such as iPods and 3GPP (third-generation) cell phones, support video encoded in the H.264 format. Two flavors of H.264 are available in the Adobe Media Encoder Format menu:

- **H.264**: This is an MPEG4–based standard for encoding for a variety of devices, including high-definition displays, 3GPP cell phones, video iPods, and PlayStation Portable (PSP) devices.

- **H.264 Blu-ray**: This is an MPEG4–based standard for encoding in high-definition for Blu-ray Disc media.

You'll be using H.264 for this exercise.

1 Make sure your Timeline sequence is selected in Lesson 20-1.prproj; then choose File > Export > Media.

2 Select H.264 as the encoding format.

3 Open the Preset menu.

Notice the variety of mobile devices set up for easy export. For example, it's easy to create video that will play on the Apple iPod by choosing the iPod preset.

Note: Adobe Media Encoder does not have to be used from Adobe Premiere Pro. You can start Adobe Media Encoder from your list of Adobe programs and add files to it that already exist on your file system.

Many popular mobile device presets are already listed, and you can create or fine-tune your own presets. You'll work with a generic preset for now.

4 Choose the 3GPP 320 x 240 15fps preset, which you can test on multiple devices.

5 Make sure the Open in Device Central option (shown here) is selected.

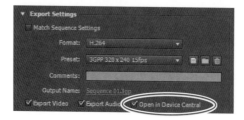

6 Name the file, and click Queue. This adds the export to the Adobe Media Encoder queue. Click Start Queue to process the file. If the files from the previous section are still encoding, the H.264 export will start when they are finished.

Adobe Device Central launches. The available devices are listed in the left panel of Adobe Device Central by category or manufacturer. If no manufacturers are listed, click the Browse button on the upper right to browse for devices online, and drag the devices (shown below) into the Test Devices panel.

7 Click Emulate Video to return to the Emulation workspace.

8 Double-click the BlackBerry Bold 9700 device. This loads your encoded video into an emulation of that device.

9   In the right panel under Scaling, experiment with the various modes, clicking the Play button under the phone emulation to see how the video will appear.

10 Choose different options from the Reflections menu under Display to see how the video might look under different lighting conditions.

11 Double-click Asus P527 to see how the video will look on this phone with a smaller screen.

12 Quit Adobe Device Central. Remember your exported encoded file is in the file location you chose in the export options.

Exporting to Final Cut Pro

At a high level, exporting from Premiere Pro to Final Cut Pro—and importing the XML file into Final Cut Pro—is simple.

1   To begin, in Adobe Premiere Pro, choose File > Export > Final Cut Pro XML. Click Yes to save your project.

2   In the Final Cut Pro XML - Save Converted Project As dialog, name the file, and click Save. Adobe Premiere Pro will let you know whether there were any issues exporting the XML.

3   In Final Cut Pro, choose File > Import > XML, locate the file, and click Choose. Final Cut Pro presents a simple dialog and will let you know whether any problems arose during import.

As always, though, the devil is in the details—specifically, the file formats supported by the two programs. If you're working in DV files in either AVI or QuickTime format, your results should be quite good. Unfortunately, if you've migrated to the HD world, which most producers have, you're probably going to run into some issues, specifically because Adobe Premiere Pro and Apple Final Cut Pro have completely different file-compatibility philosophies.

That is, Final Cut Pro can import any file that you want so long as it's in a QuickTime wrapper with an MOV format. Conversely, the Adobe way is to import all files natively. With many (if not most) HD formats, this means that files imported into Adobe Premiere Pro projects may not work in Final Cut Pro. Final Cut Pro will display the file in the Timeline with the proper In and Out points, but the media will be offline. The solution is to reimport the files into Final Cut Pro and then relink the files, which can be very time-consuming.

Working with edit decision lists

An *edit decision list* (EDL) harkens back to the days when small hard drives limited the size of your video files and slower processors meant you could not play full-resolution video. To remedy this, editors used low-resolution files in a non-linear editor like Adobe Premiere Pro, edited their project, exported that to an EDL, and then took that text file and their original tapes down to a production studio. They'd use expensive switching hardware to create the finished, full-resolution product.

These days, there isn't much call for that kind of offline work, but filmmakers still use EDLs because of the size of the files and other complexities associated with going from film to video and back to film.

CMX is gone but its EDL lives on

There is no standard EDL format. Adobe Premiere Pro uses a format compatible with the CMX 3600, a switcher created by CMX Systems, which was a pioneer of production-studio and broadcast-TV computer-controlled video editors. Formed as a joint venture by CBS and Memorex in 1971, CMX owned 90 percent of the broadcast video–editing market by the mid-1980s. It discontinued operations in 1998, but its EDL remains the de facto standard to communicate edit decisions.

If you plan to use an EDL, you need to keep your project within some narrow guidelines:

- EDLs work best with projects that contain no more than one video track, two stereo (or four mono) audio tracks, and no nested sequences.

- Most standard transitions, frame holds, and clip-speed changes work well in EDLs.

- Adobe Premiere Pro supports a key track for titles or other content. That track has to be immediately above the video track selected for export.

- You must capture and log all the source material with accurate timecodes.

- The capture card must have a device control that uses a timecode.

- Videotapes must each have a unique reel number and be formatted with the timecode before you shoot the video to ensure there are no breaks in the timecode.

To view the EDL options, choose File > Export > EDL, which opens the EDL Export Settings dialog.

Your options are as follows:

- **EDL Title**: This specifies a title to appear in the first line of the EDL file.

- **Start Timecode**: Here you set the starting timecode value for the first edit in the sequence.

- **Include Video Levels**: This includes video opacity–level comments in the EDL.

- **Include Audio Levels**: This includes audio-level comments in the EDL.

- **Audio Processing**: Here you specify when audio processing should occur. Options are Audio Follows Video, Audio Separately, and Audio At End.

- **Tracks To Export**: This specifies which tracks to export. The video track directly above the video track selected for export is designated as the key track.

● **Note:** The title can be different from the filename. After clicking OK in the EDL Export Settings dialog, you will have the opportunity to enter a filename.

Review questions

1 What are the main formats for exporting digital video if you want to be able to edit the files in the future?

2 When you click Record in the Export to Tape dialog, your camcorder remains paused. What's going on?

3 What streaming media options are available in Adobe Media Encoder?

4 What encoding format should you use when exporting to most mobile devices?

5 Must you wait for Adobe Media Encoder to finish processing its queue before working on a new project?

6 What's the biggest problem you're likely to encounter when exporting Premiere Pro projects to Final Cut Pro?

Review answers

1 The primary options for SD are Microsoft DV AVI and QuickTime MOV in DV format. For HD files, try producing a file using the Match Sequence Settings option, or H.264.

2 Before Adobe Premiere Pro can start recording a project to tape, it has to render it. You can do that in advance by opening a sequence and pressing Enter. Otherwise, when you click the Record button, you'll have to wait a while for Adobe Premiere to render the unrendered portions of your sequence.

3 This varies by platform. Both operating systems include Flash (FLV|F4V), H.264, and QuickTime, with the Windows version including Windows Media as well.

4 H.264 is the encoding format used when exporting to most mobile devices.

5 No. Adobe Media Encoder is a stand-alone application. You can work in other applications or even start a new Adobe Premiere Pro project while it's processing its render queue.

6 File incompatibilities, particularly for HD video files. Adobe Premiere Pro simply handles HD formats differently than Final Cut Pro, and many HD files that Adobe Premiere Pro can directly edit can't be imported into Final Cut Pro.

21 AUTHORING DVDS WITH ADOBE ENCORE CS5

Topics covered in this lesson

- Preparing projects for DVD authoring in Adobe Premiere Pro
- Adding Encore chapter markers to the Timeline
- Sending a sequence to Encore via Adobe Dynamic Link
- Creating an autoplay DVD
- Creating a menu DVD
- Creating a Blu-ray Disc
- Exporting DVD projects to Flash

 This lesson will take approximately 30 minutes.

Send your Adobe Premiere Pro CS5 Timeline to Adobe Encore CS5 to create DVDs, Blu-ray Discs, or Adobe Flash Professional CS5 web projects.

Getting started

DVDs are a tremendous media delivery platform. Their images and videos are full-screen (including 16:9 wide-screen), the audio quality is good, and they are interactive. Simply click a menu button to jump immediately to a video, a scene, or behind-the-scenes stills.

Creating these interactive DVDs, with all their menus and buttons, used to take a Hollywood feature-film budget and expensive hardware. With Adobe Premiere Pro and Encore, you can create professional-looking DVDs on your computer in minutes.

Adobe Encore is now included with Adobe Premiere Pro and has a collection of customizable DVD menu templates with backgrounds and buttons—static or animated. If you like, you can even use your own images or videos as backgrounds.

Adobe Encore CS5 takes DVD authoring much further than previous versions. You can use Adobe Encore to create standard-definition (SD) DVDs or high-definition (HD) Blu-ray Discs, and you can even output your DVD project to Flash.

Overview of DVD authoring in Adobe Premiere Pro

DVD authoring is the process used to create menus, buttons, and links to assets and menus. It also describes behaviors such as what the DVD player should do when it gets to the end of a video—does it return to the DVD's main menu, to some other menu, or to another video?

Each DVD-authoring application takes a different approach to creating interactive DVDs. Adobe Premiere Pro simplifies the authoring process by allowing you to send your Timeline to Adobe Encore, which is a full-featured professional authoring tool. When you author in Adobe Encore, you have two basic options for creating DVDs:

- **Autoplay DVDs**: These discs have no menus. They work best for short movies that you want your viewers to watch from start to finish. Before you create an autoplay DVD, you can add Encore chapter markers to the Timeline. Markers let viewers skip forward or backward through the movie by using the Next and Previous buttons on their DVD player's remote control.

- **Menu-based DVDs**: These DVDs have one or more menus with buttons that link to separate videos, slide shows, or scene-selection submenus. (Scene-selection submenus, as you probably know, let viewers navigate to scenes within the videos.)

Adobe Encore can output a project to any of three file formats:

- **SD DVD**: This is the traditional DVD format widely in use today for set-top DVD players.

- **Blu-ray Disc**: This is a delivery medium for HD video.

- **Flash**: With one step, Adobe Encore can export your DVD project to Flash content for the Web. Not only is the video converted to Flash Video, but the menu system and actions are converted to Flash content as well. Encore also produces a web-ready HTML page with links to the Flash content, ready to be uploaded to your website for client review or demonstration.

You have two options to get your Adobe Premiere Pro Timeline into Adobe Encore for authoring:

- **Send it via Dynamic Link to Encore**: The preferred method is to use Adobe Dynamic Link to "send" the Timeline to Adobe Encore. The advantage of this method is you don't need to create an intermediate file to load into Encore. This is a fast, efficient workflow. Another advantage of this method is that any changes you make later to your Timeline in Adobe Premiere Pro will be reflected immediately in Encore, without you having to render or even save the file. This is the method you will explore in this lesson.

- **Export it as media**: Adobe Premiere Pro allows you to export an intermediate temporary file to import into Encore. You can export an encoded file that Adobe Encore can import and use directly, or you can export an intermediate format that is editable, such as AVI or QuickTime format, and allow Encore to encode it for you. Using this method, you could author a DVD with any third-party tool; however, you lose the advantages associated with Dynamic Link. This method consumes more hard disk space for the temporary intermediate file and requires more render time.

Adding Adobe Encore chapter markers to the Timeline

● **Note:** Adobe Encore chapter markers are not clip markers or Timeline markers. Clip markers and Timeline markers help you position and trim clips. Adobe Premiere Pro uses Encore chapter markers solely for DVD menu creation and button links.

Once you have finished editing a video in Adobe Premiere Pro, you can add Encore chapter markers to the Timeline to denote chapters for the final DVD. You can move, remove, and add markers at any time in the sequence.

1   Open Lesson 21-1.prproj, and open Sequence 01 if it is not already open. You will be exporting this short video project to an autoplay DVD with no menus. But first you'll add a chapter marker so users can click ahead with the DVD remote.

2   To place an Adobe Encore chapter marker, position the current-time indicator where you want the marker to be, and then click the Set Encore Chapter Marker button (located near the top left of the Timeline). Place the marker at the beginning of the third clip (about 00;00;14;01 on the Timeline).

● **Note:** Adobe Premiere Pro automatically places an Encore chapter marker on the first frame of every sequence. You cannot move or remove this marker. You can move, remove, or rename any other chapter markers you add.

3   Name this chapter marker *Lightning*. Click OK.

Creating an autoplay DVD

Next, you'll create an autoplay DVD that will begin playing your movie automatically when a user plays the disc in a DVD player.

1   Choose File > Adobe Dynamic Link > Send to Encore. Adobe Encore launches.

2   Name the disc *Auto Play DVD*, and choose the Lesson 21 folder for the location.

3   Select DVD as the authoring mode.

4 Click OK.

Encore opens with the Adobe Premiere Pro sequence you selected in the Encore Project panel. This also creates an Encore Timeline of the same name.

5 Double-click the Timeline object in the Encore Project panel, which opens a Timeline panel in Encore and a monitor window so you can preview the video. Play or scrub the video to see it is the sequence you exported from Adobe Premiere Pro.

This video sequence is loaded into Adobe Encore via Dynamic Link. This technology allows Encore to play the Adobe Premiere Pro sequence without first having to render it anywhere. To demonstrate that this link is dynamic, you'll now make a change to the Adobe Premiere Pro sequence and see that it is reflected immediately in Encore.

6 Switch from Adobe Encore to Adobe Premiere Pro.

7 Choose Effects > Video Effects > Image Control, and drag the Black & White filter to the first clip on the Adobe Premiere Pro Timeline.

> **● Note:** If an Adobe Premiere Pro sequence is dynamically linked to an Adobe Encore project, it is not even necessary for Adobe Premiere Pro to be running for Encore to use the linked sequence.

8 Do not save the Adobe Premiere Pro project after you make this change. Switch back to Encore, and play the Timeline. You will see that the change you made appears in Encore without rendering or even saving the project.

To complete the creation of an autoplay DVD, you need to set a couple of parameters, and then you'll be ready to burn the DVD.

9 Select the Sequence 01/Lesson 21-01 Timeline object in the Project panel; notice the End Action on the Properties panel is Not Set. This means the DVD will not know what to do when the Timeline finishes playing. Set the Timeline to stop after playing by setting End Action to Stop. If the End Action is not set to Stop, Encore will warn you to set the end action when checking the project for errors.

10 A DVD player must also know what to do if the Title button is pressed on the DVD remote. Set this by clicking a blank area of the Project panel. The properties of the disc now appear in the Properties panel. Set Title Button to Sequence 01/Lesson 21-1 by using the Pickwhip tool to select the Timeline object in the Project panel.

● **Note:** To actually create a DVD, place a blank DVD in your DVD burner. If you do not have a DVD drive or do not want to burn a physical DVD, you can proceed, but you won't be able to complete the final burn process.

11 Choose File > Build > Disc.

12 You can adjust several settings in the Build panel. Typically you will leave them at the defaults to burn your DVD. Check that you have the correct DVD recorder selected if you have more than one burner in your system, and give the project an appropriate name. Click Build to start burning your DVD.

13 If there are errors in your project, Adobe Encore will prompt you with a dialog letting you know where they are so you can correct them before burning the disc. If there are no errors in your project, Adobe Encore will burn your DVD and alert you when it is complete. Leave the Encore project open; you will use it in the next exercise.

Creating a menu DVD

Adobe Premiere Pro does not have tools to create DVD menus directly. However, you can transfer the Encore chapter markers you place on the Timeline to Adobe Encore and then use them to create buttons or chapters. You use Adobe Premiere Pro to pass the video assets along with the chapter markers to Adobe Encore, and you use Encore to build the menus and burn the DVD.

For this exercise, you do not need Adobe Premiere Pro running. Switch to the Encore project that should still be open from the previous section.

You will select a DVD menu from a list of menu templates included with Adobe Encore:

1   Select the Library panel to see a list of assets. You'll see several sets of menu and button styles. Choose the General set.

2   Scroll to locate the menu named Radiant Submenu WIDE. Double-click this menu item to add it to the Project panel and display it in the Menus panel.

3   Drag the Sequence 01/Lesson 21-01 Timeline from the Project panel to the Scene 1 button on the menu.

A DVD menu with only one scene to select is a little boring, so you will add another sequence from Adobe Premiere Pro without even having to open Adobe Premiere Pro. You will add this sequence via Dynamic Link from Encore.

Remember that the first sequence was added to Encore via Dynamic Link from Adobe Premiere Pro.

4 Choose File > Adobe Dynamic Link > Import Premiere Pro Sequence. In the Import Premiere Pro Sequence dialog, navigate to the Lesson 16 folder; then click Lesson 16-4.prproj. This reveals the sequences contained in that project on the right. Click the completed sequence to select it, and then click OK.

Import Premiere Pro Sequence

Project:

Chris Randall
Desktop
Documents
▼ Class in a book
  ▶ Lesson 14
  ▼ Lesson 15
    ▶ Adobe Premiere Pro Preview
    ▶ Encoded Files
    Lesson 15-1.prproj
    Lesson 15-2.prproj
    Lesson 15-3.prproj
    Lesson 15-4.prproj
  ▼ Lesson 16
    ▶ Adobe Premiere Pro Preview
    ▶ Encoded Files
    Lesson 16-1.prproj
    Lesson 16-2.prproj
    Lesson 16-3.prproj
    Lesson 16-4.prproj
  ▶ Lesson 17

Loading Lesson 16-4

Sequence:

completed
nested complete

Cancel

5 Drag the completed/Lesson 16-4 sequence from the Project panel to the Scene 2 button on the menu.

You can add as many sequences as you want like this. In this exercise, you will stop at two and clean up the menu a little before burning it.

6 Since you don't have multiple menus, delete the Main Menu text and the navigation arrows. You can delete them by selecting them and pressing the Delete button on your keyboard.

7 Since you have only two sequences, also delete Scene 3 and Scene 4.

8 Select each scene button, and drag them to be larger and evenly spaced on the menu. The menu should look like the one shown here.

9   Click the Timelines panel to select it. This panel filters the assets so you see only the Timeline assets. Select each Timeline, and set End Action to Return to Last Menu.

Adobe Encore makes the first object you import the First Play object, meaning it's the first object the DVD player plays when the DVD is inserted. The first thing imported into this project was the Sequence 01/Lesson 21-01 object. Notice that it has a First Play status added to its icon. That worked well for an autoplay DVD. But now you want the menu to be the first thing that plays. Fortunately, this is easy to change.

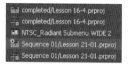

10 Right-click the menu object, and choose Set as First Play from the menu. Notice the First Play indicator is now on the menu icon.

Previewing the DVD

You can preview the menu in Adobe Encore before burning it to DVD to make sure it looks and works as you expect.

1   Choose File > Preview. Use the pointer as your DVD remote to click the buttons. Click each button to ensure they all play as expected.

2   You can burn this DVD in the same way you burned the autoplay DVD earlier. Choose File > Build > Disc, and proceed as you did in the autoplay exercise.

Creating a Blu-ray Disc

Blu-ray Disc is a format that supports HD video. HD video has a higher resolution than SD video, so it will not fit on a standard DVD. Burning a Blu-ray Disc requires a Blu-ray Disc–capable burner and Blu-ray Disc media, and to play the Blu-ray Disc, you need a Blu-ray Disc–capable player connected to a high-definition TV. Fortunately, Encore is ready to handle this new technology when you are. Burning a Blu-ray Disc is as easy as burning a standard-definition DVD.

Start where you left off with the Encore project still open, and follow these steps:

1   Select the Build panel.

2   Change Format to Blu-ray.

3   Click Build.

Yes, it *is* that easy. As with standard DVD, you can also output to a folder or image file if you do not want to burn directly to a disc.

Blu-ray Disc pop-up menus

The Blu-ray Disc standard has additional functionality not found in standard-definition DVDs. One enhancement the Blu-ray Disc format has is that menus can pop up over video when a user presses the Menu button on the remote. When creating menus for Blu-ray Disc, you will notice a Pop-up panel. Use this panel to specify the pop-up details.

Exporting DVD projects to Flash

Creating Flash content from a DVD menu is an innovative feature in Encore. Not only does Encore convert the video to Flash Video, but it converts the whole menu system to a SWF file that is viewable in a web browser. This allows you to demo DVD projects over the Web with no knowledge of Flash, HTML, or scripting—pretty amazing! The Flash controls even allow you to skip to chapter points via Flash web-friendly video controls.

In this exercise, you will export the project you just created for DVD to Flash. If you want to load that project from the included example, open the file that you created in the Lesson 21 folder called Auto Play DVD.ncor.

1   Select the Build panel.

2   Change Format to Flash.

3 Specify a location under Destination and a project name under Settings. Remember the folder and filename you use here, because you will need to navigate to the file later with a browser.

4 Leave all the other parameters at the defaults, and then click Build. You will see progress bars that provide details of the export process and a "Complete" message when it's done.

Encore converts your DVD project into an interactive Flash file that you can view in a web browser.

5 Open a web browser. (The browser needs to have the Flash plug-in to view Flash content.)

6 Navigate to the folder where you saved the Flash file.

7 Within the folder you specified, there will be an HTML file called index.html. Open this file in your browser to view your Flash application.

You will notice that the menu is fully functional, including a background, button highlights, and even semitransparent buttons. Clicking a button will play the video and then return you to the menu, preserving the end actions you set up in Adobe Encore. All this is possible without you needing to know Flash and without writing a single line of code.

As we've said before, Adobe Encore is a complete DVD-authoring and burning tool (and more!). In this lesson, you've seen a very brief example of building a fairly simple menu from Adobe Premiere Pro sequences. It is beyond the scope of this book to explore all the menu-authoring capabilities of Adobe Encore, but this lesson should have given you a taste of the amazing possibilities you have with Adobe Encore.

● **Note:** If you upload this to a web server, be sure to upload the subfolder called Sources and all its content.

Review questions

1 Why send a project to Adobe Encore via Dynamic Link rather than exporting an MPEG2 file for Encore to import?

2 What is the purpose of Encore chapter markers in Adobe Premiere Pro?

3 What is the significance of the First Play object in Encore?

4 Is it possible to export the same Encore project to DVD and Blu-ray Disc?

5 When you upload an Encore Flash project to a web server, which files must you upload?

Review answers

1 Using Dynamic Link eliminates the need to render or encode before working on a sequence in Encore. Dynamic Link allows you to make changes to the sequence in Adobe Premiere Pro and have them show up in Encore.

2 Adobe Encore chapter markers in Adobe Premiere Pro will be passed to Encore when you export. These markers can be used in Encore to set chapter points and to name buttons.

3 The First Play object in Adobe Encore is the object executed when a user inserts a DVD into a player. Typically, the First Play object is the main menu, but it can be a video Timeline that plays automatically.

4 Yes. You cannot export to the two formats simultaneously, but you can burn the same project to DVD or Blu-ray Disc.

5 You must upload the contents of the folder you specified in the Build panel, plus the Sources subfolder and its contents.

INDEX

Adobe resources
    Community Help, 4–5
    Design Center, 5
    Developer Connection, 5
    for educators, 5
    Forums, 5
    Help and Support, 5
    Labs, 5
    Marketplace & Exchange, 5
    product home page, 5
Adobe resources, consulting, 4–5
Adobe Story
    features of, 7
    script, 267
After Effects compositions, replacing
    clips with, 349–350
After Effects CS5
    animating lower third, 345–346
    described, 14
    exporting compositions from, 362
    importing projects from, 347–348
    mini-workflow, 15
    options, 343
    workspace, 343–344
alpha-channel transparencies, using in
    compositing, 278–280
analog recorder, recording to, 357–358
analog video. *See also* video
    digitizing, 66
    transferring, 74
Analyze Content dialog
    displaying, 265
    Reference Script drop-down list,
        267
anchor points, changing for clips,
    193–194
anti-aliasing, defined, 34
aperture, adjusting for cameras, 325
Area Type tool, using with Titler, 124
assets
    displaying information about, 33
    displaying properties of, 34
    finding, 41
    finding with Media Browser, 42
    importing, 32–33
    managing via batch capture, 70
    organizing in bin structure, 40
asterisk (*), using to add marker, 307
audio
    adding J-cuts, 233–234
    adding L-cuts, 235
    adjusting in Effect Controls panel,
        229–230
    analyzing with OnLocation, 331
    changing zoom level for, 223
    Constant Gain option, 230
    dragging in Source Monitor, 88
    floating-point data, 220
    importing, 32–33
    maintaining for speed changes to
        clips, 207
    playing in Source Monitor, 222
    samples per second, 220
audio and video, unlinking, 307
audio channels. *See* channels

audio clips
    applying transitions to, 229–230
    muting audio tracks for, 245
audio editing, 221–226
audio effects. *See also* mono effects;
        stereo effects
    adding in Soundbooth, 260
    Bass, 241
    Delay parameters, 241
    and editing, 12
    MultibandCompressor, 246
    PitchShifter, 242
    Reverb, 242–243
    sweetening sound with, 240–243
    Treble, 242
Audio Effects Mono folder, opening,
    240
audio feedback, dealing with, 254
audio files, transcribing to text,
    264–266
Audio Gain tool, using, 231–232
Audio Mixer
    adding effects to tracks, 249–250
    adjusting Left/Right Pan, 249
    automation modes, 251
    features of, 18
    Latch automation mode, 251
    Mute settings, 250
    Panner puck, 255
    recording voice-overs, 253–254
    Solo buttons, 250
    Touch automation mode, 251
    using to adjust volume levels,
        247–251
    VU (volume unit) meter, 249
audio noise, cleaning up, 256–259
audio peak, setting, 232
Audio preferences, setting, 31
audio problem.wav, opening in Source
        Monitor, 256
audio samples, displaying in Source
        Monitor, 222
audio tracks
    assigning to submix tracks, 220
    clips in, 247
    creating, 225
    creating fade-in effect on, 228, 235
    creating fade-out effect on, 228, 234
    determining type of, 226
    outputting to submixes, 251–253
    types of, 220
audio transitions, adding, 111
audio volume, adjusting, 227–228,
        231–232. *See also* volume levels
audio-editing tools, availability of, 220
Auto Bezier interpolation, using with
        keyframes, 176–177
Auto Color effect, using, 297
Automate to Sequence process
    following, 80–82
    using with transitions, 110
autoplay DVD
    creating, 379–381
    described, 376
autosaves, setting preferences for, 31

AVCHD media
    importing, 54
    performance of, 54
    using CUDA graphics cards, 54
    using in tapeless workflow, 48

B

backslash (\) key
    using to return to zoom level, 306
    using to zoom Timeline, 214
Bad TV 2 – old effect, locating, 350
Balance audio effect, using, 244
bars, adding for tapes, 356
Basic 3D effect, using, 180, 201
Bass audio effect, using, 241
batch capture
    clip-naming convention, 71–72
    logging tapes, 71
    performing, 70–73
    purposes of, 70
Batch list, defined, 312
batch-processing tasks, handling, 266
battery, using with camcorder, 67
Behind_The_Scenes_SD.avi clip,
        replacing, 349–350
Behind_the_scenes_SD.avi file,
        importing, 55
Beta SP video, transferring, 74
Bevel Edges Thin effect
    adding to PIP effect, 198–199
    using preset with, 198
Bezier interpolation, using with
        keyframes, 176
bins. *See also* folders
    arranging in Icon view, 80
    dragging clips between, 40–41
    managing media in, 37–40
    opening simultaneously, 40–41
    using with Project panel, 18
black video, adding to tapes, 356
blend modes
    combining layers based on,
        277–278
    using with Photoshop layers, 341
blue-screen videos, using Ultra Key
        effect with, 282
Blu-ray Disc
    creating, 385
    pop-up menus, 385
border color, changing for transitions,
    105
Breakout To Mono option, using with
        channels, 224
Bridge CS5, described, 14
brightness
    setting, 20, 31
    setting in Waveform Monitor,
        328–330
Broadcast Colors coloring effect,
        described, 294
B-roll, defined, 233
brown matte clip, using Opacity effect
        with, 276
BrowserLab, features of, 7

J

J-cuts, adding to audio, 233–234
JPEG clip, displaying in Program Monitor, 36
jump cuts, avoiding, 64

K

kerning, setting in Titler, 119
Key Color chip, using eyedropper with, 281
keyboard shortcuts
  adding audio transitions, 111
  adding marker, 307
  adding transitions, 101
  availability of, 303–304
  beginning of sequence, 307
  changing, 304–305
  Copy, 304
  end of sequence, 307
  file selection, 72
  importing folders, 308
  marquee-select, 308
  moving clips per frames, 307
  moving to beginning of clip, 307
  moving to end of clip, 307
  multifunction playback modifer key, 306
  New Title dialog, 121
  number of, 303
  opening Help, 307
  opening Import dialog, 33
  opening Titler, 307
  Out point, 91
  In and Out points for clips, 71
  playback controls, 306
  playback modifier key, 306
  In point, 91
  Redo, 304
  rendering Timeline, 55
  resizing Timeline, 306
  Rolling Edit tool, 144
  Save, 304
  selecting multiple files, 32
  sending trimmed clips to Timeline, 91
  Slide tool, 145
  toggling Snap feature, 307
  tools, 306
  undoing actions, 84, 304
  undoing duration changes, 214
  undoing edits in Program Monitor, 147
  undoing Replace Clip function, 149
  undoing ripple delete, 150
  undoing speed changes for clips, 206, 213–214
  unlinking audio and video, 307
  work area bar's end points, 307
  "keyframable" options, using in Motion, 191
keyframe adjustments, using Volume effect with, 228
keyframe controls, availability of, 13
keyframe editing, advantage of, 247
keyframe interpolation, applying in Timeline, 228
keyframes. *See also* speed keyframes
  adding interpolation, 173–178, 194–195
  adding velocity, 173–178
  adjusting on sequences, 94
  changing Rotation value for, 175
  changing time between, 190
  changing values for, 172
  creating for fade-in effects, 228
  creating for fade-out effects, 228
  editing using clip effect menu, 246–247
  relocating, 190
  using Ease Out option with, 176
  using to vary speed of clips, 209–210
keyframing effects, adding, 169–172
keyframing motion, 287
keying, improving, 281
keying effects
  Difference Matte Key, 286
  Image Matte Key, 286
  overview of, 280–281
  Remove Matte Key, 286
  using, 275
  using in compositing, 274

L

Label Colors preferences, setting, 31
Labs, consulting, 5
layers, combining based on blend mode, 277–278
L-cuts, adding to audio, 235
leading, setting in Titler, 118
Leave Color effect, using, 294–295
Lens Flare filter, using, 180
lesson files
  copying, 3
  using, 4
lesson folders, creating directory for, 15
LFE (low-frequency effects), use of, 254–255
lift edits, explained, 143
Lift option, using with clips in Timeline, 87
light_quiet.mov clip, playing, 330–331
lighting effects, adding, 178–179. *See also* specular highlight
lights, using, 65
linear editing
  managing head and tail handles, 109
  using to fine-tune transitions, 106–109
linear interpolation, using with keyframes, 176
live video, recording, 326–327. *See also* video
LL screen location, using with PIP effect, 196

logo.psd clip, adjusting position parameters, 278
Low Memory Warning alert, receiving, 31
lower third
  animating in After Effects, 345–346
  example, 340
lower third.psd, importing, 340
lower-third animation, re-creating, 341–342
LR screen location, using with PIP effect, 196
Luma Color coloring effect, described, 294
luminance, representing, 328–330

M

Mac, export formats, 359
Mac keyboard shortcuts. *See* keyboard shortcuts
Make Offline option, using with trimmed projects, 317
marker, adding, 307
Marketplace & Exchange, consulting, 5
marquee-select method
  using with files, 72
  using with still images, 214
matte clip, using Opacity effect with, 276
matte keys
  garbage, 284
  graphic, 284
  using in compositing, 283–288
media
  importing and scaling, 31
  managing in bins, 37–40
Media Browser
  expanding, 42
  features of, 18
  filtering assets in, 42
  importing OnLocation clips with, 334
  using, 49
  using to find assets, 42
Media Encoder
  choosing Format/Presets, 363
  creating watch folders, 362
  importing compositions from After Effects, 362
  launching, 266–267, 367
  managing tasks, 363
  overview of, 362–363
  using, 362–363
Media export option, using, 355
media formats, mixing, 55–56
media types, importing, 32–33
medialink label colors, changing, 31
Medieval_Axe.mp3 file, selecting, 38
Medieval_dialog_hero.wav, using Audio Gain with, 231
Medieval_Hero_01.mpeg clip
  editing, 88
  loading into Source Monitor, 90
  Speed/Duration example, 207

Production Notes

The *Adobe Premiere Pro CS5 Classroom in a Book* was created electronically using Adobe InDesign CS4. The Myriad Pro and Warnock Pro OpenType families of typefaces were used throughout this book. For more information about OpenType and Adobe fonts, visit www.adobe.com/type/opentype/.

Team credits

The following individuals contributed to the development of *Adobe Premiere Pro CS5 Classroom in a Book*:

Writers: Jan Ozer, Chris Randall, and Curt Wrigley
Senior Editor: Karyn Johnson
Developmental Editor: Stephen Nathans-Kelly
Production Editor: Myna Vladic
Technical Editor: Luisa Winters, Megan Tytler
Compositor: David Van Ness
Copyeditor: Kim Wimpsett
Proofreader: Dominic Cramp
Indexer: Valerie Perry
Cover Design: Eddie Yuen
Interior Design: Mimi Heft
Adobe Press Executive Editor: Victor Gavenda
Adobe Press Project Editor: Connie Jeung-Mills

Newly Expanded LEARN BY VIDEO Series

Learn Adobe Photoshop CS5 by Video:
Core Training in Visual Communication
(ISBN 9780321719805)

Learn Adobe Flash Professional CS5 by Video:
Core Training in Rich Media Communication
(ISBN 9780321719829)

Learn Adobe Dreamweaver CS5 by Video:
Core Training in Web Communication
(ISBN 9780321719812)

The **Learn by Video** series from video2brain and Adobe Press is the only Adobe-approved video courseware for the Adobe Certified Associate Level certification, and has quickly established itself as one of the most critically-acclaimed training products available on the fundamentals of Adobe software.

Learn by Video offers up to 19 hours of high-quality HD video training presented by experienced trainers, as well as lesson files, assessment quizzes and review materials. The DVD is bundled with a full-color printed book that provides supplemental information as well as a guide to the video topics.

Up to 19 hours of high-quality video training

Tutorials-to-Go! Transfer selected movies to your iPhone, iPod, or compatible cell phone

Table of Contents never more than a click away

Watch-and-Work mode shrinks the video into a small window while you work in the software

Video player remembers which movie you watched last

Lesson files are included on the DVD

Additional Titles

- **Learn Adobe Photoshop Elements 8 and Adobe Premiere Elements 8 by Video** (ISBN 9780321685773)
- **Learn Photography Techniques for Adobe Photoshop CS5 by Video** (ISBN 9780321734839)
- **Learn Adobe After Effects CS5 by Video** (ISBN 9780321734860)
- **Learn Adobe Flash Catalyst CS5 by Video** (ISBN 9780321734853)
- **Learn Adobe Illustrator CS5 by Video** (ISBN 9780321734815)
- **Learn Adobe InDesign CS5 by Video** (ISBN 9780321734808)
- **Learn Adobe Premiere Pro CS5 by Video** (ISBN 9780321734846)

For more information go to **www.adobepress.com/learnbyvideo**